Praise for I've Just Been Born Again

"Mike Goddard has grown in his spiritual life and ministry as God has led him into leadership of the men's group at his home church.

As he has lead them deeper in their own individual spiritual lives, he has confronted the need to teach the underlying fundamentals of the Christian faith. From that experience this book has been birthed. It is a well-thought-out presentation of the basic truths of the Christian faith in a reader-friendly format that will enable any Christian to deepen their walk with God.

I commend this book to the reader and pray that God will use it in your life, causing you to more fully understand the basis of your faith and enabling you to walk closer with our God."

– Gerry Seale, DD, *Barbados District presiding bishop, Pentecostal Assemblies of the West Indies*

"Anyone involved in the development of young Christian Believers will treasure this book, as it provides another avenue to help to disciple persons into their newfound relationship with Jesus Christ.

Mike Goddard sketches out a guideline for both instructors and converts to use to enhance the Believer's first steps and ensure their steps are firmly planted in the Word Of God. His approach is laced with a Biblical undergirding for the Believer to become a reflective, observant, and introspective student while at the same time focusing on Jesus Christ, the Author and Finisher of our faith."

– Nigel N. Henry, *World Missions director, Pentecostal Assemblies of the West Indies International*

"There are many highlights I can take from this fine work, first of which would be that it allows the Bible to speak for itself. Perhaps 80 percent of the text is a beautiful tapestry of Scripture carefully and sequentially woven together, wisely using different versions of Scripture, to outline the fundamentals of the Christian faith.

Also outstanding is the simple writing style that is easy to understand, yet the more advanced student will benefit from the well-researched information which renders the book simple in style but not simplistic in content. This text will be beneficial to the new convert and the more mature Christian."

– Rev. Dr. Orlando Seale, *Superintendent of the Barbados District of the Church of the Nazarene*

"Congratulations, Mike, on a much-needed book written from a heart that truly loves God and has a passionate desire that 'all may know Him'. Not only is it a great blessing to the new Believer but to ALL Believers.

Simply and beautifully written, Mike not only shows us how to be born again, but opens our understanding to who God really is and how He wants us to live our daily lives.

I highly recommend this book to pastors for use in the Sunday school department, Bible study, and Converts' classes, and would encourage you to make sure there are several copies in your church library."

– Pastor Rosemary Williams, *cofounder, The People's Cathedral, Barbados*

"Mike Goddard wrote this book as an aid for new Christians on their spiritual journey.

While reading the original manuscript at the author's request, I rediscovered the richness of the Scriptures.

I am glad that he arranged this book in a way that allows the Scriptures to direct, encourage, and enlighten at critical junctions of the exciting journey. Many times I found myself reflecting—instead of correcting.

The book ministered to me. May it do the same for you. I heartily recommend it."

– Harry Mayers, *retired journalist, lay preacher— Methodist Church in the Caribbean*

"The born again Believer needs to know what is involved in being born again or to experience the spiritual birth. It is the spiritual birth or renewal that equips the Believer to carry out the mandate to "go into all the world and preach the Good News to every creature."

This book outlines the basics of Christianity and what it means to be born again. The last chapter speaks to the authority given to the Believer to use the name of Jesus to heal the sick and other functions mentioned in Mark's Gospel, chapter 16, verse 18.

In spite of all your efforts to understand what it means to be born again, aided by assimilating the contents of this book, the true essence of its meaning can only be grasped when this book, based on Scripture, is read prayerfully.

Living out the experience of being born again as outlined here, enables you to better grasp its true meaning."

– Dr. DaCosta Thompson, *medical doctor and student of the Word of God*

"As one who over the years has grown disenchanted and drifted away from the Christian ethic, while I continue searching for the answer to "What're we here for?," Mike Goddard's explanation of some passages of Scripture I once found pedantic, contradictory, and gratuitously violent, brought me enticingly close to returning to the fold.

Mike's journalism training serves him well in this publication, which I'm sure is only the precursor of more. He applies his trademark wry wit and knack of gentle persuasion in dissecting and analyzing a host of Bible stories and events.

I don't get the impression here that he is on an evangelical crusade trying to convert anyone; he's only telling you that he has just been born again . . . and that it's a good feeling. And that you have nothing to lose if you try it."

– Carl Moore, *first editor,* The Nation *newspaper (Barbados); retired public affairs officer, Central Bank of Barbados; book editor*

"This book meets a relevant need in the body of Christ. Who better to write about being born again than Mike Goddard, who himself has experienced such a miraculous, life-transforming experience in his own life? Mike is a good friend, a Barnabas (an Encourager), very involved in men's Ministry and one who seeks to positively impact the spiritual landscape of Barbados. He has seen the need to educate and equip the new convert and has done so in a thorough and comprehensive manner. I commend this book not only to converts but also to those who are inquirers and seekers after truth. Teachers in New Believers classes will find this book a useful tool."

– Rev. Paul Watson, *retired senior pastor, Messiah's House, Wesleyan Holiness Church; author*

I'VE JUST BEEN BORN AGAIN

I've Just Been Born Again

A Guide for Christians, New Converts
and People Who Want to Know More
about Christianity

MICHAEL L. GODDARD

THE MESSENGER

The Messenger
22, 3rd Avenue North
Wildey Terrace
St. Michael BB11104
Barbados
E-mail: thebarbadosmessenger@yahoo.com
www.thebarbadosmessenger.com

ISBN-13: 978-976-95814-0-1
LCCN: 2017900873

Distributed by Itasca Books

Printed in the United States of America

CONTENTS

Introduction

I've Just Been Born Again is a book that every Christian should read. It reveals the awesome power and rich legacy that comes through a genuine relationship with Jesus Christ.

This is a textbook for building and sustaining the Church of Jesus Christ, the Body of Christ. It is especially helpful not only for new converts but mature Christians as well. People outside the Christian faith will also find its pages enlightening.

The new Believer will discover what it takes and means to be born again and the more experienced will be encouraged and reminded of who they are through the life, death, resurrection, and promised return of Jesus Christ.

Special emphasis is placed on some of the basic questions that confront Believers, including: "How can I be born again?," "Who is Jesus Christ?," "Who is God?," "What is sin?," "Who is the devil?," "What is prayer?," and "What are the characteristics of a Christian?"

I've Just Been Born Again is based on the premise that not all who call themselves Christians fully understand their standing and responsibility in God and the world of which they are a part. Undoubtedly, this weakness is in part responsible for the level of stagnation experienced in the lives of many Believers and by extension in many churches across the denominational spectrum. Scriptural support is thus provided to assist.

The doctrine of being born again has for more than two thousand years generated great discussion inside and outside of the Christian faith. Jesus told one of the religious leaders of His day that in order to get eternal life he had to be born again. As religious as he was, Nicodemus couldn't grasp this concept of spiritual birth, and there are many today who are just like him.

Thousands of people have become Christians in the last decade or so and it stands to reason that churches should be full. However, the majority of churches are far from overflowing.

In the United States, statistics point to a drop in church attendance, along with a decline in the number of people who identify themselves as Christians.

A Barna survey released in 2015 showed that church attendance in America between 2004 and 2014 fell from 43 percent in 2004 to 36 percent in 2014.

Another review by the Pew Research Center on the changing US religious landscape also recorded a falloff in the number of people who identify themselves as Christians. This survey, which covered 2007 to 2014, reported that the percentage of people over 18 years of age who described themselves as Christians dropped from 78.4 percent in 2007 to 70.6 percent in just seven years.

The research showed that while the falloff in affiliation was particularly significant among young adults, it occurred among Americans of all ages, all across the country.

The drop in the number of people attending church was pronounced among what are known as the mainline Protestant and Catholic denominations. Evangelical Protestants have more or less maintained their position.

The survey by The Pew Research Center revealed an increase in the number of people who refuse to identify with any organized religion. This category, dubbed "the religiously unaffiliated," jumped by more than six percentage points from just over 16 percent in 2007 to nearly 23 percent in 2014. They described themselves as atheists, agnostic, or "nothing in particular."

Statistics on religion in the USA have also revealed that the number of people of non-Christian faiths has doubled from nearly five percent in 2007 to nearly 10 percent in 2014.

Several reasons have been proffered for the falling interest in Christianity. They all seemed to be linked to people not really understanding what it means to be born again, as stated in the Bible. This situation is serious because this is the prerequisite given by Jesus Christ for eternal life.

This book should be more than useful in helping readers to increase their knowledge and understanding from a biblical perspective.

It is also a great educational tool that can be used throughout the Church, especially Mission departments, Sunday schools, Youth departments, Evangelism, and other ministries. At the personal level, it can be used as a devotional tool.

People who want to find out the basics of the Christian faith will find it an excellent source of information.

The extensive use of biblical quotations reinforces the teaching of being born again. It is hoped that this will also encourage readers to get more involved in reading and studying the Word of God.

Chapter 1

Born Again: What Do You Mean?

So you have accepted Jesus Christ as Lord and Savior and you have been told that you are born again. All this may be new and you are wondering what it means.

The word "born" speaks of beginnings and the start of something new. You start life at birth, although there is a school of thought that life starts in the womb. Being born again, however, is about a new beginning.

Simply put, there are two births: a natural and a spiritual. The first comes after a male impregnates a female and the foetus grows until it is time for it to exit the body or be born.

The second birth is spiritual and is of great significance to Christians. It relates to a person believing in Jesus Christ, repenting of his or her sins, accepting Him as Lord and Savior; a decision that leads to the forgiving of sins and the establishment of a relationship with God.

A born again Christian, then, is someone who has repented of his sins and has turned to the resurrected Christ for his salvation. As a result, he is saved and has become part of God's family and is therefore accepted to live with Him forever.

Being born again literally means born from above. It also speaks to regeneration or the beginning of new life. There are other phrases in the Bible that relate to being born again. They include being "born of the Spirit," "born of God," being "a new creation," "renewing of the Holy Spirit," and "the washing of regeneration."

Before we accept Jesus Christ as our Savior we are spiritually dead in sin. This goes back to creation where Adam, the first man, disobeyed God and was ejected from the Garden of Eden. This resulted in spiritual death for mankind. The entire story can be found in the book of Genesis, chapter three.

Man was created without sin but with the free will to choose right or wrong. Adam was given instructions by God not to eat the fruit of a specific tree, but he did it anyway. By disobeying God he sinned and was thrown out of the Garden and became spiritually separated from God. This meant that everyone born afterward was born in sin.

After the fall of the first man, God later sent His Son, Jesus Christ, to restore His relationship with mankind. The Old Testament reveals that God's people were under what is called "the law" and so were not able to enter into His presence. The chief priests had to offer animal sacrifices in order for God to forgive their sin. God, by sending His Son, Jesus, to die on the cross as a sacrifice, provided a way for man to be reconciled to Him. Jesus paid the ultimate sacrifice for sin, and His blood became the antidote, the cure or the atonement, for it.

When Jesus Christ was crucified at Calvary, the system of offering animal sacrifices ended. The way back to God for all sinners is therefore now through Jesus. He emphasised this in the Gospel of John, chapter 14 when He said:

> *"I am the way, the truth, and the life: no man cometh unto the Father, but by Me." (John 14:6 NKJV).*

There are, however, some religions that dispute this, claiming that there are several ways to get to God. That is not biblical.

Jesus also described Himself as "The Good Shepherd," stating in John's Gospel, chapter 10, that the sheep knew their owner.

> *"Then Jesus said to them again, 'Most assuredly, I say to you, I am the door of the sheep. 8 All who ever came before Me are thieves and robbers, but the sheep did not hear them. 9 I am the door. If anyone enters by Me, he will be saved, and will go in and out and find pasture. 10 The thief does not come except to steal, and to kill, and to destroy. I have come that they may have life, and that they may have it more abundantly. 11 I am the good shepherd. The good shepherd gives His life for the sheep. 12 But a hireling, he who is not the shepherd, one who does not own the sheep, sees the wolf coming and leaves the sheep and flees; and the wolf catches the sheep and scatters them. 13 The hireling flees because he is a hireling and does not care about the sheep. 14 I am the good shepherd; and I know My sheep, and am known by My own. 15 As the Father knows Me, even so I know the Father; and I lay down My life for the sheep. 16 And other sheep I have which are not of this fold; them also I must bring, and they will hear My voice; and there will be one flock and one shepherd.'" (John 10:7–16 NKJV).*

Because God has created man with the will to make decisions for himself, by becoming born again or not, he determines where he will spend eternity, or as some would say, "the afterlife".

When you repent or turn your back on sin, when you acknowledge Jesus' sacrifice and accept Him as your personal Lord and Savior, you are "washed in His blood" and "saved" or born again. His spirit, the Holy Spirit, comes to live within you, becoming your guide and teacher. The Holy Spirit, being the single most important component in the life of a Christian, transforms you. Only the presence of the Holy Spirit determines that you are born again and therefore a true Christian.

Being born again also speaks to regeneration or the beginning of a new life. When Adam sinned by disobeying God in the Garden of Eden, it resulted in spiritual death for mankind. Jesus Christ is sometimes referred to as "the second Adam" since, by His death and resurrection, man now has the opportunity to return to God by being born again, Jesus' shed blood being the saving or redeeming factor.

The Holy Bible says that those who accept Jesus Christ as Savior and who are born again will spend eternity with Him.

> *"In My Father's house are many mansions; if it were not so, I would have told you. I go to prepare a place for you. [3] And if I go and prepare a place for you, I will come again and receive you to Myself; that where I am, there you may be also." (John 14:2–3 NKJV).*

Jesus also spoke about how He will judge the world.

> *"When the Son of Man comes in His glory, and all the holy angels with Him, then He will sit on the throne of His glory. [32] All the*

> *nations will be gathered before Him, and He will separate them one from another, as a shepherd divides his sheep from the goats. [33] And He will set the sheep on His right hand, but the goats on the left. [34] Then the King will say to those on His right hand, 'Come, you blessed of My Father, inherit the kingdom prepared for you from the foundation of the world'." (Matthew 25:31–34 NKJV).*

He also had something to say about those who are not righteous.

> *"Then He will also say to those on the left hand, 'Depart from Me, you cursed, into the everlasting fire prepared for the devil and his angels'." (Matthew 25: 41 NKJV).*

So the born again will go to a place of peace and happiness; but those who reject Jesus Christ will be condemned to everlasting fire, which burns but does not consume.

John chapter three, verses 16–18, says:

> *"For God so loved the world that He gave His only begotten Son, that whoever believes in Him should not perish but have everlasting life. [17]For God did not send His Son into the world to condemn the world, but that the world through Him might be saved. [18]He who believes in Him is not condemned; but he who does not believe is condemned already, because he has not believed in the name of the only begotten Son of God." (John 3:16–18 NKJV).*

This means that when you accept Jesus as Savior you become a Christian and have received the promise of eternal life in Heaven after your natural death. When you genuinely ask Jesus to forgive you and invite Him into your heart and life, you become born again. This means that you have been given a spiritual birth and Jesus has come into your body through the agency of the Holy Spirit.

While the whole idea of being born again may seem weird or even unbelievable, it has been fuelling discussion for centuries. It was first heard way back in the days when Jesus Christ walked the earth. He used the term with Nicodemus, as recorded in the Gospel of John, chapter three.

> *"There was a man of the Pharisees, named*
> *Nicodemus, a ruler of the Jews: 2 The same*
> *came to Jesus by night, and said unto him,*
> *Rabbi, we know that thou art a teacher come*
> *from God: for no man can do these miracles*
> *that thou doest, except God be with him. 3*
> *Jesus answered and said unto him, 'Verily,*
> *verily, I say unto thee; except a man be born*
> *again, he cannot see the kingdom of God'. 4*
> *Nicodemus saith unto him, 'How can a man*
> *be born when he is old? Can he enter the*
> *second time into his mother's womb, and*
> *be born?' 5 Jesus answered, 'Verily, verily,*
> *I say unto thee, except a man be born of*
> *water and of the Spirit, he cannot enter into*
> *the kingdom of God. 6 That which is born*
> *of the flesh is flesh; and that which is born*
> *of the Spirit is spirit. 7 Marvel not that I said*
> *unto thee, Ye must be born again 8The wind*
> *bloweth where it listeth, and thou hearest*
> *the sound thereof, but canst not tell whence*
> *it cometh, and whither it goeth: so is every*

> *one that is born of the Spirit'. [9] Nicodemus answered and said unto him, 'How can these things be?' [10] Jesus answered and said unto him, 'Art thou a master of Israel, and knowest not these things? [11] Verily, verily, I say unto thee, we speak that we do know, and testify that we have seen; and ye receive not our witness. [12] If I have told you earthly things, and ye believe not, how shall ye believe, if I tell you of heavenly things?' " (John 3:1–12 KJV).*

The New Living Translation puts it this way:

> *"There was a man named Nicodemus, a Jewish religious leader who was a Pharisee. [2]After dark one evening, he came to speak with Jesus. 'Rabbi,' he said, 'we all know that God has sent you to teach us. Your miraculous signs are evidence that God is with you.' [3] Jesus replied, 'I tell you the truth, unless you are born again, you cannot see the Kingdom of God.' [4] 'What do you mean?' exclaimed Nicodemus. 'How can an old man go back into his mother's womb and be born again?' [5] Jesus replied, 'I assure you, no one can enter the Kingdom of God without being born of water and the Spirit. [6] Humans can reproduce only human life, but the Holy Spirit gives birth to spiritual life. [7] So don't be surprised when I say, You must be born again. [8]The wind blows wherever it wants. Just as you can hear the wind but can't tell where it comes from or where it is going, so you can't explain how people are born of the*

> *Spirit." [9] "How are these things possible?' Nicodemus asked. [10] Jesus replied, 'You are a respected Jewish teacher, and yet you don't understand these things? [11] I assure you, we tell you what we know and have seen, and yet you won't believe our testimony. [12] But if you don't believe me when I tell you about earthly things, how can you possibly believe if I tell you about heavenly things?' " (John 3:1–12 NLT).*

Some theologians believe that when Jesus told Nicodemus, ***"Except a man be born of water and of the Spirit, he cannot enter into the kingdom of God,"*** that He was speaking figuratively. There is, however, a strong argument that Jesus was in fact speaking literally and was indicating that you had to receive the Holy Spirit to be born again and water baptism was the outward showing of that inward transformation.

The birth of the Spirit involves a person accepting Jesus Christ as Savior, a decision that opens the way for the Holy Spirit, the Spirit of Jesus Christ, to come and live within you. Water baptism, where the person is immersed and then raised up, is the outward showing of the inward transformation from death to life eternal.

Paul the apostle made it clear in his second epistle to the Corinthians that accepting Jesus Christ as Savior is the transforming power.

> *"If anyone is in Christ, he is a new creation; old things have passed away; behold, all things have become new. [18] Now all things are of God, who has reconciled us to Himself through Jesus Christ, and has given us the ministry of reconciliation, [19] that is, that God*

was in Christ reconciling the world to Himself, not imputing their trespasses to them, and has committed to us the word of reconciliation." (2 Corinthians 5:17–19 NKJV).

The New Living Translation of that passage puts it this way:

"This means that anyone who belongs to Christ has become a new person. The old life is gone; a new life has begun! [18] And all of this is a gift from God, who brought us back to Himself through Christ. And God has given us this task of reconciling people to Him. [19] For God was in Christ, reconciling the world to Himself, no longer counting people's sins against them. And He gave us this wonderful message of reconciliation." (2 Corinthians 5:17–19 NLT).

The phrase "born again" only appears three times in the Bible: John chapter three, verses three and seven, as quoted earlier, and in the first epistle of Peter, chapter one.

"Seeing ye have purified your souls in obeying the truth through the Spirit unto unfeigned love of the brethren, see that ye love one another with a pure heart fervently: [23] Being 'born again', not of corruptible seed, but of incorruptible, by the word of God, which liveth and abideth forever. [24] For all flesh is as grass, and all the glory of man as the flower of grass. The grass withereth, and the flower thereof falleth away: [25] But the word of the Lord endureth forever. And this is the word which by the gospel is preached unto you." (1 Peter 1:22–25 KJV).

The Living Bible puts it this way:

> *"For you have a new life. It was not passed on to you from your parents, for the life they gave you will fade away. This new one will last forever, for it comes from Christ, God's ever-living Message to men. [24] Yes, our natural lives will fade as grass does when it becomes all brown and dry. All our greatness is like a flower that droops and falls; [25] but the Word of the Lord will last forever. And His message is the Good News that was preached to you." (1 Peter 1:22–25 TLB)*

The new birth allows you to see or enter the kingdom of God. This is made clear by Jesus in His conversation with Nicodemus where He said:

> *"Except a man be born of water and of the Spirit, he cannot enter into the kingdom of God." (John 3:5 KJV).*

By giving his life to Christ, the born again Christian becomes what has been termed "a new creation".

It must be understood that "the new birth" or the new creation comes from God. John explains this in chapter one, verses 12 and 13 of his Gospel, where he said:

> *"But as many as received Him, to them He gave the right to become children of God, to those who believe in His name: [13] who were born, not of blood, nor of the will of the flesh, nor of the will of man, but of God." (John 1:12–13 NKJV).*

Being born again speaks to conversion and this requires doing what is right and not just admitting what is wrong. The Bible goes even further, stressing the need for a complete spiritual transformation.

The question you must certainly be asking is, "Just how does someone become born again?" Paul speaks to this in chapter three of his epistle to Titus.

> *"For we ourselves were also once foolish, disobedient, deceived, serving various lusts and pleasures, living in malice and envy, hateful and hating one another. [4] But when the kindness and the love of God our Savior toward man appeared, [5] not by works of righteousness which we have done, but according to His mercy He saved us, through the washing of regeneration and renewing of the Holy Spirit, [6] whom He poured out on us abundantly through Jesus Christ our Savior, [7] that having been justified by His grace we should become heirs according to the hope of eternal life." (Titus 3:3–7 NKJV).*

This is made even clearer in The Living Bible translation.

> *"Once we, too, were foolish and disobedient; we were misled by others and became slaves to many evil pleasures and wicked desires. Our lives were full of resentment and envy. We hated others and they hated us. [4] But when the time came for the kindness and love of God our Savior to appear, [5] then He saved us—not because we were good enough to be saved but because of His kindness and pity—by washing away*

> *our sins and giving us the new joy of the indwelling Holy Spirit, [6] whom he poured out upon us with wonderful fullness—and all because of what Jesus Christ our Savior did [7] so that he could declare us good in God's eyes—all because of his great kindness; and now we can share in the wealth of the eternal life he gives us, and we are eagerly looking forward to receiving it. [8] These things I have told you are all true. Insist on them so that Christians will be careful to do good deeds all the time, for this is not only right, but it brings results." (Titus 3:3–8 TLB).*

The late Rev. Dr. Holmes Williams, founder and senior pastor emeritus of the People's Cathedral in Barbados, aptly described the process of being born again. He had this to say in his book, *Know What You Believe*, the church's membership manual:

"In the new Birth, the Word of God is the seed, the human heart is the soil, the preacher of the Word is the sower who drops the seed into the soil. God, by His Spirit, opens the heart to receive the seed. The hearer believes, the Spirit quickens the seed into life in the receptive heart; the new divine nature springs up out of the Divine Word—the Believer is born again, created anew, made alive, passed out of death into life."

When a person becomes born again he or she must, as in the case of natural birth, be prepared to take time to mature. Yes, you are being renewed in spirit but the process takes time. You are what is termed "a babe in Christ" and, like any baby, you will need to go through a process of growth or maturity.

The best advice that can be taken by any person who is new to Christianity or who has recently been born again, is to read and study the Bible "for yourself". As you gain knowledge you will recognize the changes that take place in you. Peter, in chapter two of his first epistle, advises the young Christian:

> *"As newborn babes, desire the sincere milk of the word that ye may grow thereby:" (1 Peter 2:2 KJV).*

This simply means that you should get to know the Word of God, the Bible.

The born again Christian must from the very outset change his way of thinking. You have to change your very mindset and this can only be done with the help of the Holy Spirit.

Paul, in the book of Romans, chapter 12, verses one and two, calls on his fellow Christians not only to treat their bodies well but to have only good thoughts and intentions.

> *"I beseech you therefore, brethren, by the mercies of God, that you present your bodies a living sacrifice, holy, acceptable to God, which is your reasonable service. [2] And do not be conformed to this world, but be transformed by the renewing of your mind, that you may prove what is that good and acceptable and perfect will of God." (Romans 12:1–2 NKJV).*

The Living Bible translates that passage this way:

> *"And so, dear brothers, I plead with you to give your bodies to God. Let them be a living sacrifice, holy—the kind He can accept.*

When you think of what He has done for you, is this too much to ask? [2] Don't copy the behaviour and customs of this world, but be a new and different person with a fresh newness in all you do and think. Then you will learn from your own experience how His ways will really satisfy you." (Romans 12:1–2 TLB).

Only those who are converted, have a spiritual transformation, and have the Holy Spirit living in them, qualify as born again Christians. Paul the apostle made this clear in chapter eight of his letter to the Romans.

"But you are not in the flesh but in the Spirit, if indeed the Spirit of God dwells in you. Now if anyone does not have the Spirit of Christ, he is not His. [10] And if Christ is in you, the body is dead because of sin, but the Spirit is life because of righteousness. [11] But if the Spirit of Him who raised Jesus from the dead dwells in you, He who raised Christ from the dead will also give life to your mortal bodies through His Spirit who dwells in you." (Romans 8:9–11 NKJV).

The Bible is the Word of God and Jesus Himself is described as "The Word". It therefore stands to reason that in order to know Jesus Christ you have to know the Word of God. This holy book, the Bible, is God's way of revealing Himself to mankind. It is the manual for Christian living.

Verse six of chapter six of Hosea says that God told the children of Israel that His people perished for lack of knowledge and that can be true of some of today's Christians.

Paul the apostle also put great emphasis on knowing the Word. In chapter two of his second letter to Timothy he gave him this advice:

> *"Study to shew thyself approved unto God, a workman that needeth not to be ashamed, rightly dividing the word of truth." (2 Timothy 2:15 KJV).*

Studying and learning the Word of God has many benefits. It helps you to get to know Jesus Christ and so allows you to create a closer relationship with Him. It also strengthens your faith. As Paul told the Roman Church:

> *"Faith comes by hearing, and hearing by the word of God." (Romans 10:17 NKJV).*

When Jesus was leaving the earth He promised the disciples that the Father would send someone to teach them.

> *"But the Helper, the Holy Spirit, whom the Father will send in My name, He will teach you all things, and bring to your remembrance all things that I said to you." (John 14:26 NKJV).*

The King James Version puts it this way:

> *"But the Comforter, which is the Holy Ghost, whom the Father will send in my name, He shall teach you all things, and bring all things to your remembrance, whatsoever I have said unto you." (John 14:26 KJV).*

There is strong evidence that a large number of Believers do not study the Bible and as a result live weak Christian lives.

The born again Believer is required to live a holy life. Peter the apostle gave this advice in the first chapter of his first epistle where he gave good reason for it:

> *"As obedient children, not conforming yourselves to the former lusts, as in your ignorance; [15] but as He who called you is holy, you also be holy in all your conduct, [16] because it is written, 'Be holy, for I am holy'." (1 Peter 1:14–15 NKJV).*

The born again Christian should have a consistent and dedicated prayer life: it is the very essence of keeping in touch with God and building and maintaining your faith. Jesus always took time to pray and this is an example to be followed. Paul encouraged the church at Thessalonica to:

> *"Rejoice always. [17]Pray continually. [18] Give thanks in all circumstances; for this is God's will for you in Christ Jesus." (I Thessalonians 5:16–18 NIV).*

Paul also encouraged the Philippians to pray, when he told them:

> *"Be careful for nothing; but in everything by prayer and supplication with thanksgiving let your requests be made known unto God." (Philippians 4:6 KJV).*

Prayer is so important that even the disciples asked Jesus to teach them how to do it. He responded by giving them what is called "The Lord's Prayer".

Although several people take this to be a prayer in itself, it is really a guideline as to how you should pray. Don't just recite it; take time to meditate on it.

The born again Christian must also strengthen his faith and his relationship with Jesus Christ through training or what is termed discipleship. Jesus' disciples learned from Him and, just before He left the earth, He instructed them to also teach others, as outlined in Matthew's Gospel.

> *"Go therefore and make disciples of all the nations, baptizing them in the name of the Father and of the Son and of the Holy Spirit, [20] teaching them to observe all things that I have commanded you; and lo, I am with you always, even to the end of the age." (Matthew 28:19–20 NKJV).*

The born again Christian should also seek out and find other Believers with whom he or she can associate. This involves becoming a member of an assembly or congregation. The Bible recommends in Hebrews 10 that there should be this relationship:

> *"And let us consider one another in order to stir up love and good works, [25] not forsaking the assembling of ourselves together, as is the manner of some, but exhorting one another, and so much the more as you see the Day approaching." (Hebrews 10:24–25 NKJV).*

Getting together to worship God is vital to the born again Christian and every effort should be made to attend church services because this strengthens faith. Jesus pointed out this to His disciples as stated in Matthew 18.

> *"Again I say to you that if two of you agree on earth concerning anything that they ask, it will be done for them by My Father in Heaven.* [20] *For where two or three are gathered together in My name, I am there in the midst of them." (Matthew 18:19–20 NKJV).*

There are some denominations that, although calling themselves Christian, do not adhere fully to the doctrine of being born again. Part of their theology or belief is reflected in a hymn written by John S. Jones in 1881. The first stanza says: "I was made a Christian when my name was giv'n, One of God's dear children, And an heir of Heaven. In the name of Christian I will glory now, Evermore remember my baptismal vow."

This has been described by some people as old theology but the hymn is still sung in some churches. Whether it is old theology or not, it is certainly not biblical and you as a Christian must ensure that everything that you do on this Christian walk is biblical or has grounding in the Bible.

Be warned: the same way that you can choose to be born again, you can decide to break the relationship with Jesus Christ and die spiritually.

> *"Therefore, brethren, we are debtors—not to the flesh, to live according to the flesh.* [13] *For if you live according to the flesh you will die; but if by the Spirit you put to death the deeds of the body, you will live.* [14] *For as many as are led by the Spirit of God, these are sons of God." (Romans 8:12–13 NKJV).*

The choice is yours. Make the right one. Either way there are consequences.

Chapter 2

Why Must I Be Born Again?

You may ask, "Why do I have to be born again?" The answer is simple: the Bible says in Romans, chapter three, verse 23 that all have sinned and come short of the glory of God. That means that we are all born as sinners. To get out of that situation or to change our status and have any hope of spending eternity with God, we must be born again.

What makes it even more important is the fact that Jesus Christ Himself said that it must be done. He told Nicodemus in chapter three of John's Gospel:

> ***"Except a man be born again, he cannot see the kingdom of God." (John 3:3 KJV).***

Before we accept Christ as our Savior we are spiritually dead to sin. This is because of the disobedience of Adam and Eve, the first people created. For their sin of disobedience, they were evicted from the Garden. Because of their sin, God cursed the ground and told Adam he would have great difficulty cultivating it with produce to feed himself. Eve's punishment was difficult childbirth.

Adam's sin caused a separation or a break in the relationship between God and man, and everyone coming after him was born a sinner or not having the Spirit of God in them. Psalm 51 shows that because man was born with a sin spirit and without God living inside of him, he has no part with God.

> *"Behold, I was brought forth in iniquity, and in sin my mother conceived me." (Psalm 51:5 NKJV).*

To be reconciled to God you must be born again. You must accept Jesus Christ as Savior, let His Holy Spirit come to live in you and thus experience spiritual birth.

You are born again or saved by grace through faith in Jesus Christ, as stated in Ephesians, chapter two.

> *"And you He made alive, who were dead in trespasses and sins, 2 in which you once walked according to the course of this world, according to the prince of the power of the air, the spirit who now works in the sons of disobedience, 3 among whom also we all once conducted ourselves in the lusts of our flesh, fulfilling the desires of the flesh and of the mind, and were by nature children of wrath, just as the others. 4 But God, who is rich in mercy, because of His great love with which He loved us, 5 even when we were dead in trespasses, made us alive together with Christ (by grace you have been saved), 6 and raised us up together, and made us sit together in the Heavenly places in Christ Jesus, 7 that in the ages to come He might show the exceeding riches of His grace in His kindness toward us in Christ Jesus. 8 For by grace you have been saved through faith, and that not of yourselves; it is the gift of*

> *God, [9] not of works, lest anyone should boast. [10] For we are His workmanship, created in Christ Jesus for good works, which God prepared beforehand that we should walk in them. [11] Therefore remember that you, once Gentiles in the flesh—who are called Uncircumcision by what is called the Circumcision made in the flesh by hands— [12] that at that time you were without Christ, being aliens from the commonwealth of Israel and strangers from the covenants of promise, having no hope and without God in the world. [13] But now in Christ Jesus you who once were far off have been brought near by the blood of Christ." (Ephesians 2:1–13 NKJV).*

Here is the same passage taken from the New Living Translation:

> *"Once you were dead because of your disobedience and your many sins. [2] You used to live in sin, just like the rest of the world, obeying the devil—the commander of the powers in the unseen world. He is the spirit at work in the hearts of those who refuse to obey God. [3] All of us used to live that way, following the passionate desires and inclinations of our sinful nature. By our very nature we were subject to God's anger, just like everyone else. [4] But God is so rich in mercy, and he loved us so much, [5] that even though we were dead because of our sins, he gave us life when he raised Christ from the dead. (It is only by God's grace that you*

have been saved!) [6] For he raised us from the dead along with Christ and seated us with him in the Heavenly realms because we are united with Christ Jesus. [7] So God can point to us in all future ages as examples of the incredible wealth of his grace and kindness toward us, as shown in all he has done for us who are united with Christ Jesus. [8] God saved you by his grace when you believed. And you can't take credit for this; it is a gift from God. [9] Salvation is not a reward for the good things we have done, so none of us can boast about it. [10] For we are God's masterpiece. He has created us anew in Christ Jesus, so we can do the good things he planned for us long ago. [11] Don't forget that you Gentiles used to be outsiders. You were called 'uncircumcised heathens' by the Jews, who were proud of their circumcision, even though it affected only their bodies and not their hearts. [12] In those days you were living apart from Christ. You were excluded from citizenship among the people of Israel, and you did not know the covenant promises God had made to them. You lived in this world without God and without hope. [13] But now you have been united with Christ Jesus. Once you were far away from God, but now you have been brought near to him through the blood of Christ." (Ephesians 2:1–13 NLT).

Some people say that they are good and don't commit sin. But even if we try to be good, we still would not qualify to spend eternity in Heaven. For your information, the only person who was without sin was Jesus Christ. He was born of a virgin and was the only begotten son of God. He was sinless because God was His father. This story can be found in Matthew 1: 18–25; Matthew 2:1–12; Luke 1:26–38, and Luke 2:1–20.

You may ask, "What is this big idea of the Spirit of God living within me?" In the book of Romans, chapter eight, verse nine, Paul says the Spirit of Christ dwells within every Believer. The King James Version puts it this way:

> *"What? Know ye not that your body is the temple of the Holy Ghost which is in you, which ye have of God, and ye are not your own? For ye are bought with a price: therefore glorify God in your body, and in your spirit, which are God's." (Romans 8:9 KJV).*

The New International Version of the Bible has this translation:

> *"Do you not know that your bodies are temples of the Holy Spirit, who is in you, whom you have received from God? You are not your own; you were bought at a price. Therefore honor God with your bodies." (Romans 8:9 NIV).*

Man is tripartite, in that he is made up of body, soul, and spirit, with the body being the temporary home of the soul and spirit. The soul is the heart or that ability to feel emotion, to think, and to make decisions. The real person inside of us is the spirit and this determines spiritual matters and, as stated in the book of Ecclesiastes, chapter 12, verse seven, when we die our spirit returns to God.

Soul and spirit may seem very similar or to be the same, but the Bible makes it clear in Hebrews chapter four, verse 12 where the writer describes the word of God as being:

> *"Quick, and powerful, and sharper than any two edged sword, piercing even to the dividing asunder of soul and spirit, and of the joints and marrow, and is a discerner of the thoughts and intents of the heart." (Hebrews 4:12 NKJV).*

So it stands to reason that in order to overcome sin we must be born again and receive the Holy Spirit or the Spirit of God. It is this Spirit which is paramount in helping us to live Christian lives.

As you start your Christian journey you will experience the battle between your wayward spirit and the Holy Spirit. There will be times when you will be tempted to do things that are not right, but through the leading of the Holy Spirit, you will know that they are wrong, and you must not give in.

Do not think that this struggle between your spirit and the Holy Spirit is unique to you. Paul the apostle, who wrote the majority of the books in the New Testament, had the same challenges and he wrote about it in Romans seven:

> *"For we know that the law is spiritual, but I am carnal, sold under sin. [15] For what I am doing, I do not understand. For what I will to do, that I do not practice; but what I hate, that I do. [16] If, then, I do what I will not to do, I agree with the law that it is good. [17] But now, it is no longer I who do it, but sin that dwells in me. [18] For I know that in me (that is, in my flesh) nothing good dwells; for to will is present with me, but how to perform*

what is good I do not find. [19] For the good that I will to do, I do not do; but the evil I will not to do, that I practice. [20] Now if I do what I will not to do, it is no longer I who do it, but sin that dwells in me. [21] I find then a law, that evil is present with me, the one who wills to do good. [22] For I delight in the law of God according to the inward man. [23] But I see another law in my members, warring against the law of my mind, and bringing me into captivity to the law of sin which is in my members. [24] O wretched man that I am! Who will deliver me from this body of death? [25] I thank God—through Jesus Christ our Lord! So then, with the mind I myself serve the law of God, but with the flesh the law of sin." (Romans 7:14–25 NKJV).

The same passage may be better understood in the New Living Translation:

"So the trouble is not with the law, for it is spiritual and good. The trouble is with me, for I am all too human, a slave to sin. [15] I don't really understand myself, for I want to do what is right, but I don't do it. Instead, I do what I hate. [16] But if I know that what I am doing is wrong, this shows that I agree that the law is good. [17] So I am not the one doing wrong; it is sin living in me that does it. [18] And I know that nothing good lives in me, that is, in my sinful nature. I want to do what is right, but I can't. [19] I want to do what is good, but I don't. I don't want to do what is wrong, but I do it anyway. [20] But if I

> *do what I don't want to do, I am not really the one doing wrong; it is sin living in me that does it. [21] I have discovered this principle of life—that when I want to do what is right, I inevitably do what is wrong. [22] I love God's law with all my heart. [23] But there is another power within me that is at war with my mind. This power makes me a slave to the sin that is still within me. [24] Oh, what a miserable person I am! Who will free me from this life that is dominated by sin and death? [25] Thank God! The answer is in Jesus Christ our Lord. So you see how it is: In my mind I really want to obey God's law, but because of my sinful nature I am a slave to sin." (Romans 7:14–25 NLT).*

Being religious does not make you born again. In other words, religion or denomination does not make you a Christian. Nicodemus, the man who was told by Jesus in John chapter three that he must be born again, was very religious. He was a Pharisee, one of the most religious sects of that day. He was a great teacher of the law and, because of his religion, would have tried to observe the Old Testament laws.

Jesus rebuked the Pharisees and the scribes for being religious and reminded them that this had been predicted way back in the Old Testament. Jesus was at the time being questioned by the Pharisees about some of the actions of His disciples in not keeping certain traditions, like washing their hands before eating.

> He said to them, ***"Well did Isaiah prophesy of you hypocrites, as it is written: 'This people honors Me with their lips, But their heart is***

> *far from Me. [7] And in vain they worship Me, teaching as doctrines the commandments of men.' [8] For laying aside the commandment of God, you hold the tradition of men—the washing of pitchers and cups, and many other such things you do'." [9] He said to them, "All too well you reject the commandment of God, that you may keep your tradition." (Mark 7:6–9 NKJV).*

There are a lot of people who say they are Christians and honestly believe that they are. They go to church, serve in the church, live upright and do all sorts of good things, but have never been born again. Some denominations that claim to be Christian even use rituals and forms of worship that are not biblical and that require no declaration of a commitment to Jesus Christ or His teachings.

Being born again or being a Christian, is based on faith and a relationship with Jesus Christ and is therefore much more than following a set of rules, traditions, and principles. Jesus told Nicodemus that in order to spend eternity with Him he had to be born again and the same goes for everyone, regardless of religion.

Living a Christian life is a daily exercise and those who are born again will face struggles. John the apostle, in chapter three of his first epistle, stressed how a born again Believer will respond to these attacks:

> *"Whoever abides in Him does not sin. Whoever sins has neither seen Him nor known Him. [7] Little children, let no one deceive you. He who practices righteousness is righteous, just as He is righteous. [8]He who sins is of the devil, for the devil has sinned from the beginning. For this purpose the Son of God*

> *was manifested, that He might destroy the works of the devil. [9] Whoever has been born of God does not sin, for His seed remains in him; and he cannot sin, because he has been born of God." (1 John 3:6–9 NKJV).*

The born again Christian will be tempted to sin but must, through the help of the Holy Spirit, resist. You can expect that the devil will continue his efforts to try to get you to return to your old ways. Be strong and be of good courage. Respond to the bidding and guidance of the Holy Spirit.

Chapter 3

How Can I Be Born Again?

To be born again you must come to the realization that you are a sinner and admit it. You must then exercise the faith to make the sincere decision to follow Jesus Christ, ask His forgiveness, and invite Him to come into your heart. This is the most significant event in the life of anyone.

Chapter 10 of the book of Romans says:

> *"That if you confess with your mouth the Lord Jesus and believe in your heart that God has raised Him from the dead, you will be saved.*
> *10 For with the heart one believes unto righteousness, and with the mouth confession is made unto salvation. 11 For the Scripture says, 'Whoever believes on Him will not be put to shame.' 12 For there is no distinction between Jew and Greek, for the same Lord over all is rich to all who call upon Him. 13 For 'whoever calls on the name of the Lord shall be saved'." (Romans 10:9–13 NKJV).*

Romans chapter eight says:

"The Spirit Himself bears witness with our spirit that we are children of God, [17] and if children, then heirs—heirs of God and joint heirs with Christ." (Romans 8:16–17 NKJV).

The Living Bible puts it this way:

"For his Holy Spirit speaks to us deep in our hearts and tells us that we really are God's children." (Romans 8:16–17 TLB).

There have been arguments and debates over just when you become born again. Some say that it is a process while others say it is immediate. The thief on the cross showed that being born again happens immediately. When he asked Jesus to remember him when He comes into His kingdom, Jesus immediately replied as recorded in verse 43, of chapter 23 in the Gospel of Luke:

"Assuredly, I say to you, today you will be with Me in Paradise." (Luke 23:43 NKJV).

In asking Jesus Christ to come into your heart you must believe that His blood was shed so that you would not have to face the terrible fate of spending eternity in hell. Jesus' blood is the only thing that can cleanse you from sin and by asking Him to cleanse you with that blood, His spirit dwells in you and you are born again.

In John chapter 14, verse six, Jesus said:

"I am the way the truth and the life, no man cometh to the father but by me." (John 14:6 KJV).

When you are born again, you receive eternal life from God Himself.

> *"Grace and peace be multiplied to you in the knowledge of God and of Jesus our Lord, [3] as His divine power has given to us all things that pertain to life and godliness, through the knowledge of Him who called us by glory and virtue, [4] by which have been given to us exceedingly great and precious promises, that through these you may be partakers of the divine nature, having escaped the corruption that is in the world through lust." (2 Peter 1:2–4 NKJV).*

The New Living Translation puts this in much simpler language.

> *"By his divine power, God has given us everything we need for living a godly life. We have received all of this by coming to know Him, the one who called us to himself by means of His marvelous glory and excellence. [4] And because of His glory and excellence, He has given us great and precious promises. These are the promises that enable you to share His divine nature and escape the world's corruption caused by human desires." (2 Peter 1:2–4 NLT).*

John, in chapter five of his first epistle, also spoke of receiving eternal life through Jesus Christ:

> *"And this is the testimony: that God has given us eternal life, and this life is in His Son. [12] He who has the Son has life; he who does not have the Son of God does not have life. [13] These things I have written to you who believe in the name of the Son of God, that you may know that you have eternal life, and that you may continue to believe in the name of the Son of God." (1 John 5:11–13 NKJV).*

Being born again, or being regenerated, makes you a new person who is righteous and holy.

> *"Therefore, if anyone is in Christ, he is a new creation; old things have passed away; behold, all things have become new. [18] Now all things are of God, who has reconciled us to Himself through Jesus Christ, and has given us the ministry of reconciliation, [19] that is, that God was in Christ reconciling the world to Himself, not imputing their trespasses to them, and has committed to us the word of reconciliation. [20] Now then, we are ambassadors for Christ, as though God were pleading through us: we implore you on Christ's behalf, be reconciled to God. [21] For He made Him who knew no sin to be sin for us, that we might become the righteousness of God in Him." (2 Corinthians 5:17–21 NKJV).*

Being born again also makes you a child of God:

> *"But as many as received Him, to them He gave the right to become children of God, to those who believe in His name: [13] who were born, not of blood, nor of the will of the flesh, nor of the will of man, but of God." (John 1:12–13 NKJV).*

In order to be born again you must repent of your sins. This means admitting to and rejecting the wrong that you have been doing and completely turning away from your present lifestyle.

To be born again also means that you are now converted and going in the opposite direction with Jesus Christ. Once you have confessed that you are a sinner, repented, and asked Jesus to come into your heart, He forgives you. Through His shed blood your sins are taken away and you are now as if you had never sinned.

Jesus told His disciples that no one can become one of His followers unless the Holy Spirit draws him.

> *"No one can come to Me unless the Father who sent Me draws him; and I will raise him up at the last day. [45] It is written in the prophets, 'And they shall all be taught by God.' Therefore everyone who has heard and learned from the Father comes to Me. [46]Not that anyone has seen the Father, except He who is from God; He has seen the Father. [47] Most assuredly, I say to you, he who believes in Me has everlasting life." (John 6:44–47 NKJV).*

Being born again is the first step in a process of regeneration or the beginning of a new spiritual life. It involves a transition from sin to a new life, believing in Jesus Christ, and doing His will, as set out in the Bible. Being born again also means that you are now willing to live righteously, avoiding sin and truly extending love to those around you.

> *When you were slaves to sin, you were free from the obligation to do right. [21] And what was the result? You are now ashamed of the things you used to do, things that end in eternal doom. [22] But now you are free from the power of sin and have become slaves of God. Now you do those things that lead to holiness and result in eternal life. [23] For the wages of sin is death, but the free gift of God is eternal life through Christ Jesus our Lord. (Romans 6:20–23 NLT).*

But living righteously is not easy, as the devil will always be after you. The good thing is that Jesus Christ, whom we know as our Savior, intercedes with the Father for us and so forgiveness is available.

> *"My little children, these things I write to you, so that you may not sin. And if anyone sins, we have an advocate with the Father, Jesus Christ the righteous. [2] And He Himself is the propitiation for our sins, and not for ours only but also for the whole world." (1 John 2:1–2 NKJV).*

The assurance that God is faithful in the midst of trials is also found in the book of Romans.

> *"Who shall bring a charge against God's elect? It is God who justifies. [34] Who is he who condemns? It is Christ who died, and furthermore*

> *is also risen, who is even at the right hand of God, who also makes intercession for us." (Romans 8:33–34 NKJV).*

Jesus has also been described as the High Priest who appeals to God on behalf of the born again Christian. This is written in chapter seven of the book of Hebrews where it is pointed out that, whereas in the past the High Priest was the one to make intercession, Jesus Christ now has that role.

> *"And inasmuch as He was not made priest without an oath [21] (for they have become priests without an oath, but He with an oath by Him who said to Him: 'The Lord has sworn and will not relent, you are a priest forever, according to the order of Melchizedek'"), [22] by so much more Jesus has become a surety of a better covenant. [23] Also there were many priests, because they were prevented by death from continuing. [24] But He, because He continues forever, has an unchangeable priesthood. [25] Therefore He is also able to save to the uttermost those who come to God through Him, since He always lives to make intercession for them. For such a High Priest was fitting for us, who is holy, harmless, undefiled, separate from sinners, and has become higher than the Heavens; [27] who does not need daily, as those high priests, to offer up sacrifices, first for His own sins and then for the people's, for this He did once for all when He offered up Himself. [28] For the law appoints as high priests men who have weakness, but the word of the oath, which*

came after the law, appoints the Son who has been perfected forever." (Hebrews 7:20–28 NKJV).

Born again Believers must at all times strive to obey God's Word, for this is a confirmation that we belong to Him. To obey God's word at all times is one objective but should not be held as the confirmation, for we do fail at times on this journey.

"Now by this we know that we know Him, if we keep His commandments. [4] He who says, 'I know Him,' and does not keep His commandments, is a liar, and the truth is not in him. [5] But whoever keeps His word, truly the love of God is perfected in him. By this we know that we are in Him. [6] He who says he abides in Him ought himself also to walk just as He walked." (1 John 2:3–6 NKJV).

The born again Believer is warned not to love the things of the world.

"If anyone loves the world, the love of the Father is not in him. [16] For all that is in the world—the lust of the flesh, the lust of the eyes, and the pride of life—is not of the Father but is of the world. [17] And the world is passing away, and the lust of it; but he who does the will of God abides forever" (1 John 2:15–17 NKJV).

Being born again requires a sustained, personal relationship with Jesus Christ. In chapter 15 of John's Gospel, Jesus likened this relationship to a grapevine. He described Himself as the True Vine and God the Father as the person who takes care of the vine.

> *"Abide in Me, and I in you. As the branch cannot bear fruit of itself, unless it abides in the vine, neither can you, unless you abide in Me. [5] "I am the vine, you are the branches. He who abides in Me, and I in him, bears much fruit; for without Me you can do nothing. [6] If anyone does not abide in Me, he is cast out as a branch and is withered; and they gather them and throw them into the fire, and they are burned. [7] If you abide in Me, and My words abide in you, you will ask what you desire, and it shall be done for you. [8] By this My Father is glorified, that you bear much fruit; so you will be My disciples. [9] "As the Father loved Me, I also have loved you; abide in My love. [10] If you keep My commandments, you will abide in My love, just as I have kept My Father's commandments and abide in His love." (John 15:4–10 NKJV).*

The fruit that is being described here relates to the type of life the Christian lives. He or she is expected to exhibit qualities that bring glory to God. What Jesus is also saying here is that like any good gardener, the Father will remove the things that are preventing spiritual growth in the Believer and provide things that help him to live a holy life. Abiding in Jesus means that in the same way the branch depends on the vine for life, so too must we depend on Him. We must therefore constantly keep His Word as a guide to our lifestyle. There must also be such an intimate relationship with Him that we constantly draw strength and direction from Him.

We must also depend on the Holy Spirit for direction in order to resist the temptation to sin.

"For if you live according to the flesh you will die; but if by the Spirit you put to death the deeds of the body, you will live. [14] For as many as are led by the Spirit of God, these are sons of God. [15] For you did not receive the spirit of bondage again to fear, but you received the Spirit of adoption by whom we cry out, 'Abba, Father.' [16] The Spirit Himself bears witness with our spirit that we are children of God, [17] and if children, then heirs—heirs of God and joint heirs with Christ, if indeed we suffer with Him, that we may also be glorified together." (Romans 8:13–17 NKJV).

This passage may be better understood in the New Living Translation:

"Therefore, dear brothers and sisters, you have no obligation to do what your sinful nature urges you to do. [13] For if you live by its dictates, you will die. But if through the power of the Spirit you put to death the deeds of your sinful nature, you will live. [14] For all who are led by the Spirit of God are children of God. [15] So you have not received a spirit that makes you fearful slaves. Instead, you received God's Spirit when He adopted you as His own children. Now we call him, 'Abba, Father.' [16] For His Spirit joins with our spirit to affirm that we are God's children. [17] And since we are His children, we are His heirs. In fact, together with Christ we are heirs of God's glory. But if we are to share His glory, we must also share His suffering." (Romans 8:12–17 NLT).

The born again Christian must do what Paul described in Galatians chapter two as becoming dead to self.

> *"For I through the law died to the law that I might live to God. [20] I have been crucified with Christ; it is no longer I who live, but Christ lives in me; and the life which I now live in the flesh I live by faith in the Son of God, who loved me and gave Himself for me." (Galatians 2:19–20 NKJV).*

The New Living Translation expresses the same passage this way:

> *"For when I tried to keep the law, it condemned me. So I died to the law—I stopped trying to meet all its requirements—so that I might live for God. [20] My old self has been crucified with Christ it is no longer I who live, but Christ lives in me. So I live in this earthly body by trusting in the Son of God, who loved me and gave himself for me." (Galatians 2:19–20 NLT).*

When we "die to self" we put aside our old sinful ways and lifestyle and Christ lives in us. Paul also speaks of being "crucified with Christ" and this pertains to strongly putting aside the sinful nature and passionately perusing what pleases God.

> *"Now the works of the flesh are evident, which are: adultery, fornication, uncleanness, lewdness, [20] idolatry, sorcery, hatred, contentions, jealousies, outbursts of wrath, selfish ambitions, dissensions, heresies,*

> *[21] envy, murders, drunkenness, revelries, and
> the like; of which I tell you beforehand, just
> as I also told you in time past, that those
> who practice such things will not inherit
> the kingdom of God. [22] But the fruit of the
> Spirit is love, joy, peace, longsuffering, kind-
> ness, goodness, faithfulness, [23] gentleness,
> self-control. Against such there is no law.
> [24] And those who are Christ's have crucified
> the flesh with its passions and desires. [25] If
> we live in the Spirit, let us also walk in the
> Spirit. [26] Let us not become conceited, pro-
> voking one another, envying one another."
> (Galatians 5:19–26 NKJV).*

The New Living Translation of this passage gives a more in-depth look at what Paul was saying:

> *"When you follow the desires of your sinful
> nature, the results are very clear: sexual
> immorality, impurity, lustful pleasures, [20] idol-
> atry, sorcery, hostility, quarreling, jealousy,
> outbursts of anger, selfish ambition, dissen-
> sion, division, [21] envy, drunkenness, wild par-
> ties, and other sins like these. Let me tell
> you again, as I have before, that anyone
> living that sort of life will not inherit the
> Kingdom of God. [22] But the Holy Spirit pro-
> duces this kind of fruit in our lives: love, joy,
> peace, patience, kindness, goodness, faith-
> fulness, [23] gentleness, and self-control. There
> is no law against these things! [24] Those who
> belong to Christ Jesus have nailed the pas-
> sions and desires of their sinful nature to
> his cross and crucified them there. [25] Since*

we are living by the Spirit, let us follow the Spirit's leading in every part of our lives. [26] Let us not become conceited, or provoke one another, or be jealous of one another." (Galatians 5:19–26 NLT).

A born again Christian can, with confidence, say like the prophet Isaiah:

"O LORD, I will praise You; Though You were angry with me, Your anger is turned away, and You comfort me. [2]Behold, God is my salvation, I will trust and not be afraid; 'For YAH, the LORD, is my strength and song; He also has become my salvation.'" [3] Therefore with joy you will draw water from the wells of salvation." (Isaiah 12:1–3 NKJV).

Chapter 4

What Is Sin?

According to biblical standards, anything that can be considered bad or not right is sin. The Bible says in 1 John, chapter five, verse 17 that all unrighteousness is sin. Sin is the transgression of God's law. Although there are many aspects of it, God condemns and hates all sin.

Sin is described in the Bible as, among other things, transgression or wrongdoing, wickedness, injustice, a lack of love, selfishness, immorality, disobedience, and not believing in God.

John the apostle was very specific in chapter three of his first epistle about those who commit sin and under whose power they operate.

> *"Whoever commits sin also commits lawlessness, and sin is lawlessness. [5] And you know that He was manifested to take away our sins, and in Him there is no sin. [6] Whoever abides in Him does not sin. Whoever sins has neither seen Him nor known Him. [7] Little children, let no one deceive you. He who practices righteousness is righteous, just as He is righteous. [8] He who sins is of the devil, for the devil has sinned from the beginning. For this purpose the Son of God was manifested, that He might destroy the works of*

> *the devil. [9] Whoever has been born of God does not sin, for His seed remains in him; and he cannot sin, because he has been born of God." (1 John 3:4–9 NKJV).*

Sin entered the world because Adam, the first man, disobeyed God. He had been instructed not to eat the fruit of the "tree of the knowledge of good and evil" but, under the urgings of his wife, Eve, he did it. For their sin of disobedience Adam and Eve were banished from the Garden of Eden. Their actions resulted in spiritual death for all mankind. Consequently we are all born sinners and that is why we sin.

Several examples of sin can be found in Galatians chapter five, verses 19 to 21.

> *"Now the works of the flesh are evident, which are: adultery, fornication, uncleanness, lewdness, [20] idolatry, sorcery, hatred, contentions, jealousies, outbursts of wrath, selfish ambitions, dissensions, heresies, [21] envy, murders, drunkenness, revelries, and the like; of which I tell you beforehand, just as I also told you in time past, that those who practice such things will not inherit the kingdom of God." (Galatians 5:19–21 NKJV).*

Romans chapter one also lists a number of sins.

> *"And even as they did not like to retain God in their knowledge, God gave them over to a debased mind, to do those things which are not fitting; [29] being filled with all unrighteousness, sexual immorality, wickedness, covetousness, maliciousness; full of envy, murder, strife, deceit, evil-mindedness;*

> *they are whisperers, [30] back-biters, haters of God, violent, proud, boasters, inventors of evil things, disobedient to parents, [31] undiscerning, untrustworthy, unloving, unforgiving, unmerciful; [32] who, knowing the righteous judgment of God, that those who practice such things are deserving of death, not only do the same but also approve of those who practice them." (Romans 1:28–32 NKJV).*

Although you may have committed your life to Jesus Christ, the sinful nature remains in the Christian and presents a constant battle with your spirit. However, although the born again Christian will sin, it will not be habitual.

The first chapter of the first epistle of John states:

> *"If we say that we have no sin, we deceive ourselves, and the truth is not in us. [9] If we confess our sins, He is faithful and just to forgive us our sins and to cleanse us from all unrighteousness. [10] If we say that we have not sinned, we make Him a liar, and His word is not in us." (1 John 1:9–10 NKJV).*

Although we must strive for perfection, it does not mean that we will be perfect. The old nature will always be at war with the new, and this battle can only be won through the power of the Holy Spirit living in you.

One of the sins that could affect the Believer is that of adultery. This relates to married people having sexual intercourse or committing immoral acts with people other than their spouse. A similar sin is fornication, which is sexual intercourse between two unmarried people. The only right sexual activity is that between a man and a woman who are married to each other.

This sin of adultery could stretch beyond physical activity to secret thoughts and desires. Jesus makes this clear in Matthew's Gospel, chapter five, verses 27 and 28. Delivering what is popularly referred to as "The Sermon on The Mount" He had this to say:

> *"You have heard that it was said to those of old, 'You shall not commit adultery.' [28] But I say to you that whoever looks at a woman to lust for her has already committed adultery with her in his heart." (Matthew 5:27–28 NKJV).*

The Bible also refers to the sin of uncleanness and lasciviousness, and these relate to sensuality and things like committing shameless acts in public.

In the Ten Commandments God specifically tells His people that they should not worship idols. This does not only relate to man-made statues or figurines, but includes the worshipping of spirits, people, or images.

To treat any person, institution, or thing as being equal to or greater than God is also a grave sin.

Witchcraft is also considered a very serious sin. This covers sorcery, spiritism, obeah, voodoo, black magic, the worshipping of demons, and using narcotic drugs to produce a spiritual experience.

The Bible lists hatred as a sin to be avoided. In fact it says in 1 John, chapter three, verse 15 that anyone who hates his brother is a murderer. Hatred is extreme dislike and also includes intense, hostile intentions and acts against other people. Similar to this is wrath, which is explosive anger that could escalate into violent words or acts.

Christians are also warned about the sin of what the Bible calls variance. This involves quarrelling and antagonism, and could even extend to struggling for superiority.

The Book of Galatians also identifies the sin of emulations, which has been described as resentfulness or even envy of the success of another person.

Christians are also cautioned against strife and the seeking of power or positions by unrighteous means.

Those Believers who would want to introduce teachings that are not supported by the Bible have been told that to do such would be to commit the sin of seditions.

Another sin that is very similar to seditions is that of heresies. This is about bringing divisions within the church and disrupting its unity.

The sin of envy could also creep in among Christians. This is resentment and dislike of someone because that person has something that you really want.

Many Christians say they still drink alcoholic beverages but they should be very careful about this activity. Galatians chapter five, verse 21 warns about drunkenness. Excessive drinking of alcoholic beverages could lead to impaired mental and physical control.

Solomon, the wisest man who ever lived, warned about imbibing too much alcohol.

> ***"Wine is a mocker, strong drink is raging: and whosoever is deceived thereby is not wise." (Proverbs 20:1 KJV).***

The Living Bible puts it in more modern language:

> ***"Wine gives false courage; hard liquor leads to brawls; what fools men are to let it master them, making them reel drunkenly down the street!" (Proverbs 20:1 TLB).***

In these times many people are falling prey to the sin of reveling or "having a good time". Christians must be careful not to be caught up in "the party spirit". You must not get involved in excessive feasting, revelry, activities that include drinking too much alcoholic beverages, using illegal narcotic drugs, engaging in immoral sex, or things of that nature.

But sin is not a modern-day thing. It has been present since the days of Adam in the Garden of Eden and has not stopped.

The Old Testament tells the story of how God chose the Israelites to be His people and how they disobeyed Him. Even while He was taking them out of Egyptian slavery they rebelled and He introduced a set of rules by which they were supposed to live. These are known as the Ten Commandments and can be found in the book of Exodus, chapter 20, verses seven to 17.

The Commandments, which apply even today, state clearly that the name of God must always be taken seriously and it should never be used obscenely or in curses or things of that nature.

God also commanded that people should honor their parents, never commit murder, never steal, never commit adultery, and never be involved in lies or deception.

He also specifically instructed that you should not lust after your neighbor's spouse, his property, or anything that belongs to him.

All those things that God advised against are sins and could be described as moral laws.

The truth of the matter is that, no matter how good we think we are, we were all born as sinners. The New King James Version of the Bible says in Romans three, verse 23:

> *"For all have sinned, and fallen short of the glory of God." (Romans 3:23 NKJV).*

Chapter six, verse 23 of the same book states:

> *"For the wages of sin is death, but the gift of God is eternal life in Christ Jesus our Lord." (Romans 6:23 NKJV).*

We are all sinners having been born without the Spirit of God in us.

The New Living Translation of the Bible sets out in Romans chapter five how the sin of Adam has affected our lives:

> *"When Adam sinned, sin entered the world.*
> *Adam's sin brought death, so death spread*
> *to everyone, for everyone sinned. [13] Yes,*
> *people sinned even before the law was*
> *given. But it was not counted as sin because*
> *there was not yet any law to break. [14] Still,*
> *everyone died—from the time of Adam to*
> *the time of Moses—even those who did not*
> *disobey an explicit commandment of God,*
> *as Adam did. Now Adam is a symbol, a rep-*
> *resentation of Christ, who was yet to come.*
> *[15] But there is a great difference between*
> *Adam's sin and God's gracious gift. For the*
> *sin of this one man, Adam, brought death to*
> *many. But even greater is God's wonderful*
> *grace and his gift of forgiveness to many*
> *through this other man, Jesus Christ. [16] And*
> *the result of God's gracious gift is very dif-*
> *ferent from the result of that one man's sin.*
> *For Adam's sin led to condemnation, but*
> *God's free gift leads to our being made right*
> *with God, even though we are guilty of many*
> *sins. [17] For the sin of this one man, Adam,*

caused death to rule over many. But even greater is God's wonderful grace and his gift of righteousness, for all who receive it will live in triumph over sin and death through this one man, Jesus Christ. [18] Yes, Adam's one sin brings condemnation for everyone, but Christ's one act of righteousness brings a right relationship with God and new life for everyone. [19] Because one person disobeyed God, many became sinners. But because one other person obeyed God, many will be made righteous.[20] God's law was given so that all people could see how sinful they were. But as people sinned more and more, God's wonderful grace became more abundant. [21] So just as sin ruled over all people and brought them to death, now God's wonderful grace rules instead, giving us right standing with God and resulting in eternal life through Jesus Christ our Lord." (Romans 5:12–21 NLT).

In the book of Galatians, Paul states clearly that all who sin and do not repent will not enter Heaven. The Bible also states that the penalty for sin is eternal death. This has been described as spending eternity in hell, a place that has been reserved for Satan and those who follow him.

We are by nature sinners condemned to eternal death. Because of our sin nature we will be tempted to sin but this is a choice. Through the death of Jesus Christ there is now room for repentance and forgiveness.

"If we confess our sins, He is faithful and just to forgive us our sins and to cleanse us from all unrighteousness." (1 John 1:9 NKJV).

While we can expect forgiveness when we repent, there is one sin that the Bible says will not be forgiven. Jesus spoke to this in chapter 12 of Matthew's Gospel. He had healed a man who was demon possessed, deaf, and mute. The religious leaders of the day accused Him of doing it through Beelzebub, the ruler of the demons. Jesus rejected their claims.

> *"Anyone who isn't with me opposes me, and anyone who isn't working with me is actually working against me. [31] So I tell you, every sin and blasphemy can be forgiven—except blasphemy against the Holy Spirit, which will never be forgiven. [32] Anyone who speaks against the Son of Man can be forgiven, but anyone who speaks against the Holy Spirit will never be forgiven, either in this world or in the world to come." (Matthew 12:30–32 NLT).*

Some theologians believe that blasphemy against the Holy Spirit relates to a persistent and willful rejection of God. This, some say, could be done through repeatedly cursing God or attributing some evil to Him.

That is certainly a sin to be avoided at all cost.

Chapter 5

Salvation: Saved from Sin

Salvation or "to be saved" as a Christian, is to be freed from sin through the grace or unmerited love and favor of God. It relates to giving up your sinful ways, committing your life to God, and following and adhering to the teachings of Jesus Christ. Until you do this you are considered "lost in sin".

Being saved means that you are in right standing with Jesus Christ, have a personal relationship with Him, and have the hope and belief that you will not spend eternity in hell. You are therefore saved to spend eternity in Heaven with God.

Salvation is not just about being spared from going to hell but involves a commitment to an intimate and holy relationship with God. It also must be reflected by love for others and doing good deeds.

The epistle to the Romans says in verse 23 of chapter three that ***"all have sinned and come short of the glory of God."*** Ezekiel chapter 18, verse 20 makes a very serious statement: ***"The soul that sinneth it shall die." (Ezekiel 18:20 KJV).*** This means that everyone needs to accept Jesus Christ as Savior.

To be saved therefore means that with God's forgiveness the Christian is now free from the bondage and conviction of sin. This brings the born again Believer into fellowship with God through Jesus Christ and the indwelling Holy Spirit.

So now there is no condemnation for those who belong to Christ Jesus. 2 And because you belong to him, the power of the life-giving Spirit has freed you from the power of sin that leads to death. 3 The law of Moses was unable to save us because of the weakness of our sinful nature. So God did what the law could not do. He sent his own Son in a body like the bodies we sinners have. And in that body God declared an end to sin's control over us by giving his Son as a sacrifice for our sins. 4 He did this so that the just requirement of the law would be fully satisfied for us, who no longer follow our sinful nature but instead follow the Spirit. 5 Those who are dominated by the sinful nature think about sinful things, but those who are controlled by the Holy Spirit think about things that please the Spirit. 6 So letting your sinful nature control your mind leads to death. But letting the Spirit control your mind leads to life and peace. 7 For the sinful nature is always hostile to God. It never did obey God's laws, and it never will. 8 That's why those who are still under the control of their sinful nature can never please God.

9 But you are not controlled by your sinful nature. You are controlled by the Spirit if you have the Spirit of God living in you. (And remember that those who do not have the Spirit of Christ living in them do not belong to him at all.) 10 And Christ lives within you, so even though your body will die because of sin, the Spirit gives you life because you

> *have been made right with God. [11] The Spirit of God, who raised Jesus from the dead, lives in you. And just as God raised Christ Jesus from the dead, he will give life to your mortal bodies by this same Spirit living within you.*
>
> *[12] Therefore, dear brothers and sisters, you have no obligation to do what your sinful nature urges you to do. [13] For if you live by its dictates, you will die. But if through the power of the Spirit you put to death the deeds of your sinful nature, you will live. [14] For all who are led by the Spirit of God are children of God. (Romans 8:1–14 NLT).*

Salvation is a gift from God and comes when, through faith, you firmly accept and trust in the crucified and risen Son of God as your personal Lord and Savior. Ephesians chapter two clearly shows that it is only by God's grace that you can achieve this status:

> *"Once you were dead because of your disobedience and your many sins. [2] You used to live in sin, just like the rest of the world, obeying the devil—the commander of the powers in the unseen world. He is the spirit at work in the hearts of those who refuse to obey God. [3] All of us used to live that way, following the passionate desires and inclinations of our sinful nature. By our very nature we were subject to God's anger, just like everyone else. [4] But God is so rich in mercy, and he loved us so much, [5] that even though we were dead because of our sins,*

> *He gave us life when He raised Christ from the dead. (It is only by God's grace that you have been saved!) [6] For He raised us from the dead along with Christ and seated us with Him in the Heavenly realms because we are united with Christ Jesus. [7] So God can point to us in all future ages as examples of the incredible wealth of His grace and kindness toward us, as shown in all He has done for us who are united with Christ Jesus. [8] God saved you by his grace when you believed. And you can't take credit for this; it is a gift from God. [9]Salvation is not a reward for the good things we have done, so none of us can boast about it. [10] For we are God's masterpiece. He has created us anew in Christ Jesus, so we can do the good things He planned for us long ago." (Ephesians 2:1–10 NLT).*

Salvation follows repentance and comes immediately on genuinely accepting Jesus Christ as Savior.

> *For Moses writes about the righteousness which is of the law, "The man who does those things shall live by them." [6] But the righteousness of faith speaks in this way; do not say in your heart, 'Who will ascend into Heaven?'" (that is, to bring Christ down from above) [7]or, 'Who will descend into the abyss?' (that is, to bring Christ up from the dead). [8] But what does it say? The word is near you, in your mouth and in your heart' (that is, the word of faith which we preach): [9] that if you confess with your mouth the*

> *Lord Jesus and believe in your heart that God has raised Him from the dead, you will be saved. [10] For with the heart one believes unto righteousness, and with the mouth confession is made unto salvation." (Romans 10:5–10 NKJV).*

The New Living Translation of that passage explains it even more:

> *"For Moses writes that the law's way of making a person right with God requires obedience to all of its commands. [6]But faith's way of getting right with God says, 'Don't say in your heart, Who will go up to Heaven?' (to bring Christ down to earth). [7]And don't say, 'Who will go down to the place of the dead?' (to bring Christ back to life again). [8]In fact, it says, 'The message is very close at hand; it is on your lips and in your heart.' And that message is the very message about faith that we preach: [9] If you confess with your mouth that Jesus is Lord and believe in your heart that God raised him from the dead, you will be saved. [10]If For it is by believing in your heart that you are made right with God, and it is by confessing with your mouth that you are saved." (Romans 10:5–10 NLT).*

While salvation can be described as a particular event occurring at a particular time, it is also a continuous attitude and way of life. Faith in Jesus Christ must therefore be strengthened to the point where we become totally devoted to and dependent on Him.

To be "saved from sin" or "saved" means that you are now free from the power of evil and that your life is now committed to God through Jesus Christ.

The Greek word for save is sozo and it means, among other things: to preserve or rescue from natural dangers and afflictions; to save from death; to bring out safely from a situation fraught with mortal danger; to save or free from disease; to save or free from demonic possession; to be restored to health, to get well; to keep preserved in good condition; to thrive, prosper, get on well; and to save or preserve from eternal death.

To be saved or to receive salvation in a biblical sense is "to be delivered from sin". The theological definition of "salvation" is "spiritual rescue from sin and death".

The Bible says clearly in Romans three that we are all sinners and therefore stand in danger of God's judgment. That judgment is spoken of in chapter 20 of the book of Revelation.

> *"And I saw a great white throne and the one sitting on it. The earth and sky fled from his presence, but they found no place to hide. [12]I saw the dead, both great and small, standing before God's throne. And the books were opened, including the Book of Life. And the dead were judged according to what they had done, as recorded in the books. [13]The sea gave up its dead, and death and the grave gave up their dead. And all were judged according to their deeds. [14]Then death and the grave were thrown into the lake of fire. This lake of fire is the second death. [15]And anyone whose name was not found recorded in the Book of Life was thrown into the lake of fire." (Revelation 20:11–15 NLT).*

The Bible teaches that we are all sinners and, therefore, God's judgment stands against us. We also have learned that through Christ, a way has been provided to lift that judgment from us.

There is a school of thought that when you are saved from sin there is a personal conviction. You are absolutely convinced that you are saved. Some people say it this way: " You know that you know that you know." Paul says it this way in the third chapter of Philippians as expressed in the New Living translation of that epistle.

> *"Therefore, brethren, we are debtors—not to the flesh, to live according to the flesh. [13] For if you live according to the flesh you will die; but if by the Spirit you put to death the deeds of the body, you will live. [14] For as many as are led by the Spirit of God, these are sons of God. [15]For you did not receive the spirit of bondage again to fear, but you received the Spirit of adoption by whom we cry out, 'Abba, Father.' [16] The Spirit Himself bears witness with our spirit that we are children of God, [17]and if children, then heirs—heirs of God and joint heirs with Christ, if indeed we suffer with Him, that we may also be glorified together." (Philippians 3:12 –17 NLT).*

Once you confess Jesus Christ as Savior you are guaranteed to be with Him in Heaven. However, salvation should also be seen as a lifetime race in which we are called to ensure that we adhere to the teachings of the Bible at all times, as you work out what God has placed in you.

> *"Dear friends, you always followed my instructions when I was with you. And now that I am away, it is even more important. Work hard to show the results of your salvation, obeying God with deep reverence and fear, [13]For God is working in you, giving you the desire and the power to do what pleases him." (Philippians 2:12–13 NLT).*

Paul the apostle on several occasions referred to the Christian life as a race. One example of this is found in Hebrews chapter 12.

> *"Therefore, since we are surrounded by such a huge crowd of witnesses to the life of faith, let us strip off every weight that slows us down, especially the sin that so easily trips us up. And let us run with endurance the race God has set before us. [2] We do this by keeping our eyes on Jesus, the champion who initiates and perfects our faith. Because of the joy awaiting him, he endured the cross, disregarding its shame. Now he is seated in the place of honor beside God's throne. [3]Think of all the hostility he endured from sinful people; then you won't become weary and give up. [4]After all, you have not yet given your lives in your struggle against sin." (Hebrews 12:1–4 NLT).*

Another example from Paul is found in 1 Corinthians, chapter nine:

> *"Do you not know that those who run in a race all run, but one receives the prize? Run in such a way that you may obtain it. [25]And everyone who competes for the prize is temperate in all things. Now they do it to obtain a perishable crown, but we for an imperishable crown. [26]Therefore I run thus: not with uncertainty. Thus I fight: not as one who beats the air. [27]But I discipline my body and bring it into subjection, lest, when I have preached to others, I myself should become disqualified." (1 Corinthians 9:24–27 NKJV).*

A third example of Paul's reference to the Christian life being a race comes from his letter to the Philippians, chapter three:

> *"But what things were gain to me, these I have counted loss for Christ. [8]Yet indeed I also count all things loss for the excellence of the knowledge of Christ Jesus my Lord, for whom I have suffered the loss of all things, and count them as rubbish, that I may gain Christ [9]and be found in Him, not having my own righteousness, which is from the law, but that which is through faith in Christ, the righteousness which is from God by faith; [10] that I may know Him and the power of His resurrection, and the fellowship of His sufferings, being conformed to His death, [11] if, by any means, I may attain to the resurrection from the dead. [12] Not that I have already attained, or am already perfected; but I press on, that I may lay hold of that for which Christ Jesus has also laid hold*

of me. [13]Brethren, I do not count myself to have apprehended; but one thing I do, forgetting those things which are behind and reaching forward to those things which are ahead, [14]I press toward the goal for the prize of the upward call of God in Christ Jesus." (Philippians 3:7–14 NKJV).

The New Living Translation makes it even simpler:

"For His sake I have discarded everything else, counting it all as garbage, so that I could gain Christ [9]and become one with Him. I no longer count on my own righteousness through obeying the law; rather, I become righteous through faith in Christ. For God's way of making us right with Himself depends on faith. [10] I want to know Christ and experience the mighty power that raised Him from the dead. I want to suffer with Him, sharing in His death, [11]so that one way or another I will experience the resurrection from the dead! [12] I don't mean to say that I have already achieved these things or that I have already reached perfection. But I press on to possess that perfection for which Christ Jesus first possessed me. [13] No, dear brothers and sisters, I have not achieved It but I focus on this one thing: Forgetting the past and looking forward to what lies ahead, [14] I press on to reach the end of the race and receive the Heavenly prize for which God, through Christ Jesus, is calling us." (Philippians 3:7–14 NLT).

You must remember and understand that in a race there are winners and losers. Some people believe that as long as you believe in God you are saved. This is far from the truth since even Satan and his evil forces believe. Rather than being saved, they already have their place allocated in hell.

> *"You believe that there is one God. You do well. Even the demons believe—and tremble!" (James 2:19 NKJV).*

Peter the apostle also had something to say about knowing that you are saved. In the first chapter of his epistle he said to the Christians living in Pontus, Galatia, Cappadocia, Asia, and Bithynia:

> *"God the Father knew you and chose you long ago, and his Spirit has made you holy. As a result, you have obeyed Him and have been cleansed by the blood of Jesus Christ. May God give you more and more grace and peace. [3]All praise to God, the Father of our Lord Jesus Christ. It is by His great mercy that we have been born again, because God raised Jesus Christ from the dead. Now we live with great expectation, [4]and we have a priceless inheritance—an inheritance that is kept in Heaven for you, pure and undefiled, beyond the reach of change and decay. [5]And through your faith, God is protecting you by His power until you receive this salvation, which is ready to be revealed on the last day for all to see." (1 Peter 1:2–5 NLT).*

Jesus, as quoted in the Gospel of John, chapter 13, verse 34, explained to His disciples exactly how people would know they are His followers.

> *"So now I am giving you a new commandment: Love each other. Just as I have loved you, you should love each other. [35]Your love for one another will prove to the world that you are my disciples." (John 13:34–35 NLT).*

The born again Believer has been promised eternal life in Christ Jesus as opposed to spending eternity in hell. Here is the explanation given to the Roman Christians.

> *"For when you were slaves of sin, you were free in regard to righteousness. [21] What fruit did you have then in the things of which you are now ashamed? For the end of those things is death. [22] But now having been set free from sin, and having become slaves of God, you have your fruit to holiness, and the end, everlasting life. [23] For the wages of sin is death, but the gift of God is eternal life in Christ Jesus our Lord." (Romans 6:20–23 NKJV).*

The New Living Translation puts it this way:

> *"When you were slaves to sin, you were free from the obligation to do right. [21] And what was the result? You are now ashamed of the things you used to do, things that end in eternal doom. [22] But now you are free from the power of sin and have become slaves of God. Now you do those things that lead to*

> *holiness and result in eternal life. [23] For the wages of sin is death, but the free gift of God is eternal life through Christ Jesus our Lord." (Romans 6:20–23 NLT).*

The term "eternal life" means more than just living forever in some endless existence. It is about knowing God the Father and Jesus Christ the Son. This is exactly what Jesus said just before His arrest and crucifixion.

> *"Jesus spoke these words, lifted up His eyes to Heaven, and said: "Father, the hour has come. Glorify Your Son, that Your Son also may glorify You, [2] as You have given Him authority over all flesh, that He should give eternal life to as many as You have given Him. [3] And this is eternal life, that they may know You, the only true God, and Jesus Christ whom You have sent." (John 17:1–3 NKJV).*

The Bible is clear in showing that eternal life comes through Jesus Christ. John the apostle gave this assurance to the early church:

> *"And this is the testimony: that God has given us eternal life, and this life is in His Son. [12] He who has the Son has life; he who does not have the Son of God does not have life. [13] These things I have written to you who believe in the name of the Son of God, that you may know that you have eternal life, and that you may continue to believe in the name of the Son of God." (1 John 5:11–12 NKJV).*

Eternal life therefore has a special quality that allows Believers to know God in a never-ending and ever-deepening relationship.

Eternal life is not just about repentance and giving your life to Jesus Christ. It requires a continuing relationship with God through the Father, Jesus Christ the Son, and the Holy Spirit. There is no eternal life without a continuing relationship with God. It depends on living by faith under the anointing and help of the Holy Spirit.

When you are saved from sin, live a life that is holy before God, love your neighbor as yourself, win others to Christ, and live according to God's Word, you will inherit eternal life.

Chapter 6

What Is a Christian?

A Christian is someone who not only believes in Jesus Christ but has committed his or her life to Him. The Christian accepts that Jesus is the only way to God and by repenting of his or her personal sins, has been born again through the Holy Spirit. A Christian, by accepting Jesus Christ as Savior, becomes a child of God.

The followers of Jesus were first called Christians at Antioch as stated in Acts chapter 11, verse 26. The word "Christian", which means "Christlike" or "like Christ", was used on two other occasions in the Bible—Acts chapter 26, verse 28 and in 1 Peter chapter four, verse 16.

The name was given to the early Christians simply because their behavior, activity, and way of life reflected that of Christ. They were therefore described as being like Christ, "belonging to Christ" or "followers of Christ".

To be a true Christian you must repent of your sins, accept Jesus Christ as your Savior, and establish a personal relationship with Him. You must truly believe that He is the only begotten Son of God, who was conceived by the Holy Spirit, born of a virgin, suffered, and was crucified for the sins of the world. You must also accept that He died and was buried, rose from the dead, ascended into Heaven, and is with God the Father.

Being a Christian also means that you must accept that Jesus Christ will return to judge both the living and the dead.

You must also believe His promise that He will come back for those who love Him and will take them to spend eternity with Him.

The born again Christian is therefore required to aspire to be like Christ.

Accepting Jesus Christ as Savior is not just about going to Heaven, it also means turning away from a sinful life. It is a higher calling than just giving up the wrong things, even though that is also required.

The Christian faith is built on the conviction that God, who loves the human race, sent His sinless Son, Jesus Christ, to earth to die for sinners so that they could be reconciled to Him. This is stated in the Gospel of John, chapter three.

> *"For God so loved the world that He gave His only begotten Son, that whoever believes in Him should not perish but have everlasting life. [17] For God did not send His Son into the world to condemn the world, but that the world through Him might be saved. [18] "He who believes in Him is not condemned; but he who does not believe is condemned already, because he has not believed in the name of the only begotten Son of God." (John 3:16–18 NKJV).*

Christianity is an outward manifestation of an inward transformation and is about a change of heart. Its very essence is love—love of and for God, and love of others. Jesus not only encouraged but commanded His disciples to show love. In the Gospel of John, chapter 13 He gave them specific instructions.

"A new commandment I give to you, that you love one another; as I have loved you, that you also love one another. [35] By this all will know that you are My disciples, if you have love for one another." (John 13:34–35 NKJV).

What Jesus was saying is that in order to be one of His followers, a Christian, you not only have to love but must also show love.

Jesus also had something to say about love in the Gospel of Matthew, chapter 22. There He was questioned by a Pharisee as to what was the greatest commandment in the law. Pharisees were people who tried to obey every aspect of Jewish law.

Jesus said to him, "You shall love the Lord your God with all your heart, with all your soul, and with all your mind." [38] This is the first and great commandment. [39] And the second is like it: "You shall love your neighbor as yourself." [40] On these two commandments hang all the Law and the Prophets. (Matthew 22:37–40 NKJV).

John in his first epistle also stressed the importance of love and loving God. In chapter four he had this to say:

"Dear friends, let us love one another, for love comes from God. Everyone who loves has been born of God and knows God. [8] Whoever does not love does not know God, because God is love. [9] This is how God showed His love among us: He sent his one and only Son into the world that we might live through Him. [10] This is love: not that we

> *loved God, but that He loved us and sent His Son as an atoning sacrifice for our sins. 11 Dear friends, since God so loved us, we also ought to love one another." (1 John: 4:7–11 NKJV).*

Paul, the apostle and writer of several New Testament books, also spoke about the importance of love. In chapter 13 of his first epistle to the Corinthians he valued love higher than any of the other spiritual gifts given to the church.

> *"Though I speak with the tongues of men and of angels, but have not love, I have become sounding brass or a clanging cymbal. 2 And though I have the gift of prophecy, and understand all mysteries and all knowledge, and though I have all faith, so that I could remove mountains, but have not love, I am nothing. 3 And though I bestow all my goods to feed the poor, and though I give my body to be burned, but have not love, it profits me nothing. 4 Love suffers long and is kind; love does not envy; love does not parade itself, is not puffed up; 5 does not behave rudely, does not seek its own, is not provoked, thinks no evil; 6 does not rejoice in iniquity, but rejoices in the truth; 7 bears all things, believes all things, hopes all things, endures all things. 8 Love never fails. But whether there are prophecies, they will fail; whether there are tongues, they will cease; whether there is knowledge, it will vanish away. 9 For we know in part and we prophesy in part. 10 But when that which is perfect has come, then that which is in part*

> *will be done away. [11]When I was a child, I spoke as a child, I understood as a child, I thought as a child; but when I became a man, I put away childish things. [12]For now we see in a mirror, dimly, but then face to face. Now I know in part, but then I shall know just as I also am known. [13]And now abide faith, hope, love, these three; but the greatest of these is love." (1 Corinthians: 13 1–13 NKJV).*

There are some people who say they love God but are at enmity with others, even fellow Christians. John says in his first epistle that this is not right.

> *"If someone says, 'I love God,' and hates his brother, he is a liar; for he who does not love his brother whom he has seen, how can he love God whom he has not seen? [21] And this commandment we have from Him: that he who loves God must love his brother also." (1 John 4:20–21 NKJV).*

Peter the apostle in the fourth chapter of his first epistle, also had some advice about love for the early church.

> *"But the end of all things is at hand; therefore be serious and watchful in your prayers. [8] And above all things have fervent love for one another, for 'love will cover a multitude of sins'. [9] Be hospitable to one another without grumbling." (1 Peter 4:7–9 NKJV).*

The signature Bible verse for all Christians is John chapter three, verse 16, which most Christians can readily quote. It reads:

> *"For God so loved the world that He gave His only begotten Son, that whoever believes in Him should not perish but have everlasting life." (John 3:16 NKJV).*

John, in the third chapter of his first epistle, also alluded to this as he counseled the early church.

> *"By this we know love, because He laid down His life for us. And we also ought to lay down our lives for the brethren. [17]But whoever has this world's goods, and sees his brother in need, and shuts up his heart from him, how does the love of God abide in him? [18]My little children, let us not love in word or in tongue, but in deed and in truth. [19] And by this we know that we are of the truth, and shall assure our hearts before Him." (1 John 3:16–19 NKJV).*

The message of love is nothing new but was handed down from God long before the start of the early church. In chapter 10 of the book of Deuteronomy, Moses spoke to the children of Israel about it after receiving the second copy of the Ten Commandments from God.

> *"And now, Israel, what does the Lord your God require of you, but to fear the Lord your God, to walk in all His ways and to love Him, to serve the Lord your God with all your heart and with all your soul, [13] and to keep the commandments of the Lord and His statutes which I command you today for your good? [14]Indeed Heaven and the highest Heavens belong to the Lord your God, also the earth*

> *with all that is in it. [15]The Lord delighted only in your fathers, to love them; and He chose their descendants after them, you above all peoples, as it is this day." (Deuteronomy 10:12–15 NKJV).*

A Christian therefore is not only someone who believes in Jesus Christ and has committed his or her life to Him, but someone who must show a genuine love for others.

There are many misconceptions about Christianity. Some people believe that if they are members of a religious denomination and have high moral values and assist others they are Christians. Some of these people do not have a personal relationship with Jesus Christ, have never really committed their lives to Him, and just live "as good people". Some believe that as long as they go to church, pray, and believe that there is a God, they are Christians.

Jesus said, in order to have a personal relationship with Him you must be born again. Unfortunately several religious denominations that call themselves Christian do not believe in, preach, or teach the concept of being born again. Some of these denominations are built on doing good works but neglect the spiritual aspects of Christianity.

Going to church does not make you a Christian and praying to God does not qualify you as a Christian. It all comes back to the encounter between Jesus and Nicodemus as recorded in the Gospel of John, chapter three. In that story Jesus told Nicodemus unless he was born again he could not see the kingdom of Heaven. Nicodemus, like many people today, was very religious, being a member of the top religious sect of the day. He, however, did not have a personal relationship with Jesus Christ.

It is simple: going to church, serving in the assembly, being a good person, trying not to sin, giving to the poor, and even praying do not make you a Christian. You must be born again and that requires confessing your sin, and asking Jesus Christ to forgive you and come into your heart. Only then can you genuinely call yourself a Christian or a Child of God.

The book of Titus reminded the early Christians to be subjected to rulers and authority and to be prepared to do good works.

> *"To speak evil of no one, to be peaceable, gentle, showing all humility to all men. [3] For we ourselves were also once foolish, disobedient, deceived, serving various lusts and pleasures, living in malice and envy, hateful and hating one another. [4] But when the kindness and the love of God our Savior toward man appeared, [5] not by works of righteousness which we have done, but according to His mercy He saved us, through the washing of regeneration and renewing of the Holy Spirit, [6] whom He poured out on us abundantly through Jesus Christ our Savior, [7] that having been justified by His grace we should become heirs according to the hope of eternal life". (Titus 3:2–7 NKJV).*

Being born again is the first step in Christianity and, like a new baby, the new convert has to grow. When you first give your life to Jesus Christ you are regarded as "a babe in Christ". Peter the Apostle refers to this in chapter two of his first epistle:

> *"Therefore, laying aside all malice, all deceit, hypocrisy, envy, and all evil speaking, [2] as newborn babes, desire the pure milk of the word, that you may grow thereby, [3] if indeed you have tasted that the Lord is gracious." (1 Peter 2:1–3 NKJV).*

This simply means that you should get to know the Word of God and that Word is contained in the Bible. This is essential if you want to mature as a Christian.

The writer of the book of Hebrews pointed out to the Christians that it was necessary that they grew and not remain as babes in Christ. They were continuing to act as new converts rather than striving for maturity.

> *"You have been Believers so long now that you ought to be teaching others. Instead, you need someone to teach you again the basic things about God's word. You are like babies who need milk and cannot eat solid food. [13] For someone who lives on milk is still an infant and doesn't know how to do what is right. [14] Solid food is for those who are mature, who through training have the skill to recognize the difference between right and wrong." (Hebrews 5:12–14 NLT).*

The Holy Spirit will help you to grow, and with time and commitment, you will become more knowledgeable in your Christianity. Studying the Word, having a consistent prayer relationship with God, and living a life of repentance will result in spiritual growth, and you becoming a strong Christian.

You will continue to grow as you allow the Word of God, the guidance of the Holy Spirit, and a personal relationship with the Lord to transform you so that you are firmly grounded in the Word and are living in accordance with the Bible. This also entails taking the Bible seriously and literally and applying it to your daily life.

The Christian, with the help of the Holy Spirit, should regularly review his or her life and work toward eradicating those things that hinder his or her walk with God.

Chapter 7

The Characteristics of a Christian

One of the main characteristics of the born again Christian is holiness. The Hebrew word for holy means set apart for God, sanctified, hallowed, or consecrated. In the Greek language it means to be without faults and set apart by God.

The Believer must also have a lifestyle that reflects the Word of God and the teachings of Jesus Christ.

Peter the apostle, in his first epistle, gave this advice to the church:

> *"Therefore gird up the loins of your mind, be sober, and rest your hope fully upon the grace that is to be brought to you at the revelation of Jesus Christ; [14] as obedient children, not conforming yourselves to the former lusts, as in your ignorance; [15] but as He who called you is holy, you also be holy in all your conduct, [16] because it is written, 'Be holy, for I am holy'." (1 Peter 1:13–15 NKJV).*

The New Living Translation puts it this way:

> *"So think clearly and exercise self-control. Look forward to the gracious salvation that will come to you when Jesus Christ is revealed to the world. [14] So you must live as God's obedient children. Don't slip back into your old ways of living to satisfy your own desires. You didn't know any better then. [15] But now you must be holy in everything you do, just as God who chose you is holy. [16] For the Scriptures say, 'You must be holy because I am holy'." (1 Peter 1:13–15 NLT).*

God is holy and so His children must be holy. Holiness comes through the work of the Holy Spirit in our lives and our faith in the redeeming blood of Jesus Christ to cleanse us from sin. Holiness begins with being truly born again and knowing and understanding our relationship with Him as a Holy God. This entails living a life that is different from those who are in the world.

We must therefore stand out by living according to the Word of God, studying the Bible, and strengthening our faith and striving to become the people that He has called us to be.

> *"But you are a chosen generation, a royal priesthood, a holy nation, His own special people, that you may proclaim the praises of Him who called you out of darkness into His marvelous light; [10] who once were not a people but are now the people of God, who had not obtained mercy but now have obtained mercy." (1 Peter 2: 9–10 NKJV).*

But while we are expected to be holy, God isn't calling us to be perfect. Rather, He wants us to be different from the unsaved.

> *"But if we walk in the light as He is in the light, we have fellowship with one another, and the blood of Jesus Christ His Son cleanses us from all sin. [8] If we say that we have no sin, we deceive ourselves, and the truth is not in us. [9] If we confess our sins, He is faithful and just to forgive us our sins and to cleanse us from all unrighteousness. [10]If we say that we have not sinned, we make Him a liar, and His word is not in us." (1 John 1:7–10 NKJV).*

Some of the main characteristics and lifestyle of a Christian are what has been described in the Bible as "the fruit of the Spirit". These qualities are stated in chapter five of Galatians as ***"love, joy, peace, longsuffering, kindness, goodness, faithfulness, gentleness and self-control."***

The person who loves is caring and looks out for others without expecting anything in return while those who have a spirit of joy express joy because of the grace, blessings, promises, and nearness of God. It is said joy flows from the inside as distinct from happiness, which is merely transferred by outside happenings.

The Christian should also be peaceful and be at peace knowing that all is well between himself or herself and God. This frees the person from anxiety and worry.

The fruit of the Spirit includes the patience to be long-suffering. With this characteristic you are able to endure tribulation and would not easily get angry or be involved in disputes.

The born again Christian also exhibits goodness and has a yearning for truth and righteousness and a strong dislike for sin and evil things. These Believers are also kindhearted and will speak out against anything that is not of God.

Faith is one of the foundations of the Christian walk and calls for a firm and unswerving loyalty and commitment to God.

Some people may object to the suggestion that they should be meek, believing in some cases that meekness is weakness. Meekness, for the Christian, could however be described as gentleness, restraint coupled with strength and courage. A meek person is also one who could be angry when necessary and humbly submissive when that quality is needed.

The ninth "fruit of the Spirit" as described in Galatians is that of temperance. With this characteristic the Christian will show self-control, faithfulness in relationships, and will be able to master his or her desires and passions.

Being a born again Christian is not only about living according to moral law, but knowing Jesus Christ and having a mutual relationship with Him. While morality could be considered a code, Christianity is a lifestyle that reflects the love of Jesus Christ.

Paul in his letter to the church at Ephesus advised the Christians there to ***"walk worthy of the vocation wherewith they were called." "With all lowliness and meekness, with long-suffering, forbearing one another in love ."***

This same advice is applicable to today's Christians.

> *Wherefore putting away lying, speak every man truth with his neighbour: for we are members one of another. 26Be ye angry, and sin not: let not the sun go down upon your wrath: 27 Neither give place to the devil. 28Let him that stole steal no more: but rather let*

> *him labour, working with his hands the thing which is good, that he may have to give to him that needeth. [29] Let no corrupt communication proceed out of your mouth, but that which is good to the use of edifying, that it may minister grace unto the hearers. [30] And grieve not the holy Spirit of God, whereby ye are sealed unto the day of redemption. [31] Let all bitterness, and wrath, and anger, and clamour, and evil speaking, be put away from you, with all malice: [32] And be ye kind one to another, tender-hearted, forgiving one another, even as God for Christ's sake hath forgiven you." (Ephesians 4:25–32 KJV).*

This portion of Scripture is expressed this way in the New Living Translation:

> *"Put on your new nature, created to be like God—truly righteous and holy. [25] So stop telling lies. Let us tell our neighbours the truth, for we are all parts of the same body. [26] And 'don't sin by letting anger control you'. Don't let the sun go down while you are still angry, [27] for anger gives a foothold to the devil. [28] If you are a thief, quit stealing. Instead, use your hands for good hard work, and then give generously to others in need. [29] Don't use foul or abusive language. Let everything you say be good and helpful, so that your words will be an encouragement to those who hear them. [30] And do not bring sorrow to God's Holy Spirit by the way you live. Remember, he has identified you as his own, guaranteeing that you will be saved on the day of redemption. [31] Get rid*

of all bitterness, rage, anger, harsh words, and slander, as well as all types of evil behaviour. [32] Instead, be kind to each other, tender-hearted, forgiving one another, just as God through Christ has forgiven you." (Ephesians 4:24–32 NLT).

The Christian is also admonished to put aside malice, deceit, hypocrisy, envy, and evil speaking. Peter, the apostle, offered this advice in chapter two of his first epistle and also appealed to Christians to reject and keep away from what he termed "fleshly lusts which war against the soul".

The early church was also told to be careful what they said.

"Having your conduct honourable among the Gentiles, that when they speak against you as evil-doers, they may, by your good works which they observe, glorify God in the day of visitation." (1 Peter 2:12 NKJV).

Christians are also expected to observe the laws of the country in which they live. This advice is given in Peter's first epistle.

"Therefore submit yourselves to every ordinance of man for the Lord's sake, whether to the king as supreme, [14] or to governors, as to those who are sent by him for the punishment of evil doers and for the praise of those who do good. [15] For this is the will of God, that by doing good you may put to silence the ignorance of foolish men— [16] as free, yet not using liberty as a cloak for vice,

> *but as bondservants of God. [17] Honour all people. Love the brotherhood. Fear God. Honour the king." (1 Peter 2:12–17 NKJV).*

Paul also had some advice for the Colossian Christians when he told them to go after Heavenly things.

> *"Therefore put to death your members which are on the earth: fornication, uncleanness, passion, evil desire, and covetousness, which is idolatry. [6] Because of these things the wrath of God is coming upon the sons of disobedience, [7]in which you yourselves once walked when you lived in them. [8] But now you yourselves are to put off all these: anger, wrath, malice, blasphemy, filthy language out of your mouth. [9] Do not lie to one another, since you have put off the old man with his deeds, [10] and have put on the new man who is renewed in knowledge according to the image of Him who created him." (Colossians 3:5–10 NKJV).*

The New Living Translation puts that passage this way:

> *"So put to death the sinful, earthly things lurking within you. Have nothing to do with sexual immorality, impurity, lust, and evil desires. Don't be greedy, for a greedy person is an idolater, worshipping the things of this world. [6] Because of these sins, the anger of God is coming. [7] You used to do these things when your life was still part of this world. [8] But now is the time to get rid of anger, rage, malicious behaviour,*

> *slander, and dirty language. [9] Don't lie to each other, for you have stripped off your old sinful nature and all its wicked deeds. [10] Put on your new nature, and be renewed as you learn to know your Creator and become like him." (Colossians 3:5–10 NLT).*

Paul did not leave it there but also identified what should be the character of the born again Christian or "New man".

> *"Therefore, as the elect of God, holy and beloved, put on tender mercies, kindness, humility, meekness, long-suffering; [13] bearing with one another, and forgiving one another, if anyone has a complaint against another; even as Christ forgave you, so you also must do. [14] But above all these things put on love, which is the bond of perfection. [15] And let the peace of God rule in your hearts, to which also you were called in one body; and be thankful. [16]Let the word of Christ dwell in you richly in all wisdom, teaching, and admonishing one another in psalms and hymns and spiritual songs, singing with grace in your hearts to the Lord. [17] And whatever you do in word or deed, do all in the name of the Lord Jesus, giving thanks to God the Father through Him." (Colossians 3:12–17 NKJV).*

Now check the same passage in the New Living Translation:

> *"Since God chose you to be the holy people he loves, you must clothe yourselves with tenderhearted mercy, kindness, humility, gentleness, and patience. [13] Make allowance for each other's faults, and forgive anyone who offends you. Remember, the Lord forgave you, so you must forgive others. [14] Above all, clothe yourselves with love, which binds us all together in perfect harmony. [15] And let the peace that comes from Christ rule in your hearts. For as members of one body you are called to live in peace. And always be thankful. [16] Let the message about Christ, in all its richness, fill your lives. Teach and counsel each other with all the wisdom he gives. Sing psalms and hymns and spiritual songs to God with thankful hearts. [17] And whatever you do or say, do it as a representative of the Lord Jesus, giving thanks through him to God the Father. (Colossians 3:12–17 NLT).*

The writer of the Book of Romans advised Christians to commit both body and spirit to Jesus Christ.

> *"And so, dear brothers and sisters, I plead with you to give your bodies to God because of all he has done for you. Let them be a living and holy sacrifice—the kind he will find acceptable. This is truly the way to worship him. [2] Don't copy the behaviour and customs of this world, but let God transform you into a new person by changing the way you think. Then you will learn to know God's will for you, which is good and pleasing*

and perfect. 3 Because of the privilege and
authority God has given me, I give each of
you this warning: Don't think you are better
than you really are. Be honest in your eval-
uation of yourselves, measuring yourselves
by the faith God has given us. 4 Just as our
bodies have many parts and each part has a
special function, 5 so it is with Christ's body.
We are many parts of one body, and we all
belong to each other. 6 In His grace, God
has given us different gifts for doing certain
things well. So if God has given you the ability
to prophesy, speak out with as much faith as
God has given you. 7 If your gift is serving
others, serve them well. If you are a teacher,
teach well. 8 If your gift is to encourage
others, be encouraging. If it is giving, give
generously. If God has given you leadership
ability, take the responsibility seriously. And
if you have a gift for showing kindness to
others, do it gladly. 9 Don't just pretend to
love others. Really love them. Hate what is
wrong. Hold tightly to what is good. 10 Love
each other with genuine affection, and take
delight in honouring each other. 11 Never
be lazy, but work hard and serve the Lord
enthusiastically. 12 Rejoice in our confident
hope. Be patient in trouble, and keep on
praying. 13 When God's people are in need,
be ready to help them. Always be eager to
practice hospitality. 14 Bless those who per-
secute you. Don't curse them; pray that God
will bless them. 15 Be happy with those who
are happy, and weep with those who weep.
16 Live in harmony with each other. Don't be

> *too proud to enjoy the company of ordinary people. And don't think you know it all! [17] Never pay back evil with more evil. Do things in such a way that everyone can see you are honourable. [18] Do all that you can to live in peace with everyone. [19] Dear friends, never take revenge. Leave that to the righteous anger of God. For the Scriptures say, 'I will take revenge; I will pay them back,' says the Lord. [20]Instead, 'If your enemies are hungry, feed them. If they are thirsty, give them something to drink. In doing this, you will heap burning coals of shame on their heads.' [21] Don't let evil conquer you, but conquer evil by doing good." (Romans 12:1–21 NLT).*

Timothy is described as Paul's protégé and his mentor encouraged him not to be too concerned about the fact that he was young; to do everything to the best of his abilities. This could apply to some Christians today.

> *"Let no one despise your youth, but be an example to the Believers in word, in conduct, in love, in spirit, in faith, in purity. [13] Till I come, give attention to reading, to exhortation, to doctrine. [14] Do not neglect the gift that is in you, which was given to you by prophecy with the laying on of the hands of the eldership. [15] Meditate on these things; give yourself entirely to them, that your progress may be evident to all." (1 Timothy 4:12–15 NKJV).*

As a born again Christian your best witness is to exhibit the characteristics of Jesus Christ and, in so doing, attract others to become His followers. Jesus told Believers, as recorded in the Gospel of Matthew, chapter five, that they were the salt of the earth and even more than that.

> *"You are the light of the world. A city that is set on a hill cannot be hidden. [15] Nor do they light a lamp and put it under a basket, but on a lampstand, and it gives light to all who are in the house. [16] Let your light so shine before men, that they may see your good works and glorify your Father in Heaven." (Matthew 5:14–16 NKJV).*

As a born again Believer you must be a Christian example. Be the "salt of the earth" and "the light of the world" as you live your life.

Paul the apostle had the following advice for the Christians at Philippi:

> *"Work hard to show the results of your salvation, obeying God with deep reverence and fear. [13] For God is working in you, giving you the desire and the power to do what pleases him. [14] Do everything without complaining and arguing, [15] so that no one can criticize you. Live clean, innocent lives as children of God, shining like bright lights in a world full of crooked and perverse people. (Philippians 2:12–15 NLT).*

Chapter 8

The Power of the Christian

The born again Christian has access to and the ability and authority to use the most awesome power available to man, the power of God. Because of his relationship with Jesus Christ, the Believer can perform even more miracles and things of that nature than the Savior Himself.

The Holy Spirit, the Spirit of Jesus Christ, lives within the Christian and it is this indwelling power that makes the Believer extraordinary. The born again Christian must therefore recognize who he or she is in Christ.

Paul the apostle told the church at Philippi:

> *"I can do all things through Christ who strengthens me." (Philippians 4:13 NKJV).*

But it was Jesus Himself who really said it all. Just before He left the earth He told His disciples about the power that they had.

> *"Most assuredly, I say to you, he who believes in Me, the works that I do he will do also; and greater works than these he will do, because I go to My Father. [13] And whatever you ask in My name, that I will do, that the*

> *Father may be glorified in the Son. [14] If you ask anything in My name, I will do it." (John 14:12–14 NKJV).*

Jesus, through His death and resurrection, conquered death and hell and therefore had full authority over all things. Just before He left the earth, He delegated authority to His disciples and instructed them to continue His work. That event is known as the Great Commission and is recorded in chapter 28 of Matthew's Gospel.

> *"And Jesus came and spoke to them, saying, 'All authority has been given to Me in Heaven and on earth. [19]Go therefore and make disciples of all the nations, baptizing them in the name of the Father and of the Son and of the Holy Spirit, [20] teaching them to observe all things that I have commanded you; and lo, I am with you always, even to the end of the age'." (Matthew 28:18–20 NKJV).*

The Gospel of Mark gives even more details of the Great Commission, showing that Jesus not only told His disciples exactly what to do but also predicted what the results would be.

> *"And He said to them, 'Go into all the world and preach the gospel to every creature. [16] He who believes and is baptized will be saved; but he who does not believe will be condemned. [17] And these signs will follow those who believe: In My name they will cast out demons; they will speak with new tongues; [18] they will take up serpents; and if they drink anything deadly, it will by*

> *no means hurt them; they will lay hands on the sick, and they will recover'." (Mark 16:15–18 NKJV).*

Earlier in His ministry, Jesus had sent out His disciples on a missionary trip and He had indicated the kind of power they had. His instructions to them left no doubt that they could perform miracles.

> *"Heal the sick, cleanse the lepers, raise the dead, cast out demons. Freely you have received, freely give. [9] Provide neither gold nor silver nor copper in your money belts, [10] nor bag for your journey, nor two tunics, nor sandals, nor staffs; for a worker is worthy of his food." (Matthew 10:8–10 NKJV).*

Jesus had given His disciples a perfect example to follow because throughout His entire ministry He performed miracles of all description. He raised the dead, healed the sick, cleansed leprous men, opened blind eyes, caused the deaf to hear, made cripples walk, turned water into wine, transformed a small meal into a feast, revealed what people were thinking, and could tell them what they were doing when He wasn't even near to them.

One miracle that would have stood out with Jesus' disciples was the time when they were caught in a storm at sea and He came to them walking on the water.

> *"Now in the fourth watch of the night Jesus went to them, walking on the sea. And when the disciples saw Him walking on the sea, they were troubled, saying, 'It is a ghost!' And they cried out for fear. [27] But immediately Jesus spoke to them, saying, 'Be of*

> *good cheer! It is I; do not be afraid.' [28] And Peter answered Him and said, 'Lord, if it is You, command me to come to You on the water.' [29] So He said, 'Come.' And when Peter had come down out of the boat, he walked on the water to go to Jesus. [30] But when he saw that the wind was boisterous, he was afraid; and beginning to sink he cried out, saying, 'Lord, save me!' [31] And immediately Jesus stretched out His hand and caught him, and said to him, 'O you of little faith, why did you doubt?' [32] And when they got into the boat, the wind ceased." (Matthew 14:25–32 NKJV).*

This event confirmed that those who accept Jesus Christ as Savior can do the things that He did. It was fear and lack of faith that curtailed Peter's miraculous walk on water, and the same could happen to born again Believers if their faith is like his.

The Bible provides us with numerous examples of Christians doing miracles similar to those carried out by Jesus. In the book of the Acts of the Apostles there is a well-known account of the healing of a lame man by Peter and John.

> *"And a certain man lame from his mother's womb was carried, whom they laid daily at the gate of the temple which is called Beautiful, to ask alms from those who entered the temple; [3] who, seeing Peter and John about to go into the temple, asked for alms. [4] And fixing his eyes on him, with John, Peter said, 'Look at us.' [5] So he gave them his attention, expecting to receive*

> *something from them. [6] Then Peter said, 'Silver and gold I do not have, but what I do have I give you: In the name of Jesus Christ of Nazareth, rise up and walk.' [7] And he took him by the right hand and lifted him up, and immediately his feet and ankle bones received strength. [8] So he, leaping up, stood and walked and entered the temple with them—walking, leaping, and praising God. [9] And all the people saw him walking and praising God. [10] Then they knew that it was he who sat begging alms at the Beautiful Gate of the temple; and they were filled with wonder and amazement at what had happened to him." (Acts 3:2–10 NKJV).*

The Acts of the Apostles also records more than one instance of people being raised from the dead. There's the account of a young man who fell through a window while Paul was preaching.

> *"Now on the first day of the week, when the disciples came together to break bread, Paul, ready to depart the next day, spoke to them and continued his message until midnight. [8] There were many lamps in the upper room where they were gathered together. [9] And in a window sat a certain young man named Eutychus, who was sinking into a deep sleep. He was overcome by sleep; and as Paul continued speaking, he fell down from the third story and was taken up dead. [10] But Paul went down, fell on him, and embracing him said, 'Do not trouble yourselves, for his life is in him.' [11] Now when he had come up,*

> *had broken bread and eaten, and talked a long while, even till daybreak, he departed. [12] And they brought the young man in alive, and they were not a little comforted." (Acts 20:7–12 NKJV).*

Peter was involved in the raising of a dead woman named Tabitha, also known as Dorcas. She was sick and subsequently died and her friends sent for Peter, who was not far away. When he got there her friends and associates were weeping and mourning her death.

> *"But Peter put them all out, and knelt down and prayed. And turning to the body he said, 'Tabitha, arise.' And she opened her eyes, and when she saw Peter she sat up. [41] Then he gave her his hand and lifted her up; and when he had called the saints and widows, he presented her alive." (Acts 9:40–41 NKJV).*

The Apostles performed numerous miracles to the point where they did not even have to touch or lay hands on the sick for them to be healed.

> *"And through the hands of the apostles many signs and wonders were done among the people. And they were all with one accord in Solomon's Porch. [13] Yet none of the rest dared join them, but the people esteemed them highly. [14] And Believers were increasingly added to the Lord, multitudes of both men and women, [15] so that they brought the sick out into the streets and laid them on beds and couches, that at least the shadow*

> *of Peter passing by might fall on some of them. [16] Also a multitude gathered from the surrounding cities to Jerusalem, bringing sick people and those who were tormented by unclean spirits, and they were all healed." (Acts 5:12–16 NKJV).*

God also worked unusual miracles through Paul to the point where even handkerchiefs or aprons were brought from his body to the sick, and the diseases left them and the evil spirits went out of them.

But there were those who were not Christians and who tried to imitate the apostles and suffered the consequences.

> *"Then some of the itinerant Jewish exorcists took it upon themselves to call the name of the Lord Jesus over those who had evil spirits, saying, 'We exorcise you by the Jesus whom Paul preaches.' [14]Also there were seven sons of Sceva, a Jewish chief priest, who did so. [15] And the evil spirit answered and said, 'Jesus I know, and Paul I know; but who are you?' [16]Then the man in whom the evil spirit was leaped on them, overpowered them, and prevailed against them, so that they fled out of that house naked and wounded." (Acts 19:13–16 NKJV).*

One of the concepts that certain born again Christians find difficult to accept or even contemplate is the idea that they can do greater things than Jesus. But, hard as this may be to believe, the mere fact that it was said by Jesus Himself should be more than enough evidence that it is possible. The challenge to achieving what God has for His children is the measure of faith that Believers possess. Remember even

Peter doubted when he was called to walk on water and he would have spent quite a lot of time with Jesus. Peter's mistake was that he took his eyes off Jesus.

Born again Believers have been given the assurance that their needs will be satisfied. Psalm 23 says:

> *"The Lord is my shepherd therefore shall I lack nothing."*

The psalmist also said that God will protect and provide for those who love Him.

> *"The angel of the Lord encamps all around those who fear Him, and delivers them. [8] Oh, taste and see that the Lord is good; Blessed is the man who trusts in Him! [9] Oh, fear the Lord, you His saints! There is no want to those who fear Him. [10] The young lions lack and suffer hunger; But those who seek the Lord shall not lack any good thing." (Psalm 34:7–10 NKJV).*

The born again Christian has been assured that God has already provided mind-boggling gifts and rewards for him or her. Paul reiterated to the Corinthian Christians what Isaiah the prophet had spoken about in the Old Testament.

> *"But as it is written: 'Eye has not seen, nor ear heard, nor have entered into the heart of man the things which God has prepared for those who love Him.' [10] But God has revealed them to us through His Spirit. For the Spirit searches all things, yes, the deep things of God. [11] For what man knows the things of a man except the spirit of the man*

> *which is in him? Even so no one knows the things of God except the Spirit of God." (1 Corinthians 2:9–11 NKJV).*

The Old Testament has numerous instances where the prophets demonstrated the power of God through outstanding and incredible miracles. Elijah stopped the rain for three and a half years (1 Kings:17); Joshua commanded the sun to stand still (Joshua 10:12); Moses parted the Red Sea (Exodus 14:21); David killed Goliath the giant with a slingshot (1 Samuel:17); the walls of Jericho fell down (Joshua 12:20); Elijah called down fire from Heaven and it even burnt up water (1 Kings 18:38); Peter and the apostles prayed and there was an earthquake (Acts 4:31).

Born again Christians walk in that same awesome power and anointing. But they must live a holy life if they want to be in the place where they may be used to perform miracles and be the people God has called them to be.

CHAPTER 9

WHO IS GOD?

God is the all-encompassing power of the universe; the supreme, supernatural being with supernatural powers. His personal attributes and characteristics show that He is also a person. God created the world and everything that is in it and has arranged everything from the rising of the sun to the operations of the oceans and the wind; the weather, night and day, the animals and time itself. This is all found and described in the first chapter of the book of Genesis.

God is spirit in existence and essence, and as such is invisible. He is eternal; having existed before the world began, He will exist forever. God is all-powerful and there is nothing in Heaven or earth that is more powerful than Him. God also knows everything, even the past, the present, and the future. He knows your thoughts even before they come into your mind. You cannot hide anything from Him, neither can you hide from Him.

David said in Psalm 139:

> *"Where can I go from Your Spirit? Or where*
> *can I flee from Your presence? [8] If I ascend*
> *into Heaven, You are there; If I make my bed*
> *in hell, behold, You are there. [9]If I take the*
> *wings of the morning, And dwell in the utter-*
> *most parts of the sea, [10] Even there Your hand*
> *shall lead me, And Your right hand shall hold*

me. [11] If I say, 'Surely the darkness shall fall on me,' Even the night shall be light about me; [12] Indeed, the darkness shall not hide from You. But the night shines as the day; The darkness and the light are both alike to You." (Psalm 139:7–12 NKJV).

God told the children of Israel that He was to be their only God. This was so important that He made it the first commandment that He gave to Moses. He did not leave it there but went on to warn against accepting idols as gods.

"You shall not make for yourself a carved image—any likeness of anything that is in Heaven above, or that is in the earth beneath, or that is in the water under the earth; [5] you shall not bow down to them nor serve them. For I, the Lord your God, am a jealous God, visiting the iniquity of the fathers upon the children to the third and fourth generations of those who hate Me, [6] but showing mercy to thousands, to those who love Me and keep My commandments." (Exodus 20:4–6 NKJV).

God, through His prophet Isaiah, again spoke to the children of Israel about worshipping idols, stressing that He alone is God.

"Remember the former things of old, For I am God, and there is no other; I am God, and there is none like Me, [10] Declaring the end from the beginning, And from ancient times things that are not yet done, Saying, 'My counsel shall stand, And I will do all My pleasure'." (Isaiah 46:9–10 NKJV).

God has been described as being all-powerful, or as the Bible puts it, omnipotent. Jesus told His disciples in Matthew's Gospel, chapter 19, verse 26 that with God all things are possible. Even before that, God the Father had said something similar to the prophet Jeremiah in the Old Testament.

> *"Then the word of the Lord came to Jeremiah, saying, [27] 'Behold, I am the Lord, the God of all flesh. Is there anything too hard for Me?'" (Jeremiah 32:26–27 NKJV).*

Isaiah, another of the old prophets, also spoke to the people about the power of God.

> *"Thus says the Lord, your Redeemer, And He who formed you from the womb: 'I am the Lord, who makes all things, Who stretches out the Heavens all alone, Who spreads abroad the earth by Myself; [25] Who frustrates the signs of the babblers, And drives diviners mad; Who turns wise men backward, And makes their knowledge foolishness'." (Isaiah 44:24–25 NKJV).*

God knows everything and this is described as being omniscient, as shown in Psalm 147.

> *"He counts the number of the stars; He calls them all by name. [5] Great is our Lord, and mighty in power; His understanding is infinite." (Psalms 147:4–5 NKJV).*

There are people who claim that God does not exist and argue that the world and everything in it evolved over the centuries. But God Himself has stressed that He created everything. He made this clear when He questioned Job.

> *"Where were you when I laid the foundations of the earth? Tell Me, if you have understanding. 5 Who determined its measurements? Surely you know! Or who stretched the line upon it? 6 To what were its foundations fastened? Or who laid its cornerstone, 7 When the morning stars sang together, And all the sons of God shouted for joy? 8 "Or who shut in the sea with doors, When it burst forth and issued from the womb; 9 When I made the clouds its garment, And thick darkness its swaddling band; 10 When I fixed My limit for it, And set bars and doors; 11 When I said, 'This far you may come, but no farther, And here your proud waves must stop!' 12 "Have you commanded the morning since your days began, And caused the dawn to know its place, 13 That it might take hold of the ends of the earth, And the wicked be shaken out of it? 14 It takes on form like clay under a seal, And stands out like a garment. 15 From the wicked their light is withheld, And the upraised arm is broken. 16 "Have you entered the springs of the sea? Or have you walked in search of the depths? 17 Have the gates of death been revealed to you? Or have you seen the doors of the shadow of death? 18 Have you comprehended the breadth of the earth? Tell Me, if you know all this. 19 "Where is the way to the dwelling*

of light? And darkness, where is its place,
[20] That you may take it to its territory, That
you may know the paths to its home? [21] Do
you know it, because you were born then, Or
because the number of your days is great?
[22] Have you entered the treasury of snow, Or
have you seen the treasury of hail, [23] Which
I have reserved for the time of trouble, For
the day of battle and war? [24] By what way
is light diffused, Or the east wind scattered
over the earth? [25] Who has divided a channel
for the overflowing water, Or a path for the
thunderbolt, [26] To cause it to rain on a land
where there is no one, A wilderness in which
there is no man; [27] To satisfy the desolate
waste, And cause to spring forth the growth
of tender grass? [28] Has the rain a father? Or
who has begotten the drops of dew? [29] From
whose womb comes the ice? And the frost
of Heaven, who gives it birth? [30] The waters
harden like stone, And the surface of the
deep is frozen. [31] Can you bind the cluster
of the Pleiades, Or loose the belt of Orion?
[32] Can you bring out Mazzaroth in its season?
Or can you guide the Great Bear with its
cubs? [33] Do you know the ordinances of the
Heavens? Can you set their dominion over
the earth? [34]Can you lift up your voice to
the clouds, That an abundance of water may
cover you? [35] Can you send out lightnings,
that they may go, And say to you, 'Here we
are!'? [36] Who has put wisdom in the mind? Or
who has given understanding to the heart?
[37] Who can number the clouds by wisdom?
Or who can pour out the bottles of Heaven,

[38] When the dust hardens in clumps, And the clods cling together? [39] "Can you hunt the prey for the lion, Or satisfy the appetite of the young lions, [40] When they crouch in their dens, Or lurk in their lairs to lie in wait?
[41] Who provides food for the raven, When its young ones cry to God, And wander about for lack of food?" (Job 38:4–41 NKJV).

God was telling Job in no uncertain terms that He is responsible for everything.

God is universal but He is still a personal God for those who trust Him. He is as much interested in the operations of everything in this earth as He is in your personal life. He hears and answers individual prayers and is open to receive your every request.

Although God is omnipotent, omnipresent, and omniscient, He is a personal God and is available to those who love Him.

"Draw close to God and He will draw close to you." (James 4:8 NKJV).

The Bible also says that God cannot change.

"For I am the LORD, I do not change; Therefore you are not consumed, O sons of Jacob." (Malachi 3:6 NKJV).

God has described Himself as being "I AM THAT I AM". It is all recorded in Exodus chapter three where He was sending Moses to free the children of Israel from enslavement in Egypt.

> *Then Moses said to God, 'Indeed, when I come to the children of Israel and say to them, The God of your fathers has sent me to you, and they say to me, 'What is His name? What shall I say to them?' And God said to Moses, 'I AM WHO I AM.' And He said, 'Thus you shall say to the children of Israel, 'I AM has sent me to you.'" [15] Moreover God said to Moses, 'Thus you shall say to the children of Israel: The Lord God of your fathers, the God of Abraham, the God of Isaac, and the God of Jacob, has sent me to you. This is My name forever, and this is My memorial to all generations. [16] Go and gather the elders of Israel together, and say to them, The Lord God of your fathers, the God of Abraham, of Isaac, and of Jacob, appeared to me, saying, I have surely visited you and seen what is done to you in Egypt; [17] and I have said I will bring you up out of the affliction of Egypt to the land of the Canaanites and the Hittites and the Amorites and the Perizzites and the Hivites and the Jebusites, to a land flowing with milk and honey." (Exodus 3:13–17 NKJV).*

God is also known as YAHWEH or JEHOVAH, which is really His proper name. The original spelling was YHWH and it is translated in English as LORD in all capital letters. This is to distinguish it from another of His names, Adonai, which also means Lord.

The name YAHWEH signifies that He is always present, available, and ready to answer those who call on Him. The name YHWH was considered to be so sacred that it was never pronounced.

God is sometimes referred to as the Godhead, which is "tripartite", triune, or three in one: God the Father, God the Son, and God the Holy Ghost, with Jesus being the Son. All three are equal yet distinct and functioning as one. Although God exists in these three, God is one and Christianity is built on this belief. Deuteronomy six, verse four says:

> *"Hear, O Israel! The LORD our God, the LORD is one!" (Deuteronomy 6:4 NKJV).*

The concept is that God is one yet God is three. The Jews threatened to stone Jesus when He tried to explain to them that He and the Father are equal or one.

John, in chapter 10 of his Gospel, recorded it this way:

> *"Now it was the Feast of Dedication in Jerusalem, and it was winter. 23 And Jesus walked in the temple, in Solomon's porch. 24 Then the Jews surrounded Him and said to Him, 'How long do You keep us in doubt? If You are the Christ, tell us plainly.' 25 Jesus answered them, 'I told you, and you do not believe. The works that I do in My Father's name, they bear witness of Me. 26 But you do not believe, because you are not of My sheep, as I said to you. 27 My sheep hear My voice, and I know them, and they follow Me. 28 And I give them eternal life, and they shall never perish; neither shall anyone snatch them out of My hand. 29 My Father, who has given them to Me, is greater than all; and no one is able to snatch them out of My Father's hand. 30 I and My Father are one'." (John 10:22–30 NKJV).*

Paul stressed the connection between God the Father and Jesus the Son to the Philippians.

> *"Let this mind be in you which was also in Christ Jesus, [6] who, being in the form of God, did not consider it robbery to be equal with God, [7]but made Himself of no reputation, taking the form of a bondservant, and coming in the likeness of men. [8] And being found in appearance as a man, He humbled Himself and became obedient to the point of death, even the death of the cross." (Philippians 2:5–8 NKJV).*

The triune nature of God was seen in operation when John baptized Jesus. All three in the trinity were active.

> *"When He had been baptized, Jesus came up immediately from the water; and behold, the Heavens were opened to Him, and He saw the Spirit of God descending like a dove and alighting upon Him. [17] And suddenly a voice came from Heaven, saying, 'This is My beloved Son, in whom I am well pleased'." (Matthew 3:16–17 NKJV).*

Paul had this to say to the church at Corinth as recorded in chapter eight of his first epistle to them:

> *"For even if there are so-called gods, whether in Heaven or on earth (as there are many gods and many lords), [6] yet for us there is one God, the Father, of whom are all things, and we for Him; and one Lord Jesus Christ, through whom are all things, and through whom we live." (1 Corinthians 8:5–6 NKJV).*

The triune nature of God is also revealed by John in his first epistle.

> *"For there are three that bear witness in Heaven: the Father, the Word, and the Holy Spirit; and these three are one." (1 John 5:7 NKJV).*

God is spirit and therefore no one has ever seen Him. But He wants people to worship Him. Jesus explained this to the Samaritan woman whom he encountered at the well at Sychar.

> *"Jesus said to her, "Woman, believe Me, the hour is coming when you will neither on this mountain, nor in Jerusalem, worship the Father. [22] You worship what you do not know; we know what we worship, for salvation is of the Jews. [23] But the hour is coming, and now is, when the true worshipers will worship the Father in spirit and truth; for the Father is seeking such to worship Him. [24] God is Spirit, and those who worship Him must worship in spirit and truth." (John 4:21–24 NKJV).*

Moses, who led the Israelites out of captivity from the Egyptians, explained to his followers the supremacy of God.

> *"For the Lord your God is God of gods and Lord of lords, the great God, mighty and awesome, who shows no partiality nor takes a bribe. [18] He administers justice for the fatherless and the widow, and loves the stranger, giving him food and clothing. [19] Therefore love the stranger, for you were*

> *strangers in the land of Egypt. [20] You shall fear the Lord your God; you shall serve Him, and to Him you shall hold fast, and take oaths in His name. [21]He is your praise, and He is your God, who has done for you these great and awesome things which your eyes have seen." (Deuteronomy 10:17–21 NKJV).*

God's attributes are too numerous to itemize. He is perfect, holy, loving, kind, merciful, gracious, truthful, faithful, dependable, just, long suffering, patient, forgiving, and not willing that any should perish.

God loves, among other things: obedience, reverence, truth, a cheerful giver, and those who honor and serve Him. He loves the sinner but hates sin. These are not the only things that He hates.

> *"These six things the Lord hates, Yes, seven are an abomination to Him: [17]A proud look, A lying tongue, Hands that shed innocent blood, [18] A heart that devises wicked plans, Feet that are swift in running to evil, [19] A false witness who speaks lies, And one who sows discord among brethren." (Proverbs 6:16–19 NKJV).*

While God has been described as loving, He is also a judge and those who die in their sins will face Him as such.

> *"I saw the dead, both great and small, standing before God's throne. And the books were opened, including the Book of Life. And the dead were judged according to what they had done, as recorded in the books. [13] The sea gave up its dead, and*

> *death and the grave gave up their dead. And all were judged according to their deeds. [14] Then death and the grave were thrown into the lake of fire. This lake of fire is the second death. [15]And anyone whose name was not found recorded in the Book of Life was thrown into the lake of fire." (Revelation 20:12–15 NLT).*

The born again Christian can find comfort in the words of Psalm 100 where the writer had this to say:

> *"Know that the Lord, He is God; It is He who has made us, and not we ourselves; We are His people and the sheep of His pasture. [4] Enter into His gates with thanksgiving, And into His courts with praise. Be thankful to Him, and bless His name. [5] For the Lord is good; His mercy is everlasting, And His truth endures to all generations." (Psalm 100:3–5 NKJV).*

God has several names and David had a special one for Him: "The King of Glory".

> *"Lift up your heads, O you gates! And be lifted up, you everlasting doors! And the King of glory shall come in. [8] Who is this King of glory? The Lord strong and mighty, The Lord mighty in battle. [9] Lift up your heads, O you gates! Lift up, you everlasting doors! And the King of glory shall come in. [10] Who is this King of glory? The Lord of hosts, He is the King of glory." (Psalm 24:7–10 NKJV).*

God is known by several names including Jehovah or God Almighty. He is Jehovah M'Kaddesh, the God who sanctifies; Jehovah Jireh, the God who provides; Jehovah Shalom the God our peace. God is Jehovah Rapha, the one who heals; Jehovah Nissi, God our banner; El-Shaddai, God the source of all blessings. He is also Adonai which means Master or Lord. God is Elohim, God of strength and power; God the Creator and Judge of the earth. This name also speaks to God's sovereignty and supreme power. God is also known as Jehovah El Elyon, God Most High; Jehovah El-Gibhor, Mighty God; Jehovah Tsidkenu, the Lord our righteousness and Jehovah El Olam, Everlasting God.

God is really a mystery to say the least. A being that defies description and goes beyond what we could ever think or imagine. He is too infinite for finite minds to comprehend. Paul the apostle, in his letter to the church at Rome, had this to say about Him.

> *Oh, how great are God's riches and wisdom and knowledge! How impossible it is for us to understand his decisions and his ways! 34 For who can know the LORD's thoughts? Who knows enough to give him advice? 35 And who has given him so much that he needs to pay it back? 36 For everything comes from him and exists by his power and is intended for his glory. All glory to him forever! Amen. (Romans 11:33-36 NLT).*

Top gospel singer Chris Tomlin, in one of his songs called God "Indescribable" and amazing.

From the highest of heights to the depths of the sea
Creation's revealing Your majesty
From the colors of fall to the fragrance of spring

Every creature unique in the song that it sings
All exclaiming
Indescribable, uncontainable,
You placed the stars in the sky and You know them by name.
You are amazing God
All powerful, untamable,
Awestruck we fall to our knees as we humbly proclaim
You are amazing God
Who has told every lightning bolt where it should go
Or seen heavenly storehouses laden with snow
Who imagined the sun and gives source to its light
Yet conceals it to bring us the coolness of night
None can fathom
Indescribable, uncontainable,
You placed the stars in the sky and You know them by name
You are amazing God
All powerful, untamable,
Awestruck we fall to our knees as we humbly proclaim
You are amazing God
You are amazing God
Indescribable, uncontainable,
You placed the stars in the sky and You know them by name.
You are amazing God
All powerful, untamable,
Awestruck we fall to our knees as we humbly proclaim
You are amazing God
Indescribable, uncontainable,
You placed the stars in the sky and You know them by name.
You are amazing God
Incomparable, unchangeable
You see the depths of my heart and You love me the same
You are amazing God
You are amazing God.

No matter the name by which you know God, never forget that He is God all by Himself and He will do what He wants to do whenever and however He likes.

Trust Him.

Chapter 10

Who Is Jesus Christ?

Jesus Christ is the Son of God. He is really Jesus the Christ, meaning that He is the Messiah, since the word Christ is not His surname but, rather, means "Anointed One" or "Messiah".

Jesus was conceived by the Holy Spirit, born of a virgin named Mary, was crucified, died, and was buried. He was resurrected from the dead and miraculously ascended into Heaven.

The story of Jesus Christ can be found in the Gospels of Matthew, Mark, Luke, and John. His birth was prophesied in the Old Testament by the prophet Isaiah where he spoke the following words as set out in chapter seven of his book:

> *"Therefore the Lord Himself will give you a sign: Behold, the virgin shall conceive and bear a Son, and shall call His name Immanuel." (Isaiah 7:14 NKJV).*

Isaiah went even further in chapter nine.

> *"For unto us a Child is born, Unto us a Son is given; And the government will be upon His shoulder. And His name will be called Wonderful, Counselor, Mighty God, Everlasting Father, Prince of Peace. [7] Of the*

> *increase of His government and peace there will be no end, Upon the throne of David and over His kingdom, To order it and establish it with judgment and justice from that time forward, even forever. The zeal of the Lord of hosts will perform this." (Isaiah 9:6–7 NKJV).*

When the Angel Gabriel announced to Mary that she would have a son, he not only gave her the baby's name but His characteristics. It is all written in Luke chapter one, verses 30 to 32.

> *"Do not be afraid, Mary, for you have found favor with God. [31] And behold, you will conceive in your womb and bring forth a Son, and shall call His name Jesus. [32] He will be great, and will be called the Son of the Highest; and the Lord God will give Him the throne of His father David." (Luke 1:30–32 NKJV).*

The birth of Jesus was announced to shepherds, not by any ordinary person but by angels. They were tending their flocks near Bethlehem where Jesus was born.

> *"Now there were in the same country shepherds living out in the fields, keeping watch over their flock by night. [9] And behold, an angel of the Lord stood before them, and the glory of the Lord shone around them, and they were greatly afraid. [10] Then the angel said to them, "Do not be afraid, for behold, I bring you good tidings of great joy which will be to all people. [11] For there is born to you this day in the city of David a*

Saviour, who is Christ the Lord. [12] And this will be the sign to you: You will find a Babe wrapped in swaddling clothes, lying in a manger." [13] And suddenly there was with the angel a multitude of the eavenly host praising God and saying: [14] 'Glory to God in the highest, And on earth peace, goodwill toward men!' [15] So it was, when the angels had gone away from them into Heaven, that the shepherds said to one another, 'Let us now go to Bethlehem and see this thing that has come to pass, which the Lord has made known to us.' [16] And they came with haste and found Mary and Joseph, and the Babe lying in a manger. [17] Now when they had seen Him, they made widely known the saying which was told them concerning this Child." (Luke 2: 8–17 NKJV).

When Jesus was taken to the temple in Jerusalem to be dedicated to the Lord, something happened which again showed that He was no ordinary child, but the Messiah.

"And behold, there was a man in Jerusalem whose name was Simeon, and this man was just and devout, waiting for the Consolation of Israel, and the Holy Spirit was upon him. [26] And it had been revealed to him by the Holy Spirit that he would not see death before he had seen the Lord's Christ. [27] So he came by the Spirit into the temple. And when the parents brought in the Child Jesus, to do for Him according to the custom of the law, [28] he took Him up in his arms and blessed God and said: [29] 'Lord, now You are letting Your

servant depart in peace, According to Your word; [30] For my eyes have seen Your salvation [31] Which You have prepared before the face of all peoples, [32] A light to bring revelation to the Gentiles, And the glory of Your people Israel'." (Luke 2:25–32 NKJV).

Jesus was both man and God, divine and human, and He sometimes referred to Himself as both the Son of God and the Son of Man. Son of Man was also a Messianic title to the Jews. He was the Son of God, not only because of His miraculous conception but also because God said He was His Son.

The story is told in Matthew chapter three concerning Jesus' baptism by John the Baptist. Verses 16 and 17 speak directly of God acknowledging that Jesus is His Son.

"When He had been baptized, Jesus came up immediately from the water; and behold, the Heavens were opened to Him, and He saw the Spirit of God descending like a dove and alighting upon Him. [17] And suddenly a voice came from Heaven, saying, 'This is My beloved Son, in whom I am well pleased'." (Matthew 3:16–17 NKJV).

John the Baptist also testified that Jesus was the Son of God. Chapter one of John's Gospel records the following:

"And John bore witness, saying, 'I saw the Spirit descending from Heaven like a dove, and He remained upon Him. [33] I did not know Him, but He who sent me to baptize with water said to me, 'Upon whom you see the Spirit descending, and remaining

on Him, this is He who baptizes with the Holy Spirit.' [34] And I have seen and testified that this is the Son of God." (John 1:32–34 NKJV).

God again acknowledged that Jesus was His Son during what is described in Matthew chapter 17 as "the transfiguration on the mount".

"While he was still speaking, behold, a bright cloud overshadowed them; and suddenly a voice came out of the cloud, saying, 'This is My beloved Son, in whom I am well pleased. Hear Him!' [6] And when the disciples heard it, they fell on their faces and were greatly afraid. (Matthew 17:5–6 NKJV).

But Jesus was not only the Son of God, He was God. John's Gospel described Him as The Word:

"In the beginning was the Word, and the Word was with God, and the Word was God. [2] He was in the beginning with God. [3]All things were made through Him, and without Him nothing was made that was made. [4] In Him was life, and the life was the light of men. [5] And the light shines in the darkness, and the darkness did not comprehend it." (John 1:1–5 NKJV).

John continued in that same chapter by describing Jesus as The Light.

"He was in the world, and the world was made through Him, and the world did not know Him. [11]He came to His own, and His own did not receive Him. [12] But as many as received Him, to them He gave the right to become children of God, to those who believe in His name: [13] who were born, not of blood, nor of the will of the flesh, nor of the will of man, but of God. [14] And the Word became flesh and dwelt among us, and we beheld His glory, the glory as of the only begotten of the Father, full of grace and truth. [15] John bore witness of Him and cried out, saying, 'This was He of whom I said, 'He who comes after me is preferred before me, for He was before me.'" [16] And of His fullness we have all received, and grace for grace. [17] For the law was given through Moses, but grace and truth came through Jesus Christ. [18]No one has seen God at any time. The only begotten Son, who is in the bosom of the Father, He has declared Him." (John 1:10–18 NKJV).

The disciples recognized Jesus as the Son of God, the first being Nathaniel. Earlier, when he was told by Philip that he had found the Messiah, Jesus of Nazareth, Nathaniel had asked the question: ***"Can any good thing come out of Nazareth?" (John 1:46 NKJV).*** When they met and Jesus identified certain traits about him, Nathaniel replied: ***"Rabbi, You are the Son of God! You are the King of Israel!" (John 1:49 NKJV).***

The other disciple who recognized Jesus as the Son of God was Peter. Here was a man who had walked with and lived closely with Jesus and saw His miracles and His lifestyle. He was the one who walked toward Jesus on water. Matthew records the event in chapter 16 of his Gospel. Jesus was speaking to the disciples, warning them about not following the doctrine of the Pharisees and Sadducees, when Peter's confession unfolded.

> *"When Jesus came into the region of Caesarea Philippi, He asked His disciples, saying, 'Who do men say that I, the Son of Man, am?' [14] So they said, 'Some say John the Baptist, some Elijah, and others Jeremiah or one of the prophets.' [15] He said to them, 'But who do you say that I am?' [16] Simon Peter answered and said, 'You are the Christ, the Son of the living God.' (Matthew 16:13–16 NKJV).*

Jesus explained that that truth was revealed to Peter by the Holy Spirit.

There were others who acknowledged that Jesus was indeed the Son of God. During the crucifixion, one of the men who killed Him confessed that, based on all that he had witnessed, Jesus certainly was the Son of God.

> *"So when the centurion and those with him, who were guarding Jesus, saw the earthquake and the things that had happened, they feared greatly, saying, 'Truly this was the Son of God!'" (Matthew 27:54 NKJV).*

Paul the apostle also acknowledged that Jesus was both God and man. In the second chapter of his epistle to the Philippians he wrote:

> *"Let this mind be in you which was also in Christ Jesus, [6] who, being in the form of God, did not consider it robbery to be equal with God, [7] but made Himself of no reputation, taking the form of a bondservant, and coming in the likeness of men. [8] And being found in appearance as a man, He humbled Himself and became obedient to the point of death, even the death of the cross. [9] Therefore God also has highly exalted Him and given Him the name which is above every name, [10] that at the name of Jesus every knee should bow, of those in Heaven, and of those on earth, and of those under the earth, [11] and that every tongue should confess that Jesus Christ is Lord, to the glory of God the Father." (Philippians 2:5–11 NKJV).*

Jesus proved He was the Son of God by His actions. Not only did He perform miracles and wonders, but He never sinned. Even when He was dying on the cross, rather than curse or seek revenge over those who were crucifying Him, He asked God the Father to forgive them.

There is no doubt that Jesus was a man. Like all human beings, He was the offspring of a woman. He lived the life of a man, experiencing all the things that humans go through. Jesus grew up in a village with family and earthly friends. He was the son of a carpenter and, based on Jewish culture, would have been trained in His father's craft. Jesus knew about sadness and tears, as shown in the story of the raising of His friend Lazarus from the dead in the Gospel of John, chapter 11. Jesus got angry when He found people in the temple doing business. He had compassion on several people who needed healing or some miracle, and even rebuked His disciples for trying to keep children from coming to Him. He experienced every emotion that is known to man, including hunger, rejection, thirst, tiredness, pain, betrayal, desertion by His friends, and finally death and burial.

Jesus, however, proved that He was the Son of God when He arose from the dead, as He had predicted in His preaching.

Jesus Christ is the Savior and was sent to earth by His Father, God, to save sinners, to redeem them to Himself so that they could have an opportunity to spend eternity with Him. God had made the first human beings, whom we know as Adam and Eve, and they shared His company and were perfect. They lived in the Garden of Eden but they disobeyed Him and sinned, as told in the book of Genesis. God, who wanted a perfect people to serve Him, decided that He would reconcile man to Him. He designed a divine plan where He would send His Son, who was perfect in every way. He had to be the ultimate sacrifice, being both God and man.

Some have questioned how someone could be both God and man at the same time. The answer can be found in Luke chapter one, verses 34 and 35, right after the angel Gabriel had announced to Mary that she had been chosen to be the mother of the Messiah or Savior of the world.

> *"Then Mary said to the angel, 'How can this be, since I do not know a man?' [35] And the angel answered and said to her, 'The Holy Spirit will come upon you, and the power of the Highest will overshadow you; therefore, also, that Holy One who is to be born will be called the Son of God'." (Luke 1:34–35 NKJV).*

The Message Bible puts it this way:

> *"Mary asked the angel, 'But how can I have a baby? I am a virgin.' [35] The angel replied, 'The Holy Spirit shall come upon you, and the power of God shall overshadow you; so the baby born to you will be utterly holy—the Son of God'." (Luke 1:34–35 TMB).*

But Mary wasn't the only one that an angel told about the birth of Jesus. The Living Bible tells the story this way in Matthew chapter one.

> *"These are the facts concerning the birth of Jesus Christ: His mother, Mary, was engaged to be married to Joseph. But while she was still a virgin she became pregnant by the Holy Spirit. [19] Then Joseph, her fiancé, being a man of stern principle, decided to break the engagement but to do it quietly, as he didn't want to publicly disgrace her. [20] As he lay awake considering this, he fell into a dream, and saw an angel standing beside him. 'Joseph, son of David,' the angel said, 'don't hesitate to take Mary as your wife! For the child within her has been conceived by the Holy Spirit. [21] And she will have a Son, and you shall name Him Jesus (meaning 'Saviour'), for he will save His people from their sins. [22] This will fulfill God's message through his prophets'." (Matthew 1:18–22 TLB).*

Jesus testified that He was the Son of God. He had healed a man by the pool of Bethesda on the Sabbath day and had claimed that God was His Father. According to John chapter five, this angered the Jews and they wanted to kill Him.

> *"Then Jesus answered and said to them, 'Most assuredly, I say to you, the Son can do nothing of Himself, but what He sees the Father do; for whatever He does, the Son also does in like manner. [20] For the Father loves the Son, and shows Him all things that He Himself does; and He will show Him greater works than these, that you may marvel. [21] For as the Father raises the dead and gives life to them, even so the Son gives life to whom He will. [22] For the Father judges no one, but has committed all judgment to the Son, [23] that all should honour the Son just as they honor the Father. He who does not honour the Son does not honor the Father who sent Him'." (John 5:19–23 NKJV).*

In the Gospel of Luke, chapter four, Jesus, without saying the actual words, declared that He was the one who was sent from the Father.

> *"So He came to Nazareth, where He had been brought up. And as His custom was, He went into the synagogue on the Sabbath day, and stood up to read. [17] And He was handed the book of the prophet Isaiah. And when He had opened the book, He found the place where it was written: [18] 'The Spirit of the Lord is upon Me, Because He has anointed Me To preach the gospel to the poor; He has sent Me to heal the broken-hearted, To proclaim liberty to the captives And recovery of sight to the blind, To set at liberty those who are oppressed; [19] To proclaim the acceptable year of the Lord.'*

> *[20] Then He closed the book, and gave it back to the attendant and sat down. And the eyes of all who were in the synagogue were fixed on Him. [21] And He began to say to them, 'Today this Scripture is fulfilled in your hearing'." (Luke 4:16–21 NKJV).*

Isaiah had made this prophecy a long time before and it is significant that Jesus was "given" this book rather than any other. This would have been the Scripture designated to be read in all synagogues on that day. By reading that specific passage, Jesus was telling the Jews that He was in fact the Messiah that Isaiah was talking about.

Jesus spent about 33 years on earth, but His ministry only spanned the last three. This was the period when He proved that He had the power of God.

He started out by turning water into wine; His miracles then went on to include opening blind eyes, curing deafness, healing the sick, casting out demons, and even raising the dead. In addition He calmed a storm, walked on water, multiplied a boy's lunch so that it fed more than five thousand people, caused a great fish catch where just before there were no fish, and He even read people's thoughts.

The New Testament records 37 miracles performed by Jesus, but John in his Gospel states that there were a lot more. According to verse 25 of chapter 21, they were too numerous to mention.

> *"And there are also many other things that Jesus did, which if they were written one by one, I suppose that even the world itself could not contain the books that would be written." (John 21:25 NKJV).*

Paul in his letter to the Colossian church explained to them some of the attributes of Jesus Christ:

> *"Christ is the visible image of the invisible God. He existed before anything was created and is supreme over all creation, [16] for through him God created everything in the Heavenly realms and on earth. He made the things we can see and the things we can't see—such as thrones, kingdoms, rulers, and authorities in the unseen world. Everything was created through him and for him. [17] He existed before anything else, and he holds all creation together. [18] Christ is also the head of the church, which is his body. He is the beginning, supreme over all who rise from the dead. So He is first in everything. [19] For God in all his fullness was pleased to live in Christ, [20] and through him God reconciled everything to himself. He made peace with everything in Heaven and on earth by means of Christ's blood on the cross." (Colossians 1:15–20 NLT).*

The part Jesus plays in the life of the Christian has also been set out in the first chapter of Paul's epistle to the Colossians where he said:

> *"This includes you who were once far away from God. You were his enemies, separated from him by your evil thoughts and actions. [22] Yet now he has reconciled you to himself through the death of Christ in his physical body. As a result, he has brought you into his own presence, and you are holy and blameless as you stand before him without a single*

> *fault. [23]But you must continue to believe this truth and stand firmly in it. Don't drift away from the assurance you received when you heard the Good News. The Good News has been preached all over the world, and I, Paul, have been appointed as God's servant to proclaim it." (Colossians 1:21–23 NLT).*

Jesus created controversy among the Jews when He declared, as recorded in John chapter 10, verse 30, that He and the Father are one. He did not say that they were alike, but rather that they are one. Jesus pointed out to the Jews in John chapter 10 that if they judged Him on the miracles that He had done they would have to conclude that He was God.

> *"If I do not do the works of My Father, do not believe Me; [38] but if I do, though you do not believe Me, believe the works, that you may know and believe that the Father is in Me, and I in Him." (John 10:37–38 NKJV).*

Jesus Christ is not only God but John chapter three, verses 16–18 show that He is the Savior of the world.

> *"For God so loved the world that He gave His only begotten Son, that whoever believes in Him should not perish but have everlasting life. [17]For God did not send His Son into the world to condemn the world, but that the world through Him might be saved.[18]'He who believes in Him is not condemned; but he who does not believe is condemned already, because he has not believed in the name of the only begotten Son of God'." (John 3:16–18 NKJV).*

Jesus categorically stated that He was indeed the Savior when He said in John chapter 14, verse six:

> *"I am the way, the truth, and the life. No one comes to the Father except through Me." (John 14:6 NKJV).*

On the day of Pentecost, Peter, filled with the Holy Ghost, made this important statement to the astonished crowd who had gathered in Jerusalem:

> *"Repent, and be baptized every one of you in the name of Jesus Christ for the remission of sins, and ye shall receive the gift of the Holy Ghost." (Acts 2:38 NKJV).*

Peter had occasion to again stress that salvation had to come through Jesus Christ when he was accused before the authorities after the healing of the crippled man at the temple gate.

> *"Let it be known to you all, and to all the people of Israel, that by the name of Jesus Christ of Nazareth, whom you crucified, whom God raised from the dead, by Him this man stands here before you whole. 11 This is the 'stone which was rejected by you builders, which has become the chief cornerstone. 12 Nor is there salvation in any other, for there is no other name under Heaven given among men by which we must be saved." (Acts 4:10–12 NKJV).*

Jesus, while He was with His disciples, explained to them that He and the Father are inseparable. His answer as given to Thomas is found in John chapter 14 starting at verse seven.

> *"If you had known Me, you would have known My Father also; and from now on you know Him and have seen Him. [8] Philip said to Him, 'Lord, show us the Father, and it is sufficient for us.' [9] Jesus said to him, 'Have I been with you so long, and yet you have not known Me, Philip? He who has seen Me has seen the Father; so how can you say, 'Show us the Father'? [10] Do you not believe that I am in the Father, and the Father in Me? The words that I speak to you I do not speak on My own authority; but the Father who dwells in Me does the works. [11] Believe Me that I am in the Father and the Father in Me, or else believe Me for the sake of the works themselves'." (John 14:7–11 NKJV).*

Romans chapter six, verse 23 also has something to say about Jesus Christ being Savior:

> *"For the wages of sin [is] death; but the gift of God [is] eternal life through Jesus Christ our Lord." (Romans 6:23 NKJV).*

Jesus has promised that He will return and there are numerous Scriptures that speak to this. This prophesy is one that Christians embrace with a passion because it is the very bedrock of their faith and belief.

Even Satan knew that Jesus was the Son of God. The devil tried to get Him to obey his evil requests during what has been described in Matthew chapter four as "the temptation of Jesus Christ". He knew if Jesus had given in, He would not have been the Son of God because that exalted One would have discerned the evil trick.

This encounter with Satan took place just as Jesus had ended a 40 day fast.

> *And when He had fasted forty days and forty nights, afterward He was hungry. [3]Now when the tempter came to Him, he said, 'If You are the Son of God, command that these stones become bread.' [4] But He answered and said, 'It is written, 'Man shall not live by bread alone, but by every word that proceeds from the mouth of God.' [5] Then the devil took Him up into the holy city, set Him on the pinnacle of the temple, [6] and said to Him, 'If You are the Son of God, throw Yourself down. For it is written: 'He shall give His angels charge over you, 'and, 'In their hands they shall bear you up, Lest you dash your foot against a stone.' [7] Jesus said to him, 'It is written again, 'You shall not tempt the Lord your God.' [8]Again, the devil took Him up on an exceedingly high mountain, and showed Him all the kingdoms of the world and their glory. [9] And he said to Him, "'All these things I will give You if You will fall down and worship me.' [10] Then Jesus said to him, 'Away with you, Satan! For it is written, 'You shall worship the Lord your God, and Him only you shall serve'." (Matthew 4:2–10 NKJV).*

The demons also knew that Jesus was the Son of God. The story is told in Matthew chapter eight where Jesus encountered two men who were demon possessed.

> *"When He had come to the other side, to the country of the Gergesenes, there met Him two demon-possessed men, coming out of the tombs, exceedingly fierce, so that no one could pass that way. [29] And suddenly they cried out, saying, 'What have we to do with You, Jesus, You Son of God? Have You come here to torment us before the time?' " (Matthew 8:28–29 NKJV).*

But that was not the only occasion where the demon-possessed recognized Jesus. Mark chapter one reveals that soon after He had called some of His disciples, He encountered a demon-possessed man.

> *"Then they went into Capernaum, and immediately on the Sabbath He entered the synagogue and taught. [22] And they were astonished at His teaching, for He taught them as one having authority, and not as the scribes. [23] Now there was a man in their synagogue with an unclean spirit. And he cried out, [24] saying, 'Let us alone! What have we to do with You, Jesus of Nazareth? Did You come to destroy us? I know who You are—the Holy One of God!' " (Mark 1:21 –24 NKJV).*

Jesus identified Himself in several ways during His ministry. According to Him, He was "The bread of Life" (John 6:35). He also described Himself as "The Light of the world"

(John 8:12). In John 10:9 He called Himself "The Door". In John 10, verses 11–14 He is characterized as "The Good Shepherd". Jesus told Martha that He was "The Resurrection and the Life" (John 11:25). To Thomas He identified Himself as "The Way, the Truth, and the Life" (John 14: 6). In John 15 Jesus announced that He was "The True Vine" and His Father the Husbandman.

The hope, belief, and expectation of every Christian is that Jesus Christ is coming again. This is the pillar on which Christianity is built.

John the apostle walked with Jesus during His three years of ministry and was so close to Him that he is sometimes referred to as "the disciple whom Jesus loved". John was present for most of the iconic events of that day and it was to him that Jesus gave the revelation of what is to come. John, as instructed, recorded the vision, which can be read in its entirety in the book of Revelation, the last book in the Bible.

> *"I was in the Spirit on the Lord's Day, and*
> *I heard behind me a loud voice, as of a*
> *trumpet, 11 saying, 'I am the Alpha and*
> *the Omega, the First and the Last,' and,*
> *'What you see, write in a book and send*
> *it to the seven churches which are in Asia:*
> *to Ephesus, to Smyrna, to Pergamos, to*
> *Thyatira, to Sardis, to Philadelphia, and to*
> *Laodicea.' 12 Then I turned to see the voice*
> *that spoke with me. And having turned I*
> *saw seven golden lampstands, 13 and in the*
> *midst of the seven lampstands One like the*
> *Son of Man, clothed with a garment down*
> *to the feet and girded about the chest with*
> *a golden band. 14 His head and hair were*
> *white like wool, as white as snow, and His*

> *eyes like a flame of fire; [15] His feet were like fine brass, as if refined in a furnace, and His voice as the sound of many waters; [16] He had in His right hand seven stars, out of His mouth went a sharp two-edged sword, and His countenance was like the sun shining in its strength. [17] And when I saw Him, I fell at His feet as dead. But He laid His right hand on me, saying to me, "Do not be afraid; I am the First and the Last. [18] I am He who lives, and was dead, and behold, I am alive forevermore. Amen." (Revelation 1:10–18 NKJV).*

Jesus has promised that He will return to earth for His chosen people, the Church, or if you prefer, all Christians. He made this promise to His disciples as He was preparing to be crucified.

> *"Let not your heart be troubled; you believe in God, believe also in Me. [2] In My Father's house are many mansions; if it were not so, I would have told you. I go to prepare a place for you. [3] And if I go and prepare a place for you, I will come again and receive you to Myself; that where I am, there you may be also." (John 14: 1–3 NKJV).*

After His resurrection Jesus was with His disciples, instructing them what they should do after He left the earth. This included the command to wait for the Holy Spirit, or the Comforter as He is sometimes called.

> *"Now when He had spoken these things, while they watched, He was taken up, and a cloud received Him out of their sight. [10] And while they looked steadfastly toward Heaven as He went up, behold, two men stood by them in white apparel, [11] who also said, 'Men of Galilee, why do you stand gazing up into Heaven? This same Jesus, who was taken up from you into Heaven, will so come in like manner as you saw Him go into Heaven'." (Acts 1:10–11 NKJV).*

The first epistle to the Thessalonians, chapter four also speaks to the return of Jesus Christ.

> *"For the Lord Himself will descend from Heaven with a shout, with the voice of an archangel, and with the trumpet of God. And the dead in Christ will rise first. [17] Then we who are alive and remain shall be caught up together with them in the clouds to meet the Lord in the air. And thus we shall always be with the Lord." (1 Thessalonians 4:16–17 NKJV).*

Every Christian lives with the hope, the faith, and the confident expectation that Jesus Christ will return.

Chapter 11

The Name of Jesus

Jesus emphasized that there is power in His name and has given His followers the authority to use it. As a born again Christian you have been given the right to call on and use the name of Jesus.

> *"Most assuredly, I say to you, he who believes in Me, the works that I do he will do also; and greater works than these he will do, because I go to My Father. [13] And whatever you ask in My name, that I will do, that the Father may be glorified in the Son. [14] If you ask anything in My name, I will do it." (John 14:12–14 NKJV).*

He repeated this as recorded in chapter 16 of the same Gospel of John:

> *"And in that day you will ask Me nothing. Most assuredly, I say to you, whatever you ask the Father in My name He will give you. [24] Until now you have asked nothing in My name. Ask, and you will receive, that your joy may be full." (John 16:23–24 NKJV).*

Jesus' name is the only one through which a sinner can be saved. He told His disciple Thomas, as recorded in the Gospel of John, chapter 14:

> *"I am the way, the truth, and the life. No one comes to the Father except through Me." (John 14:6 NKJV).*

When Jesus gave what is known as "the Great Commission", He outlined the power that would come by using His name. And He said to them,

> *"Go into all the world and preach the gospel to every creature. [16] He who believes and is baptized will be saved; but he who does not believe will be condemned. [17] And these signs will follow those who believe: In My name they will cast out demons; they will speak with new tongues; [18] they will take up serpents; and if they drink anything deadly, it will by no means hurt them; they will lay hands on the sick, and they will recover." (Mark 16:15 –18 NKJV).*

To say that Jesus' name is powerful is a great understatement. In fact, His name is all-powerful. At the announcement of his birth, the angels told Joseph exactly what He should be called and why He should be given that name.

> *"But while he thought about these things, behold, an angel of the Lord appeared to him in a dream, saying, "Joseph, son of David, do not be afraid to take to you Mary your wife, for that which is conceived in her is of the Holy Spirit. [21] And she will bring forth a Son,*

and you shall call His name Jesus, for He will save His people from their sins." (Matthew 1:20–21 NKJV).

Paul, in chapter two of his letter to the Philippians, told them that God had given Jesus a name that was above all others.

"Let this mind be in you which was also in Christ Jesus, [6] who, being in the form of God, did not consider it robbery to be equal with God, [7] but made Himself of no reputation, taking the form of a bondservant, and coming in the likeness of men. [8] And being found in appearance as a man, He humbled Himself and became obedient to the point of death, even the death of the cross. [9] Therefore God also has highly exalted Him and given Him the name which is above every name, [10] that at the name of Jesus every knee should bow, of those in Heaven, and of those on earth, and of those under the earth, [11] and that every tongue should confess that Jesus Christ is Lord, to the glory of God the Father." (Philippians 2:5–11 NKJV).

This is how the New Living Translation expresses that same passage:

You must have the same attitude that Christ Jesus had. [6] Though he was God, he did not think of equality with God as something to cling to. [7] Instead, he gave up his divine privileges; he took the humble position of a slave and was born as a human being. When he appeared in human form, [8] he humbled himself in obedience to God and died a criminal's death on a cross. [9] Therefore, God elevated him to the place of highest honor and gave him the name above all other names, [10] that at the name of Jesus every knee should bow, in heaven and on earth and under the earth,[11] and every tongue declare that Jesus Christ is Lord, to the glory of God the Father. (Philippians 2:5–11 NLT).

Paul, in his letter to the church at Ephesus, again emphasized the importance of the name of Jesus.

"Therefore I also, after I heard of your faith in the Lord Jesus and your love for all the saints, [16] do not cease to give thanks for you, making mention of you in my prayers: [17] that the God of our Lord Jesus Christ, the Father of glory, may give to you the spirit of wisdom and revelation in the knowledge of Him, [18] the eyes of your understanding being enlightened; that you may know what is the hope of His calling, what are the riches of the glory of His inheritance in the saints, [19] and what is the exceeding greatness of His power toward us who believe, according to the working of His mighty power [20] which He worked in Christ when He raised Him from the dead and seated Him at His right hand in the Heavenly places, [21] far above all principality and power and might and dominion, and every name that is named, not only in this age but also in that which is to come. [22] And He put all things under His feet, and gave Him to be

> *head over all things to the church, [23] which is His body, the fullness of Him who fills all in all." (Ephesians 1:15–23 NKJV).*

It is significant that even evil spirits know and respect the name of Jesus. There is the story in Acts chapter 19 where Paul was visiting the church at Ephesus. A group of people who were not Christians, attempted to use the name of Jesus for their own purposes.

> *"Then some of the itinerant Jewish exorcists took it upon themselves to call the name of the Lord Jesus over those who had evil spirits, saying, 'We exorcise you by the Jesus whom Paul preaches.' [14] Also there were seven sons of Sceva, a Jewish chief priest, who did so. [15] And the evil spirit answered and said, 'Jesus I know, and Paul I know; but who are you?' [16] Then the man in whom the evil spirit was leaped on them, overpowered them, and prevailed against them, so that they fled out of that house naked and wounded. [17] This became known both to all Jews and Greeks dwelling in Ephesus; and fear fell on them all, and the name of the Lord Jesus was magnified. [18] And many who had believed came confessing and telling their deeds." (Acts 19:13–18 NKJV).*

But there is more to using the name of Jesus than just calling it. In order to ignite the power in that name there must be a connection between the person using it and Jesus Himself. You cannot just use the power without having a relationship with the power source. Remember Jesus said that to be able to use His name, you must believe on Him.

> *"And these signs will follow those who believe: In My name they will cast out demons; they will speak with new tongues; [18] they will take up serpents; and if they drink anything deadly, it will by no means hurt them; they will lay hands on the sick, and they will recover." (Mark 16:17–18 NKJV).*

The sons of Sceva, as described in an earlier passage of Scripture, tried using the names of Jesus and Paul, but the demons recognized that they did not have the power. Because of the absence of the Holy Spirit the demons were not afraid. Paul talked about this power in chapter four of his second letter to the Corinthian church.

> *"But we have this treasure in earthen vessels, that the excellence of the power may be of God and not of us. [8] We are hard-pressed on every side, yet not crushed; we are perplexed, but not in despair; [9] persecuted, but not forsaken; struck down, but not destroyed— [10] always carrying about in the body the dying of the Lord Jesus, that the life of Jesus also may be manifested in our body. [11] For we who live are always delivered to death for Jesus' sake, that the life of Jesus also may be manifested in our mortal flesh." (2 Corinthians 4:7–11 NKJV).*

The New Living Translation quotes verse seven this way:

> *"We now have this light shining in our hearts, but we ourselves are like fragile clay jars containing this great treasure. This makes it clear that our great power is from God, not from ourselves." (2 Corinthians 4:7 NLT).*

The born again Christian can use the name of Jesus Christ because he or she has the Holy Spirit living within and it is the Holy Spirit who gives the authority to call on that powerful and anointed name.

The story is told in Acts chapter three of the lame man who sat at the temple gate in Jerusalem and who encountered Peter and John. He begged these apostles for money but through the name of Jesus Christ he got something worth much more.

> *"And fixing his eyes on him, with John, Peter said, 'Look at us.' [5] So he gave them his attention, expecting to receive something from them. [6] Then Peter said, 'Silver and gold I do not have, but what I do have I give you: In the name of Jesus Christ of Nazareth, rise up and walk.' [7] And he took him by the right hand and lifted him up, and immediately his feet and ankle bones received strength. [8] So he, leaping up, stood and walked and entered the temple with them—walking, leaping, and praising God. [9] And all the people saw him walking and praising God." (Acts 3:4–9 NKJV).*

Jesus Christ has been described as the King of kings and the Lord of lords. Paul the apostle spoke to this in the sixth chapter of his first epistle to Timothy.

> *"I urge you in the sight of God who gives life to all things, and before Christ Jesus who witnessed the good confession before Pontius Pilate, [14] that you keep this commandment without spot, blameless until our Lord Jesus Christ's appearing, [15] which*

He will manifest in His own time, He who is the blessed and only Potentate, the King of kings and Lord of lords, [16] who alone has immortality, dwelling in unapproachable light, whom no man has seen or can see, to whom be honour and everlasting power. Amen." (1 Timothy 6:13–16 NKJV).

These titles are also revealed in the book of Revelation, chapter 19 where John spoke of his vision of Jesus Christ in Heaven.

"He had a name written that no one knew except Himself. [13] He was clothed with a robe dipped in blood, and His name is called The Word of God. [14] And the armies in Heaven, clothed in fine linen, white and clean, followed Him on white horses. [15] Now out of His mouth goes a sharp sword, that with it He should strike the nations. And He Himself will rule them with a rod of iron. He Himself treads the winepress of the fierceness and wrath of Almighty God. [16] And He has on His robe and on His thigh a name written: KING OF KINGS AND LORD OF LORDS." (Revelation 19:12–16 NKJV).

Chapter 12
The Blood of Jesus

The blood of Jesus is the powerful vehicle that transforms a repentant sinner into a child of God or a born again Christian. It is the means by which God grants forgiveness and pardon for transgressions against His law.

The principle of blood being the element for cleansing sin goes back to Old Testament times and the Mosaic Law, and is referred to as atonement. God made a covenant or sacred agreement with His chosen people Israel which was so solemn that it was confirmed in blood. There had to be a sacrifice and the shedding of blood. Once a year, the priest was required to offer the blood of animals on the altar of the temple for the sins of the people.

God emphasized the sanctity and importance of blood in Leviticus chapter 17 when He told the Israelites that they shouldn't eat blood nor the flesh of animals whose blood hadn't been drained.

> *"For the life of the flesh is in the blood, and I have given it to you upon the altar to make atonement for your souls; for it is the blood that makes atonement for the soul." (Leviticus 17:11 NKJV).*

This blood offering was limited in its effectiveness in that it had to be done repeatedly but it was considered necessary at that time.

> *"Therefore not even the first covenant was dedicated without blood. [19] For when Moses had spoken every precept to all the people according to the law, he took the blood of calves and goats, with water, scarlet wool, and hyssop, and sprinkled both the book itself and all the people, [20] saying, 'This is the blood of the covenant which God has commanded you.' [21] Then likewise he sprinkled with blood both the tabernacle and all the vessels of the ministry. [22] And according to the law almost all things are purified with blood, and without shedding of blood there is no remission." (Hebrews 9:18–22 NKJV).*

The Mosaic sacrifice was the forerunner of the ultimate sacrifice that was to come through the crucifixion of Jesus Christ. Because of Adam's sin of disobedience, God had to find a way to restore His relationship with man. The blood of animals wasn't good enough. Animal blood covered the sins, but a better offering was needed to cleanse or remove the sin. There had to be the offering of a sinless sacrifice, and that was Jesus.

Conceived by the Holy Spirit and born of a virgin, Jesus Christ was no ordinary man, He was the Son of God. Not having an earthly father, there was no sin to be transferred. He was the perfect sacrifice, holy, not having the sin nature. He was also morally pure.

"But Christ came as High Priest of the good things to come, with the greater and more perfect tabernacle not made with hands, that is, not of this creation. [12]Not with the blood of goats and calves, but with His own blood He entered the Most Holy Place once for all, having obtained eternal redemption. [13] For if the blood of bulls and goats and the ashes of a heifer, sprinkling the unclean, sanctifies for the purifying of the flesh, [14] how much more shall the blood of Christ, who through the eternal Spirit offered Himself without spot to God, cleanse your conscience from dead works to serve the living God? [15] And for this reason He is the Mediator of the new covenant, by means of death, for the redemption of the transgressions under the first covenant, that those who are called may receive the promise of the eternal inheritance." (Hebrews 9:11–15 NKJV).

This passage may be better understood from the New Living Translation of the Bible:

"So Christ has now become the High Priest over all the good things that have come. He has entered that greater, more perfect Tabernacle in Heaven, which was not made by human hands and is not part of this created world. [12] With his own blood—not the blood of goats and calves—he entered the Most Holy Place once for all time and secured our redemption forever. [13] Under the old system, the blood of goats and bulls and the ashes of a heifer could cleanse people's bodies from

ceremonial impurity. [14] Just think how much more the blood of Christ will purify our consciences from sinful deeds so that we can worship the living God. For by the power of the eternal Spirit, Christ offered himself to God as a perfect sacrifice for our sins. [15] That is why he is the one who mediates a new covenant between God and people, so that all who are called can receive the eternal inheritance God has promised them. For Christ died to set them free from the penalty of the sins they had committed under that first covenant." (Hebrews 9:11–15 NLT).

John the Baptist hailed Jesus as extraordinary and identified Him for who He was, the Lamb of God. John was at the time baptizing people in the River Jordan.

The next day John saw Jesus coming toward him, and said, 'Behold! The Lamb of God who takes away the sin of the world! [30] This is He of whom I said, 'After me comes a Man who is preferred before me, for He was before me.' [31] I did not know Him; but that He should be revealed to Israel, therefore I came baptizing with water.' [32] And John bore witness, saying, 'I saw the Spirit descending from Heaven like a dove, and He remained upon Him. [33] I did not know Him, but He who sent me to baptize with water said to me, 'Upon whom you see the Spirit descending, and remaining on Him, this is He who baptizes with the Holy Spirit.' [34] And I have seen and testified that this is the Son of God." (John 1:29–34 NKJV).

Jesus went to John to be baptized but John objected.

> *"And John tried to prevent Him, saying, 'I need to be baptized by You, and are You coming to me?'* [15] *But Jesus answered and said to him, 'Permit it to be so now, for thus it is fitting for us to fulfill all righteousness.' Then he allowed Him.* [16] *When He had been baptized, Jesus came up immediately from the water; and behold, the Heavens were opened to Him, and He saw the Spirit of God descending like a dove and alighting upon Him.* [17] *And suddenly a voice came from Heaven, saying, 'This is My beloved Son, in whom I am well pleased'." (Matthew 3: 14–17 NKJV).*

It is important to recognize that, as is written in Hebrews chapter nine, it was Jesus' real blood that was shed at Calvary, which washes away sin.

> *"Not with the blood of goats and calves, but with His own blood He entered the Most Holy Place once for all, having obtained eternal redemption." (Hebrews 9:12 NKJV).*

Man had sinned and the sentence was spiritual death. According to Mosaic Law, a substitute could be provided but the blood of animals would not do. The sacrifice had to be innocent and sinless and, because He was the Son of God, only Jesus could die in our place. His blood was the atonement for our sins. Jesus alluded to this when He administered the last supper to His disciples in the Upper Room.

> *"Then He took the cup, and gave thanks, and gave it to them, saying, 'Drink from it, all of you. [28] For this is My blood of the new covenant, which is shed for many for the remission of sins'." (Matthew 26:27–28 NKJV).*

Earlier, Jesus had angered the Jews when He told them that He was the Bread of Life that had come down from Heaven.

> *"Whoever eats My flesh and drinks My blood has eternal life, and I will raise him up at the last day. [55] For My flesh is food indeed, and My blood is drink indeed. [56] He who eats My flesh and drinks My blood abides in Me, and I in him. [57] As the living Father sent Me, and I live because of the Father, so he who feeds on Me will live because of Me." (John 6:54–57 NKJV).*

Jesus, being the perfect sacrifice, was prophesied in the Old Testament and Peter testified to this.

> *"And if you call on the Father, who without partiality judges according to each one's work, conduct yourselves throughout the time of your stay here in fear; [18] knowing that you were not redeemed with corruptible things, like silver or gold, from your aimless conduct received by tradition from your fathers, [19] but with the precious blood of Christ, as of a lamb without blemish and without spot. [20] He indeed was foreordained before the foundation of the world,*

> *but was manifest in these last times for you [21] who through Him believe in God, who raised Him from the dead and gave Him glory, so that your faith and hope are in God." (1 Peter 1:17–21 NKJV).*

Jesus was indeed the fulfillment of the New Covenant and this is confirmed in Hebrews chapter 10.

> *"Behold, I have come to do Your will, O God." He takes away the first that He may establish the second. [10] By that will we have been sanctified through the offering of the body of Jesus Christ once for all. [11] And every priest stands ministering daily and offering repeatedly the same sacrifices, which can never take away sins. [12] But this Man, after He had offered one sacrifice for sins forever, sat down at the right hand of God, [13] from that time waiting till His enemies are made His footstool. [14] For by one offering He has perfected forever those who are being sanctified." (Hebrews 10:9–14 NKJV).*

The blood of Jesus has numerous powerful qualities. It cleanses, as recorded in John's epistle.

> *"But if we walk in the light as He is in the light, we have fellowship with one another, and the blood of Jesus Christ His Son cleanses us from all sin." (1 John 1:7 NKJV).*

The cleansing power of Jesus' blood is also referenced in Revelation chapter one.

"And from Jesus Christ, the faithful witness, the firstborn from the dead, and the ruler over the kings of the earth. To Him who loved us and washed us from our sins in His own blood." (Revelation 1:5 NKJV).

The blood of Jesus is available for the remission of sins.

"For Christ has not entered the holy places made with hands, which are copies of the true, but into Heaven itself, now to appear in the presence of God for us; [25] not that He should offer Himself often, as the high priest enters the Most Holy Place every year with blood of another— [26] He then would have had to suffer often since the foundation of the world; but now, once at the end of the ages, He has appeared to put away sin by the sacrifice of Himself. [27] And as it is appointed for men to die once, but after this the judgment, [28] so Christ was offered once to bear the sins of many. To those who eagerly wait for Him He will appear a second time, apart from sin, for salvation." (Hebrews 9:24–28 NKJV).

The blood of Jesus brings peace.

"For it pleased the Father that in Him all the fullness should dwell, [20] and by Him to reconcile all things to Himself, by Him, whether things on earth or things in Heaven, having made peace through the blood of His cross." (Colossians 1:19–20 NKJV).

Jesus' blood also gives the born again Christian boldness and the power to draw nearer to God.

> *"Therefore, brethren, having boldness to enter the Holiest by the blood of Jesus, [20] by a new and living way which He consecrated for us, through the veil, that is, His flesh, [21] and having a high priest over the house of God, [22] let us draw near with a true heart in full assurance of faith, having our hearts sprinkled from an evil conscience and our bodies washed with pure water." (Hebrews 10:19–22 NKJV).*

Christians also have the assurance that the blood of Jesus gives them the power to overcome adversity.

> *"Then I heard a loud voice saying in Heaven, 'Now salvation, and strength, and the kingdom of our God, and the power of His Christ have come, for the accuser of our brethren, who accused them before our God day and night, has been cast down. [11] And they overcame him by the blood of the Lamb and by the word of their testimony, and they did not love their lives to the death'." (Revelation 12:10–11 NKJV).*

The blood of Jesus sanctifies the born again Christian.

> *"For the bodies of those animals, whose blood is brought into the sanctuary by the high priest for sin, are burned outside the camp. [12] Therefore Jesus also, that He might sanctify the people with His own blood, suffered outside the gate." (Hebrews 13:11–12 NKJV).*

The blood of the Lamb of God, Jesus Christ, also has redemptive and forgiving powers.

> *"In Him we have redemption through His blood, the forgiveness of sins, according to the riches of His grace [8] which He made to abound toward us in all wisdom and prudence, [9] having made known to us the mystery of His will, according to His good pleasure which He purposed in Himself, [10] that in the dispensation of the fullness of the times He might gather together in one all things in Christ, both which are in Heaven and which are on earth—in Him." (Ephesians 1:7–10 NKJV).*

The blood of Jesus has purchasing power, as Paul indicated to the church leaders at Ephesus.

> *"Therefore take heed to yourselves and to all the flock, among which the Holy Spirit has made you overseers, to shepherd the church of God which He purchased with His own blood." (Acts 20:28 NKJV).*

The shedding of Jesus' blood on the cross should never be taken lightly. His dying declaration "It is finished" is considered His final step in opening the way for man's redemption. Matthew chapter 27, verse 51 says the veil of the temple was torn in two from top to bottom, indicating that the way to God was now clear.

> *"Then he said, 'Look, I have come to do your will.' He cancels the first covenant in order to put the second into effect. [10] For God's*

> *will was for us to be made holy by the sacrifice of the body of Jesus Christ, once for all time." (Hebrews 10:9–10 NLT).*

We are warned that there are dire consequences if we return to our sinful ways.

> *"For it is impossible for those who were once enlightened, and have tasted the Heavenly gift, and have become partakers of the Holy Spirit, [5] and have tasted the good word of God and the powers of the age to come, [6] if they fall away, to renew them again to repentance, since they crucify again for themselves the Son of God, and put Him to an open shame." (Hebrews 10:4–6 NKJV).*

The writer of the book of Hebrews further emphasizes how horrible it would be for those who after being converted, willfully reject their born again status and completely turn away from the faith.

> *"For if we sin willfully after we have received the knowledge of the truth, there no longer remains a sacrifice for sins, [27] but a certain fearful expectation of judgment, and fiery indignation which will devour the adversaries. [28] Anyone who has rejected Moses' law dies without mercy on the testimony of two or three witnesses. [29] Of how much worse punishment, do you suppose, will he be thought worthy who has trampled the Son of God underfoot, counted the blood of the covenant by which he was sanctified a common thing, and insulted the Spirit of grace? [30] For*

we know Him who said, 'Vengeance is Mine, I will repay,' says the Lord. And again, 'The Lord will judge His people.' [31]It is a fearful thing to fall into the hands of the living God." (Hebrews 10:26–31 NKJV).

The Living Bible quotes that same Scripture this way:

"If anyone sins deliberately by rejecting the Saviour after knowing the truth of forgiveness, this sin is not covered by Christ's death; there is no way to get rid of it. [27] There will be nothing to look forward to but the terrible punishment of God's awful anger, which will consume all his enemies. [28] A man who refused to obey the laws given by Moses was killed without mercy if there were two or three witnesses to his sin. [29] Think how much more terrible the punishment will be for those who have trampled underfoot the Son of God and treated his cleansing blood as though it were common and unhallowed, and insulted and outraged the Holy Spirit who brings God's mercy to his people. [30] For we know him who said, 'Justice belongs to me; I will repay them'; who also said, 'The Lord himself will handle these cases.' [31] It is a fearful thing to fall into the hands of the living God." (Hebrews 10:26–31 TLB).

Chapter 13

Who Is The Holy Spirit?

The Holy Spirit is the Power that transforms from sin to salvation and from sinner to born again Christian. He is the connection between God and the Christian and is God, being part of the Godhead. His characteristics show that He is also a person. When a sinner accepts Jesus Christ as Savior, the Holy Spirit comes into him and he is transformed.

In the first chapter of his letter to the Ephesian Christians, Paul told them that when they believed, they received the Holy Spirit.

> *"In Him you also trusted, after you heard the word of truth, the gospel of your salvation; in whom also, having believed, you were sealed with the Holy Spirit of promise, [14] who is the guarantee of our inheritance until the redemption of the purchased possession, to the praise of His glory." (Ephesians 1:13–14 NKJV).*

The New Living Translation explains this passage more clearly:

> *"And now you Gentiles have also heard the truth, the Good News that God saves you. And when you believed in Christ, he identified you as his own by giving you the Holy Spirit,*

> *whom he promised long ago. [14] The Spirit is God's guarantee that he will give us the inheritance he promised and that he has purchased us to be his own people. He did this so we would praise and glorify him." (Ephesians 1:13–14 NLT).*

This idea or thinking about the Holy Spirit living inside a person may seem strange, but Paul explains it beautifully in chapter six of his first epistle to the Corinthians.

> *"Or do you not know that your body is the temple of the Holy Spirit who is in you, whom you have from God, and you are not your own? [20] For you were bought at a price; therefore glorify God in your body and in your spirit, which are God's." (1 Corinthians 6:19–20 NKJV).*

This is how the New Living Translation puts it:

> *"Don't you realize that your body is the temple of the Holy Spirit, who lives in you and was given to you by God? You do not belong to yourself, [20] for God bought you with a high price. So you must honour God with your body. (1 Corinthians 6:19–20 NLT).*

When the sinner is converted, his soul that is dead in sin, is made alive by the Holy Spirit.

> *"For we ourselves were also once foolish, disobedient, deceived, serving various lusts and pleasures, living in malice and envy, hateful and hating one another. [4] But*

when the kindness and the love of God our Saviour toward man appeared, [5] not by works of righteousness which we have done, but according to His mercy He saved us, through the washing of regeneration and renewing of the Holy Spirit, [6] whom He poured out on us abundantly through Jesus Christ our Saviour, [7] that having been justified by His grace we should become heirs according to the hope of eternal life." (Titus 3:3–7 NKJV).

The New Living Translation says it this way:

"Once we, too, were foolish and disobedient. We were misled and became slaves to many lusts and pleasures. Our lives were full of evil and envy, and we hated each other. [4] But—When God our Saviour revealed His kindness and love, [5] He saved us, not because of the righteous things we had done, but because of His mercy. He washed away our sins, giving us a new birth and new life through the Holy Spirit. [6] He generously poured out the Spirit upon us through Jesus Christ our Saviour. [7] Because of His grace He declared us righteous and gave us confidence that we will inherit eternal life." (Titus 3:3–7 NLT).

The Holy Spirit is also known as the Holy Ghost, the Spirit of God, the Spirit of Jesus, the Spirit of Truth, the Comforter, the Spirit of Life, the Teacher, the Witness, the Counselor, and the Helper.

When Jesus was about to leave the earth He promised His disciples that He would not leave them alone but would send someone to be with them. John recorded this in chapter 14 of his Gospel.

> *"If you love Me, keep My commandments. [16] And I will pray the Father, and He will give you another Helper, that He may abide with you forever— [17] the Spirit of truth, whom the world cannot receive, because it neither sees Him nor knows Him; but you know Him, for He dwells with you and will be in you. [18] I will not leave you orphans; I will come to you. [19] A little while longer and the world will see Me no more, but you will see Me. Because I live, you will live also. [20] At that day you will know that I am in My Father, and you in Me, and I in you." (John 14:15–20 NKJV).*

The New Living Translation puts that same passage this way:

> *"If you love me, obey my commandments. [16] And I will ask the Father, and he will give you another Advocate, who will never leave you. [17] He is the Holy Spirit, who leads into all truth. The world cannot receive him, because it isn't looking for him and doesn't recognize him. But you know him, because he lives with you now and later will be in you. [18] No, I will not abandon you as orphans—I will come to you. [19] Soon the world will no longer see me, but you will see me. Since I live, you also will live. [20] When I am raised to life again, you will know that I am in my Father, and you are in me, and I am in you." (John 14:15–20 NLT).*

The last phrase of this passage, *"I will come to you"*, indicates that the Holy Spirit is the Spirit of Jesus.

Jesus also spoke about the coming of the Holy Spirit in chapter 15 of John's Gospel.

> *"But when the Helper comes, whom I shall send to you from the Father, the Spirit of truth who proceeds from the Father, He will testify of Me. [27] And you also will bear witness, because you have been with Me from the beginning." (John 15:26–27 NKJV).*

That promise of the coming of the Holy Spirit was fulfilled as described in chapter two of the Acts of the Apostles in what is known as the events on "The Day of Pentecost". This was an experience of empowerment.

> *"When the Day of Pentecost had fully come, they were all with one accord in one place. [2] And suddenly there came a sound from Heaven, as of a rushing mighty wind, and it filled the whole house where they were sitting. [3] Then there appeared to them divided tongues, as of fire, and one sat upon each of them. [4] And they were all filled with the Holy Spirit and began to speak with other tongues, as the Spirit gave them utterance." (Acts 2:1–4 NKJV).*

Some religious denominations describe the Holy Spirit as a force, but the Scriptures show that He is a divine person. The pronoun "He" is used in the Bible in reference to Him. All the characteristics of the Holy Spirit show that He is in fact a person. He thinks; He guides; He can be grieved; He makes decisions; He has a mind, a will, and emotions and He makes intercession for us.

The Holy Spirit is God and the story of Ananias and Sapphira in the book of Acts, chapter five clearly shows this. Peter the apostle had reason to question the couple about not being fully truthful in their dealings with the church.

> *"But a certain man named Ananias, with Sapphira his wife, sold a possession. [2] And he kept back part of the proceeds, his wife also being aware of it, and brought a certain part and laid it at the apostles' feet. [3] But Peter said, 'Ananias, why has Satan filled your heart to lie to the Holy Spirit and keep back part of the price of the land for yourself? [4] While it remained, was it not your own? And after it was sold, was it not in your own control? Why have you conceived this thing in your heart? You have not lied to men but to God'." (Acts 5:1–4 NKJV).*

The Holy Spirit plays a vital role in not only drawing sinners to salvation but, along with God the Father and God the Son, is also intimately involved in the life of the Christian.

> *"There is therefore now no condemnation to those who are in Christ Jesus, who do not walk according to the flesh, but according to the Spirit. [2] For the law of the Spirit of life in Christ Jesus has made me free from the law of sin and death. [3] For what the law could not do in that it was weak through the flesh, God did by sending His own Son in the likeness of sinful flesh, on account of sin: He condemned sin in the flesh, [4] that the righteous requirement of the law might be fulfilled in us who do not walk according to the flesh*

*but according to the Spirit. [5] For those who
live according to the flesh set their minds on
the things of the flesh, but those who live
according to the Spirit, the things of the Spirit.
[6] For to be carnally minded is death, but to be
spiritually minded is life and peace. [7] Because
the carnal mind is enmity against God; for it
is not subject to the law of God, nor indeed
can be. [8] So then, those who are in the flesh
cannot please God. [9] But you are not in the
flesh but in the Spirit, if indeed the Spirit of
God dwells in you. Now if anyone does not
have the Spirit of Christ, he is not His. [10] And
if Christ is in you, the body is dead because of
sin, but the Spirit is life because of righteousness. [11] But if the Spirit of Him who raised
Jesus from the dead dwells in you, He who
raised Christ from the dead will also give life
to your mortal bodies through His Spirit who
dwells in you. [12] Therefore, brethren, we are
debtors—not to the flesh, to live according
to the flesh. [13] For if you live according to
the flesh you will die; but if by the Spirit you
put to death the deeds of the body, you will
live. [14] For as many as are led by the Spirit of
God, these are sons of God. [15] For you did
not receive the spirit of bondage again to
fear, but you received the Spirit of adoption
by whom we cry out, 'Abba, Father.' [16] The
Spirit Himself bears witness with our spirit
that we are children of God, [17] and if children,
then heirs—heirs of God and joint heirs with
Christ, if indeed we suffer with Him, that we
may also be glorified together." (Romans
8:1–17 NKJV).*

The Holy Spirit is a significant help to the Christian, especially in a moment of weakness. Romans chapter eight shows His response:

> *"For we do not know what we should pray for as we ought, but the Spirit Himself makes intercession for us with groanings which cannot be uttered. [27] Now He who searches the hearts knows what the mind of the Spirit is, because He makes intercession for the saints according to the will of God." (Romans 8:26–27 NKJV).*

The Holy Spirit speaks to Christians in many ways. People, in explaining or relating events, would sometimes say, "Something told me to do such and such". If it was something positive, rest assured that it was the Holy Spirit. He speaks in thought, through the Word of God, through people, and even through events.

> *"For the Spirit searches all things, yes, the deep things of God. [11] For what man knows the things of a man except the spirit of the man which is in him? Even so no one knows the things of God except the Spirit of God. [12] Now we have received, not the spirit of the world, but the Spirit who is from God, that we might know the things that have been freely given to us by God. [13] These things we also speak, not in words which man's wisdom teaches but which the Holy Spirit teaches, comparing spiritual things with spiritual. [14] But the natural man does not receive the things of the Spirit of God, for they are foolishness to him; nor can he know them,*

> *because they are spiritually discerned. [15] But he who is spiritual judges all things, yet he himself is rightly judged by no one. [16] For 'who has known the mind of the Lord that he may instruct Him?' But we have the mind of Christ." (1 Corinthians 2:10–16 NKJV).*

There have been occasions where people have heard the voice of God speak to them audibly. This is all the work of the Holy Spirit.

The book of the Acts of the Apostles tells the story of Saul's encounter with the Holy Spirit, an event that led to his transformation to Paul the apostle. He was on his way to persecute the early Christians when he was literally stopped in his tracks by the Holy Spirit.

> *"As he journeyed he came near Damascus, and suddenly a light shone around him from Heaven. [4] Then he fell to the ground, and heard a voice saying to him, 'Saul, Saul, why are you persecuting Me?' [5] And he said, 'Who are You, Lord?' Then the Lord said, 'I am Jesus, whom you are persecuting. It is hard for you to kick against the goads.' [6] So he, trembling and astonished, said, 'Lord, what do You want me to do?' Then the Lord said to him, 'Arise and go into the city, and you will be told what you must do.' [7] And the men who journeyed with him stood speechless, hearing a voice but seeing no one. [8] Then Saul arose from the ground, and when his eyes were opened he saw no one. But they led him by the hand and brought him into Damascus. [9] And he was three days without sight, and neither ate nor drank." (Acts 9:3–9 NKJV).*

Do not be confused by the terms "Holy Ghost" and "Holy Spirit", as they are the same. It all has to do with the translation from the Greek and Hebrew languages. Research shows that the King James Version of the Bible, one of the earliest or the earliest translation into English, uses the term Holy Ghost. This term occurs no fewer than 90 times, while the term "Holy Spirit" is also used seven times.

Researchers say that the same Greek and Hebrew words are translated "ghost" and "spirit" in the King James Version on different instances. The more modern translations of the Bible more often than not use the term "Holy Spirit".

Jesus has warned that we should not commit blasphemy against the Holy Spirit. This is referred to as the unpardonable sin. The Jews were criticizing Him for a number of acts that He performed on the Sabbath Day. These included healing a woman and a demon-possessed man. The people accused Him of casting out demons by the power of Beelzebub, the ruler of demons. But Jesus stressed if He did it by the power of the Holy Spirit then the Kingdom of God was there. He went on to say that every sin and blasphemy committed by men will be forgiven, but not blasphemy against the Holy Spirit.

> *"Anyone who speaks a word against the Son of Man, it will be forgiven him; but whoever speaks against the Holy Spirit, it will not be forgiven him, either in this age or in the age to come." (Matthew 12:32 NKJV).*

We should never want to be without the Holy Spirit. His constant companionship is the bedrock to maintaining our spiritual strength. The psalmist David was one who craved the constant presence of the Holy Spirit.

Create in me a clean heart, O God, and renew a steadfast spirit within me. [11] Do not cast me away from Your presence, And do not take Your Holy Spirit from me. (Psalm 51:10–11 NKJV).

CHAPTER 14

WHO IS THE DEVIL?

There is one person who is against everything that God, Jesus Christ, and the Holy Spirit stand for. He is the author of all that is bad and his sole purpose is to keep you from spending eternity with God. He is the devil, a spiritual being who is the archenemy of God and everything that is good. He is especially bent on destroying people who give their lives to Jesus Christ.

This devil is known by several names and has been in existence from before Adam and Eve. He has been called Satan, which means adversary, and is also known as Lucifer, Beelzebub, the serpent, the dragon, the tempter, the wicked one, the accuser of the brethren, and the prince of this world, among others.

Satan is the architect of rebellion against God. It all started when he tempted Adam and Eve to disobey God. The story in Genesis chapter three reveals that God had forbidden the couple from eating the fruit of a certain tree, but Satan in the form of a serpent, enticed them to do otherwise. Because of their disobedience Adam and Eve were expelled from the Garden of Eden and the serpent was cursed. Ever since then mankind has been under attack from this devil who tries in all sorts of ways to get human beings to do the things that do not please God.

Satan was once an angel in Heaven but was cast out. Isaiah chapter 14 talks about the fall of the king of Babylon, but theologians and Bible scholars say this really relates to the fall of Satan from Heaven.

> *"How you are fallen from Heaven, O Lucifer, son of the morning! How you are cut down to the ground, You who weakened the nations! [13] For you have said in your heart: 'I will ascend into Heaven, I will exalt my throne above the stars of God; I will also sit on the mount of the congregation On the farthest sides of the north; [14] I will ascend above the heights of the clouds, I will be like the Most High.' [15] Yet you shall be brought down to Sheol, To the lowest depths of the Pit." (Isaiah 14:12–15 NKJV).*

The prophet Ezekiel also made reference to the fall of the prince of Tyre and this too has been argued by theologians and Bible scholars as being a reference to the fall of Satan.

> *"Moreover the word of the Lord came to me, saying, [12] 'Son of man, take up a lamentation for the king of Tyre, and say to him, 'Thus says the Lord God: You were the seal of perfection, Full of wisdom and perfect in beauty. [13] You were in Eden, the garden of God; Every precious stone was your covering: The sardius, topaz, and diamond, Beryl, onyx, and jasper, Sapphire, turquoise, and emerald with gold. The workmanship of your timbrels and pipes was prepared for you on the day you were created. [14] You*

> *were the anointed cherub who covers; I established you; You were on the holy mountain of God; You walked back and forth in the midst of fiery stones. [15] You were perfect in your ways from the day you were created, Till iniquity was found in you. [16] By the abundance of your trading You became filled with violence within, And you sinned; Therefore I cast you as a profane thing Out of the mountain of God; And I destroyed you, O covering cherub, From the midst of the fiery stones. [17] Your heart was lifted up because of your beauty; You corrupted your wisdom for the sake of your splendor; I cast you to the ground, I laid you before kings, That they might gaze at you'." (Ezekiel 29: 11– 17 NKJV).*

There is also what is believed to be a reference to the final fall of Satan in chapter 12 of the book of Revelation.

> *"And war broke out in Heaven: Michael and his angels fought with the dragon; and the dragon and his angels fought, [8] but they did not prevail, nor was a place found for them in Heaven any longer. [9] So the great dragon was cast out, that serpent of old, called the Devil and Satan, who deceives the whole world; he was cast to the earth, and his angels were cast out with him.[10] Then I heard a loud voice saying in Heaven, 'Now salvation, and strength, and the kingdom of our God, and the power of His Christ have come, for the accuser of our brethren, who accused them before our God day and night, has*

> *been cast down. [11] And they overcame him by the blood of the Lamb and by the word of their testimony, and they did not love their lives to the death. [12] Therefore rejoice, O Heavens, and you who dwell in them! Woe to the inhabitants of the earth and the sea! For the devil has come down to you, having great wrath, because he knows that he has a short time'." (Revelation 12:7–12 NKJV).*

Jesus also made reference to Satan being expelled from Heaven. In the Gospel of Luke, chapter 10 He was talking to His disciples, who had just returned from a missionary trip, and they were overjoyed at being able to do great miracles. Jesus, however, had a warning for them while at the same time stressing that His power was stronger than that of the devil.

> *"And He said to them, 'I saw Satan fall like lightning from Heaven. [19] Behold, I give you the authority to trample on serpents and scorpions, and over all the power of the enemy, and nothing shall by any means hurt you. [20] Nevertheless do not rejoice in this, that the spirits are subject to you, but rather rejoice because your names are written in Heaven'." (Luke 10:18–20 NKJV).*

On another occasion Jesus was debating with the Jews over His being the son of God and they were arguing that they were in fact the children of Abraham. But Jesus told them in no uncertain terms that they were children of the devil.

> *"I know that you are Abraham's descendants, but you seek to kill Me, because My word has no place in you. 38 I speak what I have seen with My Father, and you do what you have seen with your father." 39 They answered and said to Him, 'Abraham is our father.' Jesus said to them, 'If you were Abraham's children, you would do the works of Abraham. 40 But now you seek to kill Me, a Man who has told you the truth which I heard from God. Abraham did not do this. 41 You do the deeds of your father.' Then they said to Him, 'We were not born of fornication; we have one Father—God.' 42 Jesus said to them, 'If God were your Father, you would love Me, for I proceeded forth and came from God; nor have I come of Myself, but He sent Me. 43 Why do you not understand My speech? Because you are not able to listen to My word. 44 You are of your father the devil, and the desires of your father you want to do. He was a murderer from the beginning, and does not stand in the truth, because there is no truth in him. When he speaks a lie, he speaks from his own resources, for he is a liar and the father of it. 45 But because I tell the truth, you do not believe Me. 46 Which of you convicts Me of sin? And if I tell the truth, why do you not believe Me? 47 He who is of God hears God's words; therefore you do not hear, because you are not of God'." (John 8:37–47 NKJV).*

Satan is also known as the tempter and he is no respecter of persons. Matthew chapter four reveals that he attacked Jesus immediately after His baptism.

> *Then Jesus was led up by the Spirit into*
> *the wilderness to be tempted by the devil.*
> *2 And when He had fasted forty days and*
> *forty nights, afterward He was hungry.*
> *3 Now when the tempter came to Him, he*
> *said, 'If You are the Son of God, command*
> *that these stones become bread. 4But He*
> *answered and said, It is written, Man shall*
> *not live by bread alone, but by every word*
> *that proceeds from the mouth of God.*
> *5 Then the devil took Him up into the holy*
> *city, set Him on the pinnacle of the temple,*
> *6 and said to Him, If You are the Son of God,*
> *throw Yourself down. For it is written: He*
> *shall give His angels charge over you, and,*
> *In their hands they shall bear you up, Lest*
> *you dash your foot against a stone. 7 Jesus*
> *said to him, It is written again, You shall not*
> *tempt the Lord your God. 8 Again, the devil*
> *took Him up on an exceedingly high moun-*
> *tain, and showed Him all the kingdoms of*
> *the world and their glory. 9 And he said to*
> *Him, All these things I will give You if You*
> *will fall down and worship me. 10 Then Jesus*
> *said to him, Away with you, Satan! For it*
> *is written, You shall worship the Lord your*
> *God, and Him only you shall serve. 11 Then*
> *the devil left Him, and behold, angels*
> *came and ministered to Him." (Matthew*
> *4:1–11 NKJV).*

This encounter between Jesus and Satan also enforced what James said in chapter four of his letter to the early church. He told them that they should "submit to God. Resist the devil and he will flee from you." (James 4:7 NKJV).

Jesus also spoke about how He will judge the nations and what would happen to those who follow the devil.

> *"When the Son of Man comes in His glory,*
> *and all the holy angels with Him, then He*
> *will sit on the throne of His glory. 32 All the*
> *nations will be gathered before Him, and*
> *He will separate them one from another,*
> *as a shepherd divides his sheep from the*
> *goats. 33 And He will set the sheep on His*
> *right hand, but the goats on the left. 34 Then*
> *the King will say to those on His right hand,*
> *'Come, you blessed of My Father, inherit the*
> *kingdom prepared for you from the foun-*
> *dation of the world: 35 for I was hungry and*
> *you gave Me food; I was thirsty and you*
> *gave Me drink; I was a stranger and you*
> *took Me in; 36 I was naked and you clothed*
> *Me; I was sick and you visited Me; I was in*
> *prison and you came to Me.' 37 Then the*
> *righteous will answer Him, saying, 'Lord,*
> *when did we see You hungry and feed You,*
> *or thirsty and give You drink? 38 When did*
> *we see You a stranger and take You in, or*
> *naked and clothe You? 39 Or when did we*
> *see You sick, or in prison, and come to You?'*
> *40 And the King will answer and say to them,*
> *'Assuredly, I say to you, inasmuch as you did*
> *it to one of the least of these My brethren,*
> *you did it to Me.' 41 Then He will also say*
> *to those on the left hand, 'Depart from Me,*

> *you cursed, into the everlasting fire prepared for the devil and his angels: [42] for I was hungry and you gave Me no food; I was thirsty and you gave Me no drink; [43] I was a stranger and you did not take Me in, naked and you did not clothe Me, sick and in prison and you did not visit Me.' " (Matthew 25:31–43 NKJV).*

James, in his epistle, warned against friendship with the devil and explained how to fight against him.

> *"Adulterers and adulteresses! Do you not know that friendship with the world is enmity with God? Whoever therefore wants to be a friend of the world makes himself an enemy of God. [5] Or do you think that the Scripture says in vain, 'The Spirit who dwells in us yearns jealously?' [6] But He gives more grace. Therefore He says: 'God resists the proud, But gives grace to the humble." [7] Therefore submit to God. Resist the devil and he will flee from you. [8]Draw near to God and He will draw near to you. Cleanse your hands, you sinners; and purify your hearts, you double-minded. [9] Lament and mourn and weep! Let your laughter be turned to mourning and your joy to gloom. [10] Humble yourselves in the sight of the Lord, and He will lift you up.' " (James 4:4–10 NKJV).*

Peter also advised in his first epistle that Christians should resist the devil.

> *"Be sober, be vigilant; because your adversary the devil walks about like a roaring lion, seeking whom he may devour. [9] Resist him, steadfast in the faith, knowing that the same sufferings are experienced by your brotherhood in the world. [10] But may the God of all grace, who called us to His eternal glory by Christ Jesus, after you have suffered awhile, perfect, establish, strengthen, and settle you. [11] To Him be the glory and the dominion forever and ever. Amen." (1 Peter 5:8–11 NKJV).*

Satan is sometimes portrayed as an ugly creature with horns, long teeth, a tail, and carrying a three-pronged fork. This is mythical and there is nothing in the Bible to support this theory. Rather, second Corinthians, chapter 11 says the devil can transform himself into something beautiful.

> *"For such are false apostles, deceitful workers, transforming themselves into the apostles of Christ. [14] And no marvel; for Satan himself is transformed into an angel of light. [15] Therefore it is no great thing if his ministers also be transformed as the ministers of righteousness; whose end shall be according to their works." (2 Corinthians 11:13–15 KJV).*

While Satan is the enemy of God, the Bible shows that on occasion he had access to God. In the book of Job we read how these two spiritual beings had a conversation that resulted in the well-documented, much-discussed, and much-debated trials of Job.

> *"Now there was a day when the sons of God came to present themselves before the Lord, and Satan came also among them. [7] And the Lord said unto Satan, Whence comest thou? Then Satan answered the Lord, and said, From going to and fro in the earth, and from walking up and down in it.' [8] And the Lord said unto Satan, Hast thou considered my servant Job, that there is none like him in the earth, a perfect and an upright man, one that feareth God, and escheweth evil? [9] Then Satan answered the Lord, and said, Doth Job fear God for nought? [10] Hast not thou made an hedge about him, and about his house, and about all that he hath on every side? thou hast blessed the work of his hands, and his substance is increased in the land. [11] But put forth thine hand now, and touch all that he hath, and he will curse thee to thy face. [12]And the Lord said unto Satan, Behold, all that he hath is in thy power; only upon himself put not forth thine hand. So Satan went forth from the presence of the Lord." (Job 1: 6–12 NKJV).*

Satan, unlike God, cannot be everywhere at the same time and so he has associates known as demons. These evil spirits follow his instructions and influence human beings. They can torment and even kill and can invade or possess the bodies of human beings. Jesus had encounters with these demons on several occasions and one well-known incident is reported in Matthew's Gospel, chapter eight:

> *"When He had come to the other side, to the country of the Gergesenes, there met Him two demon-possessed men, coming out of the tombs, exceedingly fierce, so that no one could pass that way. [29] And suddenly they cried out, saying, "What have we to do with You, Jesus, You Son of God? Have You come here to torment us before the time?" [30] Now a good way off from them there was a herd of many swine feeding.*
> *[31] So the demons begged Him, saying, 'If You cast us out, permit us to go away into the herd of swine.' [32] And He said to them, 'Go'" So when they had come out, they went into the herd of swine. And suddenly the whole herd of swine ran violently down the steep place into the sea, and perished in the water." (Matthew 8:28–32 NKJV).*

Christians have been given the power to resist and overcome demons. When Jesus was on earth He sent out a group of His disciples to teach and preach. According to Matthew chapter 10, He gave them authority over unclean spirits, to cast them out, and to heal every kind of disease and every kind of sickness.

> *These twelve Jesus sent out after instructing them: 'Do not go in the way of the Gentiles, and do not enter any city of the Samaritans;*
> *[6] but rather go to the lost sheep of the house of Israel. [7] And as you go, preach, saying, The kingdom of Heaven is at hand. [8] Heal the sick, raise the dead, cleanse the lepers, cast out demons. Freely you received, freely give'." (Matthew 10:5–8 NKJV).*

The apostles demonstrated how Christians have power over evil spirits and there are several instances in the Bible where the apostles cast them out. The story is told in Acts 16 of a demon-possessed girl who encountered them.

> *"Now it happened, as we went to prayer, that a certain slave girl possessed with a spirit of divination met us, who brought her masters much profit by fortune-telling. [17] This girl followed Paul and us, and cried out, saying, 'These men are the servants of the Most High God, who proclaim to us the way of salvation.' [18] And this she did for many days. But Paul, greatly annoyed, turned and said to the spirit, 'I command you in the name of Jesus Christ to come out of her.' And he came out that very hour." (Acts 16:16–18 NKJV).*

Christians must however understand that they cannot stand up to Satan and his demonic forces unless they are in good standing with God. They must have a strong prayer life. Both Matthew and Mark report on an incident where Jesus had just returned from what is known as "The transfiguration on the mount". He was met by a man who explained that he had brought his demon-possessed son to be healed but the disciples could not get the evil spirit to come out of the youth. Jesus rebuked the demon and the boy was cured. His disciples later asked Him why they had failed. Mark's account of the event shows that Jesus gave them this response:

> *"So He said to them, 'This kind can come out by nothing but prayer and fasting'." (Mark 9:29 NKJV).*

Matthew's account in chapter 19 of his Gospel gives more details of the conversation between Jesus and his followers.

> *So Jesus said to them, 'Because of your unbelief; for assuredly, I say to you, if you have faith as a mustard seed, you will say to this mountain, Move from here to there, and it will move; and nothing will be impossible for you. [21] However, this kind does not go out except by prayer and fasting." (Matthew 19:20–21 NKJV).*

Jesus twice referred to Satan as the ruler of this world. The first instance came shortly after His triumphant ride into Jerusalem. He was talking to His disciples, predicting His death, when there was a voice from Heaven.

> *"Now My soul is troubled, and what shall I say? 'Father, save Me from this hour'? But for this purpose I came to this hour. [28] Father, glorify Your name. Then a voice came from Heaven, saying, 'I have both glorified it and will glorify it again.' [29] Therefore the people who stood by and heard it said that it had thundered. Others said, 'An angel has spoken to Him.' [30] Jesus answered and said, 'This voice did not come because of Me, but for your sake. [31] Now is the judgment of this world; now the ruler of this world will be cast out'." (John 12:27–31 NKJV).*

Jesus' second reference to Satan as the ruler of this world came shortly after He had promised His disciples that after His death He would send them a comforter.

"I will no longer talk much with you, for the ruler of this world is coming, and he has nothing in Me." (John 14:30 NKJV).

The reference to Satan as "the ruler of this world" does not mean that he is in complete control but rather that those who don't belong to Jesus Christ are under his rule.

Paul referred to the devil as "the god of this world". In his first letter to the Corinthians, he warned about his deceptive ways:

"Satan, who is the god of this world, has blinded the minds of those who don't believe. They are unable to see the glorious light of the Good News. They don't understand this message about the glory of Christ, who is the exact likeness of God." (2 Corinthians 4:4 NLT).

Paul, when writing to the church at Ephesus to encourage the Christians there, had another moniker for the devil:

"And you He made alive, who were dead in trespasses and sins, [2] in which you once walked according to the course of this world, according to the prince of the power of the air, the spirit who now works in the sons of disobedience, [3] among whom also we all once conducted ourselves in the lusts of our flesh, fulfilling the desires of the flesh and of the mind, and were by nature children of wrath, just as the others." (Ephesians 2:1–3 NKJV).

Satan is strong but not strong enough to withstand the power of God. That power has been given to every Christian through Jesus Christ and the Holy Spirit who lives within the Believer. The power comes through the shed blood of Jesus and the individual experience of the Believer. Revelation chapter 12 speaks to this:

> *"And war broke out in Heaven: Michael and*
> *his angels fought with the dragon; and the*
> *dragon and his angels fought, 8 but they*
> *did not prevail, nor was a place found*
> *for them in Heaven any longer. 9 So the*
> *great dragon was cast out, that serpent*
> *of old, called the Devil and Satan, who*
> *deceives the whole world; he was cast to*
> *the earth, and his angels were cast out with*
> *him. 10 Then I heard a loud voice saying in*
> *Heaven, 'Now salvation, and strength, and*
> *the kingdom of our God, and the power*
> *of His Christ have come, for the accuser*
> *of our brethren, who accused them before*
> *our God day and night, has been cast down.*
> *11 And they overcame him by the blood of*
> *the Lamb and by the word of their testi-*
> *mony, and they did not love their lives to*
> *the death. 12 Therefore rejoice, O Heavens,*
> *and you who dwell in them! Woe to the*
> *inhabitants of the earth and the sea! For*
> *the devil has come down to you, having*
> *great wrath, because he knows that he has*
> *a short time'." (Revelation 12:7–12 NKJV).*

Isaiah's prophecy relating to the fall of the king of Babylon reveals that in the end Satan will be a pitiful figure.

> *"Those who see you will gaze at you, And consider you, saying: 'Is this the man who made the earth tremble, Who shook kingdoms, [17] Who made the world as a wilderness And destroyed its cities, Who did not open the house of his prisoners?' [18] "All the kings of the nations, All of them, sleep in glory, Everyone in his own house; [19] But you are cast out of your grave Like an abominable branch, Like the garment of those who are slain, Thrust through with a sword, Who go down to the stones of the pit, Like a corpse trodden underfoot. [20] You will not be joined with them in burial, Because you have destroyed your land And slain your people. The brood of evildoers shall never be named. [21] Prepare slaughter for his children Because of the iniquity of their fathers, Lest they rise up and possess the land, And fill the face of the world with cities." (Isaiah 14:16–21 NKJV).*

As a Believer and born again Christian you have the assurance that you can stand up to Satan, but you cannot do it in your own strength. Trust God through Jesus Christ and the Holy Spirit to empower you to fight the powers of darkness, led by the devil.

Chapter 15

What Is Heaven?

The hope and dream of every born again Believer is to spend eternity in Heaven with God. But the question has always been: What and where is this Heaven?

The Bible indicates that there are three heavens. The first is the earth's immediate atmosphere and the second is outer space, where you find the sun, moon, and the planets. The third Heaven is the place where God dwells with the angels and the spirits of those saints who have passed on. This third Heaven has at one time or another been referred to as Paradise, the Father's House, and the Kingdom of God.

The third Heaven is where every child of God hopes to spend eternity. Paul the apostle spoke about this place in his second letter to the Corinthian church:

> *"This boasting will do no good, but I must go on. I will reluctantly tell about visions and revelations from the Lord. [2] I was caught up to the third Heaven fourteen years ago. Whether I was in my body or out of my body, I don't know—only God knows. [3] Yes, only God knows whether I was in my body or outside my body. But I do know [4] that I was caught up to paradise and heard things so astounding that*

> *they cannot be expressed in words, things no human is allowed to tell." (2 Corinthians 12:1–4 NLT).*

The Bible shows that Heaven is an eternal city and is sometimes called the New Jerusalem. No exact location has been given for this great city but it is definitely a place because, according to the Bible, God is there. Psalm 115 identifies where God is:

> *"Why should the Gentiles say, 'So where is their God?' [3] But our God is in Heaven; He does whatever He pleases." (Psalm 115:2–3 NKJV).*

The prophet Isaiah in chapter 66 of his book told the people what God had to say about Heaven:

> *"Thus says the Lord: 'Heaven is My throne, And earth is My footstool. Where is the house that you will build Me? And where is the place of My rest?'" (Isaiah 66:1–2 NKJV).*

Stephen the martyr, in his address at his trial, is recorded in the book of Acts as referring his accusers to this same passage.

Jesus revealed that God is in Heaven when, as stated in Matthew chapter five, verse 16, He told his followers that they had to stand out from the rest of the world.

> *"Let your light so shine before men, that they may see your good works and glorify your Father in Heaven." (Matthew 5:15 NKJV).*

Jesus on another occasion indicated that there is such a place as Heaven. The story is written in Luke chapter 10 where He had sent out 70 people to evangelize the cities where He had planned to visit. The disciples had just returned and were reporting great success. But Jesus had this to say to them:

> *"And He said to them, 'I saw Satan fall like lightning from Heaven. [19] Behold, I give you the authority to trample on serpents and scorpions, and over all the power of the enemy, and nothing shall by any means hurt you. [20] Nevertheless do not rejoice in this, that the spirits are subject to you, but rather rejoice because your names are written in Heaven'." (Luke 10:18–20 NKJV).*

Jesus also said He came from Heaven and, based on the fact that He is not a liar, there must be such a place.

> *"All that the Father gives Me will come to Me, and the one who comes to Me I will by no means cast out. [38]For I have come down from Heaven, not to do My own will, but the will of Him who sent Me. [39] This is the will of the Father who sent Me, that of all He has given Me I should lose nothing, but should raise it up at the last day." (John 6:37–39 NKJV).*

Jesus did not only come from Heaven, He returned there, as described in what is termed "The Ascension" as documented in Luke chapter 24:

> *"And He led them out as far as Bethany, and He lifted up His hands and blessed them. [51] Now it came to pass, while He blessed them, that He was parted from them and carried up into Heaven." (Luke 24:50 NKJV).*

There is also evidence in the Bible that God the Father and Jesus the Son are in Heaven. During the trial before the council on charges of blasphemy, Stephen stressed that God did not live in buildings made by man.

> *"As the prophet says: [49] 'Heaven is My throne, And earth is My footstool. What house will you build for Me? says the Lord, Or what is the place of My rest? [50] Has My hand not made all these things?' " (Acts 7:48–50 NKJV).*

Stephen went even further, charging his accusers with murdering Jesus Christ:

> *"When they heard these things they were cut to the heart, and they gnashed at him with their teeth. [55] But he, being full of the Holy Spirit, gazed into Heaven and saw the glory of God, and Jesus standing at the right hand of God, [56] and said, 'Look! I see the Heavens opened and the Son of Man standing at the right hand of God!' " (Acts 7:54–56 NKJV).*

In the ninth chapter of Hebrews the writer stressed that Jesus is in Heaven.

> *"For Christ has not entered the holy places made with hands, which are copies of the true, but into Heaven itself, now to appear in the presence of God for us; [25] not that He should offer Himself often, as the high priest enters the Most Holy Place every year with blood of another— [26] He then would have had to suffer often since the foundation of the world; but now, once at the end of the ages, He has appeared to put away sin by the sacrifice of Himself." (Hebrews 9:24–26 NKJV).*

Questions have been raised about what happens in Heaven. John, in the book of Revelation, identified several aspects of Heaven and what he saw there in a vision. He talked about a crystal-clear river, streets of gold so pure that they are like glass. John described the walls of the city as being adorned with all sorts of precious jewels and the tree of life bearing 12 kinds of fruit every month. John also wrote about activity in Heaven:

> *"After these things I looked, and behold, a door standing open in Heaven. And the first voice which I heard was like a trumpet speaking with me, saying, 'Come up here, and I will show you things which must take place after this.' [2] Immediately I was in the Spirit; and behold, a throne set in Heaven, and One sat on the throne. [3] And He who sat there was like a jasper and a sardius stone in appearance; and there was a rainbow around the throne, in appearance like an emerald. [4] Around the throne were twenty-four thrones, and on the thrones I saw*

> *twenty-four elders sitting, clothed in white robes; and they had crowns of gold on their heads. [5] And from the throne proceeded lightnings, thunderings, and voices. Seven lamps of fire were burning before the throne, which are the seven Spirits of God. [6] Before the throne there was a sea of glass, like crystal. And in the midst of the throne, and around the throne, were four living creatures full of eyes in front and in back. [7] The first living creature was like a lion, the second living creature like a calf, the third living creature had a face like a man, and the fourth living creature was like a flying eagle. [8] The four living creatures, each having six wings, were full of eyes around and within. And they do not rest day or night, saying: 'Holy, holy, holy, Lord God Almighty, Who was and is and is to come!' [9] Whenever the living creatures give glory and honor and thanks to Him who sits on the throne, who lives forever and ever, [10] the twenty-four elders fall down before Him who sits on the throne and worship Him who lives forever and ever, and cast their crowns before the throne, saying: [11]'You are worthy, O Lord, To receive glory and honor and power; For You created all things, And by Your will they exist and were created.' " (Revelation 4:1–11 NKJV).*

John also wrote that there will be no night in Heaven:

> *"The city had no need of the sun or of the moon to shine in it, for the glory of God illuminated it. The Lamb is its light. [24] And the*

> *nations of those who are saved shall walk in its light, and the kings of the earth bring their glory and honor into it. [25] Its gates shall not be shut at all by day (there shall be no night there). [26] And they shall bring the glory and the honor of the nations into it. [27] But there shall by no means enter it anything that defiles, or causes an abomination or a lie, but only those who are written in the Lamb's Book of Life." (Revelation 21:23–27 NKJV).*

When Jesus was about to leave earth He told His disciples that He was going away but He would return.

> *"Let not your heart be troubled; you believe in God, believe also in Me. [2] In My Father's house are many mansions; if it were not so, I would have told you. I go to prepare a place for you. [3] And if I go and prepare a place for you, I will come again and receive you to Myself; that where I am, there you may be also." (John 14:1–3 NKJV).*

The hope and prayer of every Christian is that we will spend eternity in Heaven with God. Location does not matter, so do not get caught up in where it is. The good thing is that the Bible says that there is a place called Heaven where God is and where Jesus is sitting at His right hand, making intercession for us. Let us do everything in our power to make it to that place where we get the opportunity to spend eternity praising and worshipping Him.

Chapter 16

What Is Hell?

The greatest fear of every born again Christian and even some sinners is ending up in hell. The Bible teaches that there is a place called hell and that it is the opposite of everything that will be found in Heaven.

The names and description of hell are many, but all of the conditions speak to a fate worse than death. Bible references identify it is a place of everlasting suffering and punishment for those who do not accept Jesus Christ as Lord and Savior.

Hell has been called hell fire, outer darkness, the fiery furnace, the fire of hell, the lake of fire, eternal fire, the pit, Sheol, Hades, and Gehenna among others. Words like weeping, wailing, gnashing of teeth, burning, torment, and no death describe what can be expected of this place.

The New Testament gives over 160 warnings about hell and more than half of these have come from Jesus. Several times He referred to "the judgment" and the punishment that would follow.

In Matthew's Gospel, chapter 13, Jesus related the parable of the man who sowed good seed in his ground but this was sabotaged by an enemy who sowed bad seed in the same field. According to the parable, the landowner's employees asked him how they should handle this problem and he told them to let the plants grow and make the separation at harvest time. The disciples were puzzled by this parable of "the Sower" and asked Jesus to explain.

> *"He answered and said to them: 'He who sows the good seed is the Son of Man. [38] The field is the world, the good seeds are the sons of the kingdom, but the tares are the sons of the wicked one. [39] The enemy who sowed them is the devil, the harvest is the end of the age, and the reapers are the angels. [40] Therefore as the tares are gathered and burned in the fire, so it will be at the end of this age. [41] The Son of Man will send out His angels, and they will gather out of His kingdom all things that offend, and those who practice lawlessness, [42] and will cast them into the furnace of fire. There will be wailing and gnashing of teeth. [43] Then the righteous will shine forth as the sun in the kingdom of their Father. He who has ears to hear, let him hear!' " (Matthew 13:37–43 NKJV).*

As if this was not enough, Jesus had a similar parable for His followers as He warned about the judgment of those who follow Him and those who reject Him.

> *"Again, the kingdom of Heaven is like a dragnet that was cast into the sea and gathered some of every kind, [48] which, when it was full, they drew to shore; and they sat down and gathered the good into vessels, but threw the bad away. [49] So it will be at the end of the age. The angels will come forth, separate the wicked from among the just, [50]and cast them into the furnace of fire. There will be wailing and gnashing of teeth." (Matthew 13:47–50 NKJV).*

These passages of Scripture really put into context what can be expected at the end of the age when Jesus, as He has promised, returns for His people.

Jesus also had a serious warning indicating that just by contemplating an action you could sin and end up in hell.

> *"You have heard that it was said to those of old, 'You shall not murder, and whoever murders will be in danger of the judgment.' [22] But I say to you that whoever is angry with his brother without a cause shall be in danger of the judgment. And whoever says to his brother, 'Raca!' shall be in danger of the council. But whoever says, 'You fool!' shall be in danger of hell fire." (Matthew 5:21–22 NKJV).*

Jesus went even further when He stressed that this "hell fire" will have no end.

> *"If your hand or foot causes you to sin, cut it off and cast it from you. It is better for you to enter into life lame or maimed, rather than having two hands or two feet, to be cast into the everlasting fire. [9] And if your eye causes you to sin, pluck it out and cast it from you. It is better for you to enter into life with one eye, rather than having two eyes, to be cast into hell fire." (Matthew 18:8–9 NKJV).*

This statement from Jesus was a reiteration of a similar one that He had made in that same chapter.

> *"If your right eye causes you to sin, pluck it out and cast it from you; for it is more profitable for you that one of your members perish, than for your whole body to be cast into hell. [30]And if your right hand causes you to sin, cut it off and cast it from you; for it is more profitable for you that one of your members perish, than for your whole body to be cast into hell." (Matthew 5:29–30 NKJV).*

The unbearable conditions of hell are emphasized throughout the New Testament. Chapter nine of Mark's Gospel states no fewer than three times that hell is a place of "unquenchable fire" and yet there is no death.

> *"If your hand causes you to sin, cut it off. It is better for you to enter into life maimed, rather than having two hands, to go to hell, into the fire that shall never be quenched— [44] where 'Their worm does not die and the fire is not quenched. [45] And if your foot causes you to sin, cut it off. It is better for you to enter life lame, rather than having two feet, to be cast into hell, into the fire that shall never be quenched— [46] where their worm does not die, and the fire is not quenched. [47] And if your eye causes you to sin, pluck it out. It is better for you to enter the kingdom of God with one eye, rather than having two eyes, to be cast into hell fire— [48] where their worm does not die and the fire is not quenched." (Mark 9:43–48 NKJV).*

The Bible says in chapter 25 of Matthew's Gospel that man will be judged after death. This is sometimes called the final judgment and will be done by Jesus Himself. In this passage Jesus says the guilty will be sentenced to everlasting fire.

> *"Then the righteous will answer Him, saying, 'Lord, when did we see You hungry and feed You, or thirsty and give You drink? [38] When did we see You a stranger and take You in, or naked and clothe You? [39] Or when did we see You sick, or in prison, and come to You?' [40] And the King will answer and say to them, 'Assuredly, I say to you, inasmuch as you did it to one of the least of these My brethren, you did it to Me.'*
>
> *[41] "Then He will also say to those on the left hand, 'Depart from Me, you cursed, into the everlasting fire prepared for the devil and his angels: [42] for I was hungry and you gave Me no food; I was thirsty and you gave Me no drink; [43] I was a stranger and you did not take Me in, naked and you did not clothe Me, sick and in prison and you did not visit Me.'*
>
> *[44] "Then they also will answer Him, saying, 'Lord, when did we see You hungry or thirsty or a stranger or naked or sick or in prison, and did not minister to You?' [45] Then He will answer them, saying, 'Assuredly, I say to you, inasmuch as you did not do it to one of the least of these, you did not do it to Me.' [46] And these will go away into everlasting punishment, but the righteous into eternal life." (Matthew 25:37–46 NKJV).*

It must be noted, as stated in verse 41 of the above passage, that hell has been prepared for the devil and his angels; not mankind.

The authority to judge the world has been given to Jesus by God the Father.

> *"Most assuredly, I say to you, he who hears My word and believes in Him who sent Me has everlasting life, and shall not come into judgment, but has passed from death into life. [25] Most assuredly, I say to you, the hour is coming, and now is, when the dead will hear the voice of the Son of God; and those who hear will live. [26] For as the Father has life in Himself, so He has granted the Son to have life in Himself, [27] and has given Him authority to execute judgment also, because He is the Son of Man. [28] Do not marvel at this; for the hour is coming in which all who are in the graves will hear His voice [29] and come forth—those who have done good, to the resurrection of life, and those who have done evil, to the resurrection of condemnation. [30] I can of Myself do nothing. As I hear, I judge; and My judgment is righteous, because I do not seek My own will but the will of the Father who sent Me." (John 5:24–30 NKJV).*

The book of Revelation also speaks of the final judgment and how those who have not accepted Jesus Christ will be punished. In chapter 20 John outlines what he saw in his vision of the end time:

> *"The devil, who deceived them, was cast into the lake of fire and brimstone where the beast and the false prophet are. And they will be tormented day and night forever and ever. [11] Then I saw a great white throne and Him who sat on it, from whose face the earth and the Heaven fled away. And there was found no place for them. [12]And I saw the dead, small and great, standing before God, and books were opened. And another book was opened, which is the Book of Life. And the dead were judged according to their works, by the things which were written in the books. [13] The sea gave up the dead who were in it, and Death and Hades delivered up the dead who were in them. And they were judged, each one according to his works. [14] Then Death and Hades were cast into the lake of fire. This is the second death. [15] And anyone not found written in the Book of Life was cast into the lake of fire." (Revelation 20:10–15 NKJV).*

John in chapter 21 of Revelation again spoke about the unrighteous being cast into a lake of fire.

> *"And He said to me, 'It is done! I am the Alpha and the Omega, the Beginning and the End. I will give of the fountain of the water of life freely to him who thirsts. [7] He who overcomes shall inherit all things, and I will be his God and he shall be My son. [8] But the cowardly, unbelieving, abominable, murderers, sexually immoral, sorcerers, idolaters, and all liars shall have*

> *their part in the lake which burns with fire and brimstone, which is the second death'." (Revelation 21:6–8 NKJV).*

There continues to be discussion on the location of hell. Some say it is below the ground and at the center of the earth. The Bible refers to "going down to hell" and "hell and the grave", to name a few. Jesus, in His parable of the rich man and Lazarus the beggar, gave some indication as to what will happen in hell:

> *"And it came to pass, that the beggar died, and was carried by the angels into Abraham's bosom: the rich man also died,*
> *and was buried; 23 And in hell he lift up his eyes, being in torments, and seeth Abraham*
> *afar off, and Lazarus in his bosom. 24 And he cried and said, Father Abraham, have mercy on me, and send Lazarus, that he may dip the tip of his finger in water, and cool my tongue; for I am tormented in this*
> *flame. 25 But Abraham said, Son, remember that thou in thy lifetime receivedst thy good things, and likewise Lazarus evil things: but now he is comforted, and thou art tormented.*
> *26 And beside all this, between us and you there is a great gulf fixed: so that they which would pass from hence to you cannot; neither can they pass to us, that would come*
> *from thence. 27 Then he said, I pray thee therefore, father, that thou wouldest send*
> *him to my father's house: 28 For I have five brethren; that he may testify unto them, lest they also come into this place of tor-*
> *ment. 29 Abraham saith unto him, They have*

> *Moses and the prophets; let them hear them. [30] And he said, 'Nay, father Abraham: but if one went unto them from the dead, they will repent. [31] And he said unto him, If they hear not Moses and the prophets, neither will they be persuaded, though one rose from the dead." (Luke 16:22–31 KJV).*

The location of hell is certainly not as important as trying to avoid that terrible place.

Chapter 17

The Bible Is The Word of God

The Bible is God's Word and can be considered to be the blueprint for righteous living. It contains what God has said directly and what He has said through his prophets and apostles. The Bible is therefore not only the Word of God but the inspired Word of God. This Holy Book, sometimes called "The Scriptures", reveals His plan for humanity and is also a written record of what Jesus, the prophets, and the apostles said and did.

An unidentified man has been quoted as saying this about the Bible: "Never compare this Book with other books. Never think or say that this Book contains the Word of God. It is the Word of God. It is supernatural in origin, eternal in duration, inexpressible in value, infinite in scope, regenerative in power, infallible in authority, universal in interest, personal in application, inspired in totality. Read it through. Write it down. Pray it in. Work it out. Pass it on."

Because it is God's Word, the Bible is even more important than the name of God. David said in Psalm 138:

> *"I will worship toward Your holy temple, And praise Your name For Your loving kindness and Your truth; For You have magnified Your word above all Your name." (Psalm 138: 2 NKJV).*

The Bible is called the Word of God because that is exactly what it is. You may say that this Holy Book shows the mind of God and what He wants for His people. This is made clear in verse 16 and 17 of second Timothy, chapter three:

> *"All Scripture is given by inspiration of God, and is profitable for doctrine, for reproof, for correction, for instruction in righteousness,*
> [17] *that the man of God may be complete, thoroughly equipped for every good work." (2 Timothy 3:16–17 NKJV).*

Verses 14 and 15 of that same chapter also stress the importance of knowing the Scriptures:

> *"But you must continue in the things which you have learned and been assured of, knowing from whom you have learned them,*
> [15] *and that from childhood you have known the Holy Scriptures, which are able to make you wise for salvation through faith which is in Christ Jesus." (2 Timothy 3:14–15 NKJV).*

The Bible is made up of 66 books and is divided into two parts, known as the Old Testament and the New Testament. The first comprises 39 books and the other 27. It is considered a sacred book inspired by God and written by people who were guided and instructed by Him.

The word Bible means "book" or "books" and is really a collection of books written over the course of more than one thousand years. It reveals God's work in the world from creation and includes a history of the Israelites, who are God's chosen people.

The Bible has been described by some as the ultimate history book, chronicling the lives of several influential people, some of them good and some bad. The Bible, among other things, includes biographies, poetry, legal documents, songs, letters, eyewitness accounts, people stories, historical documents, and advice literature.

The Old Testament contains an account of things that happened before Jesus Christ was born and tells how God dealt with the ancient Hebrew world and its people. It documents the creation of the universe and has recorded significant historic events.

The New Testament writings relate to the time that Jesus was on the earth. It talks about His birth, life, teachings, death, and resurrection. The New Testament also documents the establishment of the Christian Church, the lives of its early leaders, letters from these early Church leaders, and their advice to the early Christians.

The Bible is such a powerful and dynamic book, that it speaks to every topic that you can think about and provides answers to whatever problem you may be facing. It is considered the manual for the way people should behave, setting out clear guidelines for what is right and what is wrong.

Although the Bible is over a thousand years old, it remains the most widely read book and has been translated into hundreds of languages, the King James Version being the first English translation. In 1604 King James of England commissioned the translation of the Bible and in 1611 the first edition was published. For the first time, ordinary people could read the Bible for themselves, considering that before it was available only in Latin. Since then, there have been numerous other translations mainly geared toward giving readers a better understanding of what was written as "old English" in the King James Version.

Revered evangelist Dr. Billy Graham has described the Bible as the greatest document available for the human race. According to him, it is old yet ever new and is the most modern book in the world today.

"There is a false notion that a book as old as the Bible cannot speak to modern needs. People somehow think that in an age of scientific achievement, when knowledge has increased more in the past 25 years than in all preceding centuries put together, this ancient book is out of date. But to all who read and love the Bible, it is relevant for our generation."

Dr. Graham added that it is in these Holy Scriptures that the answers to life's ultimate questions can be found. Questions like "Where did I come from?", "Why am I here?", "Where am I going?", and "What is the purpose of my existence?"

Which translation you use is strictly a personal choice. Select one with which you feel comfortable and one that gives you a good understanding of what it's saying. Make sure you ask the Holy Spirit to assist you in making your choice and ask Him to reveal the Word of God to you as you read and study.

To the newly born again, the Bible must be the ultimate textbook in your training as a Christian. It should be read thoroughly and carefully studied since it contains information that shows God's plan for humanity. Studying the Bible reveals who Jesus Christ is and the reason for His coming to earth. As you get to know Him better, your faith is strengthened and this leads to a better understanding of His gift of eternal life.

Paul in his second epistle to Timothy gave his protégé some important advice:

> *"Study to shew thyself approved unto God, a workman that needeth not to be ashamed, rightly dividing the word of truth." (2 Timothy 2:15 KJV).*

God had something to say about those who did not know His word. The prophet Hosea in chapter four of his book quoted Him as making this comment about the Israelites:

> *"My people are destroyed for lack of knowledge. Because you have rejected knowledge, I also will reject you from being priest for Me; Because you have forgotten the law of your God." (Hosea 4:6 NKJV).*

Paul in his letter to the Ephesians told them that as leaders it was their job to teach Believers to grow in the Christian faith:

> *"And He Himself gave some to be apostles, some prophets, some evangelists, and some pastors and teachers, 12 for the equipping of the saints for the work of ministry, for the edifying of the body of Christ, 13 till we all come to the unity of the faith and of the knowledge of the Son of God, to a perfect man, to the measure of the stature of the fullness of Christ; 14 that we should no longer be children, tossed to and fro and carried about with every wind of doctrine, by the trickery of men, in the cunning craftiness of deceitful plotting, 15 but, speaking the truth in love, may grow up in all things into Him who is the head—Christ." (Ephesians 4:11–15 NKJV).*

Peter told the early church that some parts of the Scriptures may be hard to understand. He warned that some people who are not taught or are unstable sometimes give incorrect interpretations:

> *"You therefore, beloved, since you know this beforehand, beware lest you also fall from your own steadfastness, being led away with the error of the wicked; [18] but grow in the grace and knowledge of our Lord and Saviour Jesus Christ." (2 Peter 3:17–18 NKJV).*

Knowing the Word of God helps the young Christian not to sin unwittingly. David said in Psalm 119:

> *"Your word I have hidden in my heart, that I might not sin against You." (Psalm 119: 11 NKJV).*

Verse 12 of Hebrews chapter four shows that the word of God is not ordinary:

> *"For the word of God is living and powerful, and sharper than any two-edged sword, piercing even to the division of soul and spirit, and of joints and marrow, and is a discerner of the thoughts and intents of the heart." (Hebrews 4:12 NKJV).*

In John's Gospel, chapter 15, verse seven, it is shown that if you are born again and you are fully equipped with the Holy Scriptures, you have full access to God's provision.

> *"If ye abide in me, and my words abide in you, ye shall ask what ye will, and it shall be done unto you." (John 15:7 NKJV).*

Jesus also stressed the importance of His word. Talking to a crowd, He had this to say, as written in chapter eight of John's Gospel:

> *"If you abide in My word, you are My disciples indeed. [32] And you shall know the truth, and the truth shall make you free." (John 8:31–32 NKJV).*

Jesus told His disciples, as quoted in Matthew 24, that His words are everlasting:

> *"Heaven and earth will pass away, but My words will by no means pass away." (Matthew 24:35 NKJV).*

Peter also testified that God's Word is for all time:

> *"The grass withers, And its flower falls away, [25] But the word of the Lord endures forever." (1 Peter 1:24–25 NKJV).*

In the very next chapter Peter advises the young Christians to do everything to learn it.

> *"Therefore, laying aside all malice, all deceit, hypocrisy, envy, and all evil speaking, [2] as newborn babes, desire the pure milk of the word, that you may grow thereby, [3] if indeed you have tasted that the Lord is gracious." (1 Peter 2:1–3 NKJV).*

Legendary evangelist the late Smith Wigglesworth has also given his opinion on the Word of God. He is quoted as describing it as very precious.

"God has made His Word so precious that, if I could not get another copy, I would not part with my Bible for all the world. There is life in the Word. There is virtue in It. I find Christ in It; and He is the One I need for spirit, soul, and body. It tells me of the power of His name and of the power of His blood for cleansing."

The Bible is complete and Proverbs chapter 30 warns about tampering with it.

> *"Every word of God is pure; He is a shield to those who put their trust in Him. [6] Do not add to His words, Lest He rebuke you, and you be found a liar." (Proverbs 30:5–6 NKJV).*

This warning against trying to change or alter the Word of God is even stronger in Revelation chapter 22:

> *"For I testify to everyone who hears the words of the prophecy of this book: If anyone adds to these things, God will add to him the plagues that are written in this book; [19] and if anyone takes away from the words of the book of this prophecy, God shall take away his part from the Book of Life, from the holy city, and from the things which are written in this book". (Revelation 22:18–19 NKJV).*

God has made several promises to His people in the Bible and His Word says that He is not a liar. These promises could bring comfort, joy, and a sense of victory to the Christian. Isaiah chapter 55, verses 10 to 11 show that God fulfills His promises:

> *"For as the rain comes down, and the snow from Heaven, And do not return there,*

> *But water the earth, And make it bring forth and bud, That it may give seed to the sower And bread to the eater, [11] So shall My word be that goes forth from My mouth; It shall not return to Me void, But it shall accomplish what I please, And it shall prosper in the thing for which I sent it." (Isaiah 55:10–11 NKJV).*

The Bible is God's inspired Word and is the final authority for everything pertaining to righteousness and godliness. It is the strict rule by which the Believer should live. It is the basis for teaching, preaching, and correcting and even speaks to the subject of discipline in the Church.

Paul had strong words for the Christians at Corinth who were in the Church but still living in sin:

> *"I can hardly believe the report about the sexual immorality going on among you—something that even pagans don't do. I am told that a man in your church is living in sin with his stepmother. [2] You are so proud of yourselves, but you should be mourning in sorrow and shame. And you should remove this man from your fellowship. [3] Even though I am not with you in person, I am with you in the Spirit. And as though I were there, I have already passed judgment on this man [4] in the name of the Lord Jesus. You must call a meeting of the church. I will be present with you in spirit, and so will the power of our Lord Jesus. [5] Then you must throw this man out and hand him over to Satan so that his sinful nature will be destroyed and he himself will*

> *be saved on the day the Lord returns." (1 Corinthians 5:1–5 NLT).*

Paul admonished them for bragging about this indiscipline, warning that this could negatively impact the whole body of Christ, the Church.

> *"Get rid of the old 'yeast' by removing this wicked person from among you. Then you will be like a fresh batch of dough made without yeast, which is what you really are. Christ, our Passover Lamb, has been sacrificed for us. [8] So let us celebrate the festival, not with the old bread of wickedness and evil, but with the new bread of sincerity and truth. [9] When I wrote to you before, I told you not to associate with people who indulge in sexual sin. [10] But I wasn't talking about unbelievers who indulge in sexual sin, or are greedy, or cheat people, or worship idols. You would have to leave this world to avoid people like that. [11] I meant that you are not to associate with anyone who claims to be a Believer yet indulges in sexual sin, or is greedy, or worships idols, or is abusive, or is a drunkard, or cheats people. Don't even eat with such people." (1 Corinthians 5:7–11 NLT).*

The Bible has been translated into over two thousand languages and has been published in several versions. It is still the best-selling book in the world.

Although the Bible is the most available book, it is not as widely utilized as it should be. Statistics show that less than 15 percent of the people who said they believe the

Bible do not read it every day. Fewer than 35 percent read it only once a week and 42 percent say they read it "once in a great while".

The new convert must make it a priority to get a copy of the Bible, and start reading and studying it. This will be the beginning of a new and exciting life.

Let God speak to you through His Word.

Chapter 18

What Is God's Grace?

God's grace is another very important foundation on which the Christian stands. It has been described as His unmerited and undeserved divine favor. It is a gift freely given and therefore cannot be bought or earned. But grace is even more than that.

God's grace is the power through which people are saved from sin and inherit eternal life. Paul spoke to this in his epistle to the church at Ephesus:

> *"But God, who is rich in mercy, because of His great love with which He loved us, [5] even when we were dead in trespasses, made us alive together with Christ (by grace you have been saved), [6] and raised us up together, and made us sit together in the Heavenly places in Christ Jesus, [7] that in the ages to come He might show the exceeding riches of His grace in His kindness toward us in Christ Jesus. [8] For by grace you have been saved through faith, and that not of yourselves; it is the gift of God, [9] not of works, lest anyone should boast. [10] For we are His workmanship, created in Christ Jesus for good works, which God prepared beforehand that we should walk in them." (Ephesians 2:4–10 NKJV).*

The grace of God came through Jesus Christ. The Gospel of John, chapter one says that Jesus is the Word. John says that this Word, Jesus, was full of grace:

> *And the Word became flesh and dwelt among us, and we beheld His glory, the glory as of the only begotten of the Father, full of grace and truth. [15] John bore witness of Him and cried out, saying, 'This was He of whom I said, He who comes after me is preferred before me, for He was before me.' [16] And of His fullness we have all received, and grace for grace. [17] For the law was given through Moses, but grace and truth came through Jesus Christ." (John 1:14–17 NKJV).*

The Bible speaks of saving grace. This comes through Jesus Christ, whom God sent to the cross to redeem sinners. It was this grace that paid the price for everyone who will receive Jesus as Lord and Savior. This is aptly stated in the signature quotation of the Christian faith.

> *"For God so loved the world that He gave His only begotten Son, that whoever believes in Him should not perish but have everlasting life. [17] For God did not send His Son into the world to condemn the world, but that the world through Him might be saved." (John 3:16–17 NKJV).*

Every unbeliever is given a measure of grace that enables him or her to accept Jesus Christ as Savior.

> *"For the grace of God that brings salvation has appeared to all men, [12] teaching us that, denying ungodliness and worldly lusts, we should live soberly, righteously, and godly in the present age, [13]looking for the blessed hope and glorious appearing of our great God and Savior Jesus Christ, [14] who gave Himself for us, that He might redeem us from every lawless deed and purify for Himself His own special people, zealous for good works." (Titus 2:11–14 NKJV).*

Once you have repented of your sins and have given your life to Jesus Christ, the grace of God enables you to continue to live and grow in Christ.

> *"You therefore, beloved, since you know this beforehand, beware lest you also fall from your own steadfastness, being led away with the error of the wicked; [18] but grow in the grace and knowledge of our Lord and Saviour Jesus Christ." (2 Peter 3:17–18 NKJV).*

God gives grace to those who work for Him and this results in powerful ministry by His followers.

> *"And with great power the apostles gave witness to the resurrection of the Lord Jesus. And great grace was upon them all. [34] Nor was there anyone among them who lacked; for all who were possessors of lands or houses sold them, and brought the proceeds of the things that were sold, [35] and laid them at the apostles' feet; and they distributed to each as anyone had need." (Acts 4:33–35 NKJV).*

God's grace is extremely diverse and comes in many forms, ways, and manifestations.

> *"And God is able to make all grace abound toward you, that you, always having all sufficiency in all things, may have an abundance for every good work." (2 Corinthians 9:8 NKJV).*

God's grace allows the Christian to do great works, as was shown in the Acts of the Apostles:

> *"And the word of God increased; and the number of the disciples multiplied in Jerusalem greatly; and a great company of the priests were obedient to the faith. [8] And Stephen, full of faith and power, did great wonders and miracles among the people." (Acts 6:7–8 KJV).*

God gives His children grace to withstand the toughest challenges. Paul testified to this in his second epistle to the Corinthians:

> *"And lest I should be exalted above measure by the abundance of the revelations, a thorn in the flesh was given to me, a messenger of Satan to buffet me, lest I be exalted above measure. [8] Concerning this thing I pleaded with the Lord three times that it might depart from me. [9] And He said to me, 'My grace is sufficient for you, for My strength is made perfect in weakness.' Therefore most gladly I will rather boast in my infirmities, that the power of Christ may rest upon*

> *me. [10] Therefore I take pleasure in infirmities, in reproaches, in needs, in persecutions, in distresses, for Christ's sake. For when I am weak, then I am strong." (2 Corinthians 12:7–10 NKJV).*

It is through God's grace that we are able to hold on in faith to His Word and the power that is in Jesus Christ.

> *"Jesus Christ is the same yesterday, today, and forever. [9] Do not be carried about with various and strange doctrines. For it is good that the heart be established by grace, not with foods which have not profited those who have been occupied with them." (Hebrews 13:8–9 NKJV).*

The Christian needs to be strong, and it is God's grace that enables that characteristic in the Believer, as indicated by Paul to his protégé, Timothy:

> *"You therefore, my son, be strong in the grace that is in Christ Jesus." (2 Timothy 2:1 NKJV).*

God's grace is the power that enables the child of God to use his or her spiritual gifts. This is shown in Romans chapter 12, which is probably the book that best exemplifies the characteristics of a Christian:

> *"For as we have many members in one body, but all the members do not have the same function, [5] so we, being many, are one body in Christ, and individually members of one another. [6] Having then gifts differing*

according to the grace that is given to us, let us use them: if prophecy, let us prophesy in proportion to our faith; [7] or ministry, let us use it in our ministering; he who teaches, in teaching; [8] he who exhorts, in exhortation; he who gives, with liberality; he who leads, with diligence; he who shows mercy, with cheerfulness. [9] Let love be without hypocrisy. Abhor what is evil. Cling to what is good." (Romans 12:4–9 NKJV).

The declaration that we have been saved from sin by the blood of Jesus Christ is known as justification, and this can only come through the grace of God.

"For all have sinned and fall short of the glory of God, [24] being justified freely by His grace through the redemption that is in Christ Jesus, [25] whom God set forth as a propitiation by His blood, through faith, to demonstrate His righteousness, because in His forbearance God had passed over the sins that were previously committed, [26] to demonstrate at the present time His righteousness, that He might be just and the justifier of the one who has faith in Jesus." (Romans 3:23–26 NKJV).

That same passage is expressed this way in the New Living Translation:

"For everyone has sinned; we all fall short of God's glorious standard. [24] Yet God freely and graciously declares that we are righteous. He did this through Christ Jesus

> *when He freed us from the penalty for our sins. [25] For God presented Jesus as the sacrifice for sin. People are made right with God when they believe that Jesus sacrificed His life, shedding His blood. This sacrifice shows that God was being fair when He held back and did not punish those who sinned in times past, [26] for He was looking ahead and including them in what He would do in this present time. God did this to demonstrate His righteousness, for He himself is fair and just, and He declares sinners to be right in His sight when they believe in Jesus." (Romans 3:23–26 NLT).*

God's grace is sometimes linked to mercy, but like justice, it is different. While grace is about getting something that we don't deserve, mercy is about being spared what we deserve. Justice, on the other hand, is getting what is deserved.

Although the grace of God is freely given to the undeserving, it can also be sought after. The Hebrew church was encouraged to go after it.

> *"So let us come boldly to the throne of our gracious God. There we will receive his mercy, and we will find grace to help us when we need it most." (Hebrews 4:16 NLT).*

The "Throne of Grace" that Paul is speaking about could be described as such because it is the reservoir of God's gifts and all that His children need. From that "Throne of Grace" the Believer can expect God's love, mercy, forgiveness, wisdom, spiritual power, and everything else that the Christian needs to live a life committed to Him.

God gives His grace to those who humble themselves before Him and keep away from sin.

> *"Adulterers and adulteresses! Do you not know that friendship with the world is enmity with God? Whoever therefore wants to be a friend of the world makes himself an enemy of God. [5] Or do you think that the Scripture says in vain, 'The Spirit who dwells in us yearns jealously'? [6] But He gives more grace. Therefore He says: 'God resists the proud, but gives grace to the humble.' [7] Therefore submit to God. Resist the devil and he will flee from you. [8] Draw near to God and He will draw near to you. Cleanse your hands, you sinners; and purify your hearts, you double-minded. [9] Lament and mourn and weep! Let your laughter be turned to mourning and your joy to gloom. [10] Humble yourselves in the sight of the Lord, and He will lift you up." (James 4:4–10 NKJV).*

The previous passage shows that it is possible for us to get even more grace from God and sets out the requirements for receiving such grace. According to verse seven, we must submit to God and submission comes with humility. Submission, therefore, qualifies the humble for that grace. Resisting the devil and all his evil ploys can also lead to more of God's grace.

Verse eight of that Bible passage also advises the Believer to draw nigh to God. This can be done by intensifying your prayer life, increasing your studying of the Word, offering up more worship and praise, and by generally enhancing your walk with God.

James also told the saints that in trying to get more of God's grace they should "cleanse their hands" and "purify their minds". This seems to suggest putting an end to, and removing, any sins that may be in their lives. Things like adultery, lying, envy, evil thoughts, backbiting, greed, and things of that nature. Confessing these sins, repenting, and inviting the Holy Spirit to help you to overcome them could lead to even more of God's grace.

In the book of Hebrews, Christians are taught to encourage one another to live lives that would not cause them to miss out on the grace of God.

> *"Pursue peace with all people, and holiness, without which no one will see the Lord: 15 looking carefully lest anyone fall short of the grace of God; lest any root of bitterness springing up cause trouble, and by this many become defiled; 16 lest there be any fornicator or profane person like Esau, who for one morsel of food sold his birthright." (Hebrews 12:14–16 NKJV).*

Another expression of this portion of Scripture is found in the New Living Translation:

> *"Work at living in peace with everyone, and work at living a holy life, for those who are not holy will not see the Lord. 15 Look after each other so that none of you fails to receive the grace of God. Watch out that no poisonous root of bitterness grows up to trouble you, corrupting many. 16 Make sure that no one is immoral or godless like Esau, who traded his birthright as the firstborn son for a single meal." (Hebrews 12:14–16 NLT).*

Christians have been warned not to receive the grace of God in vain, but to hold on to their salvation.

> *"Now then, we are ambassadors for Christ, as though God were pleading through us: we implore you on Christ's behalf, be reconciled to God. [21] For He made Him who knew no sin to be sin for us, that we might become the righteousness of God in Him. [1]We then, as workers together with Him also plead with you not to receive the grace of God in vain. [2] For He says: 'In an acceptable time I have heard you, And in the day of salvation I have helped you.' Behold, now is the accepted time; behold, now is the day of salvation. (2 Corinthians 5:20–21; 2 Corinthians 6:1–2 NKJV).*

Paul also described himself as a good example of not receiving the grace of God in vain:

> *"For I am the least of the apostles, who am not worthy to be called an apostle, because I persecuted the church of God. [10] But by the grace of God I am what I am, and His grace toward me was not in vain; but I laboured more abundantly than they all, yet not I, but the grace of God which was with me." (1 Corinthians 15:9–10 NKJV).*

Titus, one of Paul's protégés, was encouraged by his mentor to remind the Christians to be subject to rulers and authorities and to obey. They were also not to speak evil of anyone, be peaceable and gentle to everyone, and do good works because of the grace of God.

> *"For we ourselves were also once foolish, disobedient, deceived, serving various lusts and pleasures, living in malice and envy, hateful and hating one another.. [4] But when the kindness and the love of God our Saviour toward man appeared, [5] not by works of righteousness which we have done, but according to His mercy He saved us, through the washing of regeneration and renewing of the Holy Spirit, [6] whom He poured out on us abundantly through Jesus Christ our Saviour, [7] that having been justified by His grace we should become heirs according to the hope of eternal life." (Titus 3:3–7 NKJV).*

So it is only by the grace of God that the Believer becomes born again. But to maintain that status we have to continue to desire and do the things that His Word says we must do.

Paul commended the grace of God to the Corinthian church in his benediction, a portion of Scripture that is well used at the end of services even today:

> *"The grace of the Lord Jesus Christ, and the love of God, and the communion of the Holy Spirit be with you all. Amen." (2 Corinthians 13:14 NKJV).*

This verse certainly puts into context the working and interaction of the Trinity: God the Father, God the Son, and God the Holy Spirit. Some theologians believe that the reference to the grace of Jesus Christ in this passage relates to His mercy, power, nearness, and love for the Christian.

God's grace has come to us through Jesus Christ. He was sent to redeem sinners because Adam had failed. God sent His own Son to be the atonement and Jesus' death on the cross made up for Adam's failure in the Garden of Eden.

> *"When Adam sinned, sin entered the world. Adam's sin brought death, so death spread to everyone, for everyone sinned. [13] Yes, people sinned even before the law was given. But it was not counted as sin because there was not yet any law to break. [14] Still, everyone died—from the time of Adam to the time of Moses—even those who did not disobey an explicit commandment of God, as Adam did. Now Adam is a symbol, a representation of Christ, who was yet to come. [15] But there is a great difference between Adam's sin and God's gracious gift. For the sin of this one man, Adam, brought death to many. But even greater is God's wonderful grace and his gift of forgiveness to many through this other man, Jesus Christ. [16] And the result of God's gracious gift is very different from the result of that one man's sin. For Adam's sin led to condemnation, but God's free gift leads to our being made right with God, even though we are guilty of many sins. [17] For the sin of this one man, Adam, caused death to rule over many. But even greater is God's wonderful grace and his gift of righteousness, for all who receive it will live in triumph over sin and death through this one man, Jesus Christ." (Romans 5:12–17 NLT).*

Yes, Adam's sin brought condemnation for everyone, but because of Jesus' sacrifice and God's grace, mankind can now have a right relationship with God.

> *"God's law was given so that all people could see how sinful they were. But as people sinned more and more, God's wonderful grace became more abundant. [21] So just as sin ruled over all people and brought them to death, now God's wonderful grace rules instead, giving us right standing with God and resulting in eternal life through Jesus Christ our Lord." (Romans 5:20–21 NLT).*

The grace of God opens the way for Believers to have peace with God.

> *"Therefore being justified by faith, we have peace with God through our Lord Jesus Christ: [2] By whom also we have access by faith into this grace wherein we stand, and rejoice in hope of the glory of God." (Romans 5:1–2 NKJV).*

God's grace sanctifies and strengthens His children.

> *"So now, brethren, I commend you to God and to the word of His grace, which is able to build you up and give you an inheritance among all those who are sanctified." (Acts 20:32 NKJV).*

We really must thank God for His grace, which He has freely given. We are truly blessed because of it.

> *"All praise to God, the Father of our Lord Jesus Christ, who has blessed us with every spiritual blessing in the heavenly realms because we are united with Christ. [4] Even before he made the world, God loved us and chose us in Christ to be holy and without fault in his eyes. [5] God decided in advance to adopt us into his own family by bringing us to himself through Jesus Christ. This is what he wanted to do, and it gave him great pleasure. [6] So we praise God for the glorious grace he has poured out on us who belong to his dear Son. [7] He is so rich in kindness and grace that he purchased our freedom with the blood of his Son and forgave our sins. [8] He has showered his kindness on us, along with all wisdom and understanding. (Ephesians 1:3–8 NLT).*

You may be wondering what all this talk about the grace of God means to you personally in your daily living. Think of the times when you have encountered difficult or even dangerous situations and, through no effort of your own, you miraculously escaped or overcame. That certainly was God's grace extended to you. That is just one instance of the marvelous grace of God.

It was God's grace that inspired the captain of a slave ship to write the hymn "Amazing Grace". John Newton, who later became an abolitionist, wrote the words of this well known and loved hymn in 1772. It is understood that some time before that, his ship was caught in a powerful storm and was about to sink. He prayed to God for deliverance and the ship, cargo and crew were saved. He later became an Anglican priest and wrote nearly 300 hymns including "Amazing Grace".

Chapter 19

What Is Prayer?

Prayer is simply talking to and with God and listening to Him. It is the way Believers communicate with their Heavenly Father. It is vital for every Christian and opens the way for a host of blessings.

Prayer is sometimes referred to as "calling on God", "seeking the Lord", "drawing near to God", and "going before the throne of grace".

The born again Christian must maintain constant contact with God by frequent prayer. This helps to develop a closer relationship with Him and builds faith. The Bible is clear that we should pray. The psalmist David in 1 Chronicles, chapter 16 told his people that they have to pray:

> *Oh, give thanks to the Lord! Call upon His name; Make known His deeds among the peoples! [9] Sing to Him, sing psalms to Him; Talk of all His wondrous works! [10] Glory in His holy name; Let the hearts of those rejoice who seek the Lord! [11] Seek the Lord and His strength; Seek His face evermore! [12] Remember His marvelous works which He has done, His wonders, and the judgments of His mouth, [13] O seed of Israel His servant, you children of Jacob, His chosen ones!" (1 Chronicles 16:8–13 NKJV).*

The Bible shows that prayer can produce miraculous, powerful, and dramatic results. Elijah the prophet prayed that it wouldn't rain and there was a three-and-a-half-year drought. He prayed again for rain and it fell.

Acts chapter four tells the story of how Peter and John were arrested for preaching about Jesus. They were later released and told to stop preaching. The story says that they met their colleagues and related their experience and prayed, asking God for boldness to speak His word.

> *"And when they had prayed, the place where they were assembled together was shaken; and they were all filled with the Holy Spirit, and they spoke the word of God with boldness." (Acts 4:31 NKJV).*

The story is told in John chapter 11 of the death of Lazarus, Jesus' friend. When Jesus went to his grave he had been dead four days. But Jesus prayed and something incredible happened.

> *"Then they took away the stone from the place where the dead man was lying. And Jesus lifted up His eyes and said, 'Father, I thank You that You have heard Me. 42 And I know that You always hear Me, but because of the people who are standing by I said this, that they may believe that You sent Me.'*
> *43 Now when He had said these things, He cried with a loud voice, 'Lazarus, come forth!'*
> *44 And he who had died came out bound hand and foot with grave clothes, and his face was wrapped with a cloth. Jesus said to them, 'Loose him, and let him go'." (John 11:41–44 NKJV).*

Prayer must be sincere and must be done in and with faith. This means that you must believe that what you are praying for will become a reality. Jesus explained this to His disciples after He had cursed a fig tree for not producing. His disciples were amazed at this event but He had a word of advice for them.

> *"So Jesus answered and said to them, 'Have faith in God. [23] For assuredly, I say to you, whoever says to this mountain, Be removed and be cast into the sea, and does not doubt in his heart, but believes that those things he says will be done, he will have whatever he says. [24] Therefore I say to you, whatever things you ask when you pray, believe that you receive them, and you will have them." (Mark 11:22–24 NKJV).*

Jesus also gave His disciples the assurance, as written in John chapter 14, verses 13 and 14, that effective prayer must be in His name:

> *"And whatever you ask in My name, that I will do, that the Father may be glorified in the Son. [14] If you ask anything in My name, I will do it." (John 14:13–14 NKJV).*

Not all prayers are answered instantly. Jesus said in Matthew chapter six that we sometimes need to be persistent. But while God is willing to answer prayer, we must be in a right relationship with Him.

> *"Therefore do not worry, saying, 'What shall we eat?' or 'What shall we drink?' or 'What shall we wear?' [32] For after all these things*

the Gentiles seek. For your Heavenly Father knows that you need all these things. [33] But seek first the kingdom of God and His righteousness, and all these things shall be added to you." (Matthew 6:31–33 NKJV).

John, in chapter three of his first epistle, also spoke about getting positive answers from God when we have a close relationship with Him.

"Beloved, if our heart does not condemn us, we have confidence toward God. [22] And whatever we ask we receive from Him, because we keep His commandments and do those things that are pleasing in His sight. [23] And this is His commandment: that we should believe on the name of His Son Jesus Christ and love one another, as He gave us commandment." (1 John 3:21–22 NKJV).

The result of your prayer is therefore dependent on obeying the word of God, loving and pleasing Him. James said in chapter five of his epistle:

"The effective, fervent prayer of a righteous man avails much." (James 5: 16 NKJV).

Be warned that if there is sin in your life God will not hear your prayers. If you doubt this then hear what David said in Psalms 66:

"If I regard iniquity in my heart, The Lord will not hear. [19] But certainly God has heard me; He has attended to the voice of my prayer.

> [20] *Blessed be God, Who has not turned away my prayer, nor His mercy from me!" (Psalms 66:18–20 NKJV).*

But David was not the only one to give this warning. James the apostle reiterated it in chapter four of his epistle:

> *"You lust and do not have. You murder and covet and cannot obtain. You fight and war. Yet you do not have because you do not ask. [3] You ask and do not receive, because you ask amiss, that you may spend it on your pleasures. [4] Adulterers and adulteresses! Do you not know that friendship with the world is enmity with God? Whoever therefore wants to be a friend of the world makes himself an enemy of God." (James 4:2–4 NKJV).*

Peter warned husbands in chapter three of his first epistle that they could run the risk of not having their prayers answered if they are not in a good relationship with their wives:

> *"Husbands, likewise, dwell with them with understanding, giving honour to the wife, as to the weaker vessel, and as being heirs together of the grace of life, that your prayers may not be hindered." (1 Peter 3:7 NKJV).*

The Bible emphasizes the role and significance of prayer, showing that it can be done individually or in groups, sometimes referred to as corporate prayer. It is not something reserved for church leaders and clergy only, but can and must be done by anyone and everyone. The Christian can sincerely pray from the heart.

Prayer need not involve any special language. It can be simple, in your own words, spontaneous, and even as down to earth as talking to a friend. But it must be sincere. Jesus made this clear in His parable of the Pharisee and the publican in the Gospel of Luke, chapter 18.

> *"Two men went up to the temple to pray, one a Pharisee and the other a tax collector. [11]The Pharisee stood and prayed thus with himself, 'God, I thank You that I am not like other men—extortioners, unjust, adulterers, or even as this tax collector. [12] I fast twice a week; I give tithes of all that I possess.' [13] And the tax collector, standing afar off, would not so much as raise his eyes to Heaven, but beat his breast, saying, 'God, be merciful to me a sinner!' [14] I tell you, this man went down to his house justified rather than the other; for everyone who exalts himself will be humbled, and he who humbles himself will be exalted." (Luke 18:10–14 NKJV).*

The Living Bible puts it this way:

> *"Two men went to the Temple to pray. One was a proud, self-righteous Pharisee, and the other a cheating tax collector. [11] The proud Pharisee 'prayed' this prayer: 'Thank God, I am not a sinner like everyone else, especially like that tax collector over there! For I never cheat, I don't commit adultery, [12] I go without food twice a week, and I give to God a tenth of everything I earn.' [13] But the corrupt tax collector stood at a distance and dared not even lift his eyes to Heaven as he prayed, but beat upon his chest in sorrow, exclaiming, 'God, be*

> *merciful to me, a sinner.' [14] I tell you, this sinner, not the Pharisee, returned home forgiven! For the proud shall be humbled, but the humble shall be honoured." (Luke 18:10–14 TLB).*

Jesus was known to be a man who prayed. He regularly spoke to His Father in prayer and was also known to go off by Himself to pray. He also gave instructions to His followers not to pray like unbelievers.

> *But you, when you pray, go into your room, and when you have shut your door, pray to your Father who is in the secret place; and your Father who sees in secret will reward you openly. [7] And when you pray, do not use vain repetitions as the heathen do. For they think that they will be heard for their many words. [8] Therefore do not be like them. For your Father knows the things you have need of before you ask Him." (Matthew 6:6–8 NKJV).*

Jesus did not stop there but went on to give the disciples clear guidelines on how they should pray. This model prayer is usually referred to as "The Lord's Prayer". Here is what He told them, as recorded in Luke's Gospel, chapter 11.

> *"When you pray, say: Our Father in Heaven, Hallowed be Your name. Your kingdom come. Your will be done On earth as it is in Heaven. [3] Give us day by day our daily bread. [4] And forgive us our sins, For we also forgive everyone who is indebted to us. And do not lead us into temptation, but deliver us from the evil one." (Luke 11:2–4 NKJV).*

Although a lot of people recite "The Lord's Prayer", it must be understood that this is a guide to what should go into prayer.

The first parts relate to God and His glory, and the others deal with our needs.

The first phrase, "Our Father", recognizes the God to whom we are praying and reflects the personal relationship between the person praying and the One to whom they are praying.

Having established a relationship by calling God Father, we identify His location when we say "Who art in Heaven".

These two phrases—"Our Father, who art in Heaven"—when put together show that we are not dealing with just any god but our Heavenly Father, God Almighty.

With this in mind we give Him the honor and worship He deserves when we say: "hallowed be thy name." The word "hallow" could be interpreted as holy; therefore "hallowed be your name" is telling us to worship God and to praise Him for who He is.

"Thy Kingdom come" relates to the promise by Jesus Christ that He will return to earth to establish His kingdom. It also shows that the Believer is longing for that day.

When we pray "Thy will be done, on earth as it is in Heaven," it means that we really want and desire God's will and purpose to be fulfilled in our lives.

The plea to "give us this day our daily bread" opens the door for the Christian to ask for his or her individual daily needs to be met.

"Forgive us our sins" is our confession to God that we have sinned and we need His forgiveness.

The second part of this phrase "as we forgive those who trespass against us" shows willingness on our part to forgive those who do us wrong. This is especially important since Jesus warned in Matthew chapter six that God would only forgive those who forgive others. Failure to forgive means that your prayers will not be answered.

> *"For if you forgive men their trespasses, your Heavenly Father will also forgive you. [15] But if you do not forgive men their trespasses, neither will your Father forgive your trespasses." (Luke 11:14–15 NKJV).*

"The Lord's Prayer" also indicates that we should ask God to protect us from Satan and his evil forces.

The Bible stresses that we must pray with the faith that God will answer our requests. Jesus gave the assurance in John 14 that if we ask anything in His name He would grant it. But one should not pray frivolously. We must be living the Christian life and Jesus stressed this when in Matthew six He taught His disciples that they should first get right with God before they could expect Him to give them the desires of their heart.

> *"Therefore do not worry, saying, 'What shall we eat?' or 'What shall we drink?' or 'What shall we wear?' [32] For after all these things the Gentiles seek. For your Heavenly Father knows that you need all these things. [33] But seek first the kingdom of God and His righteousness, and all these things shall be added to you. [34] Therefore do not worry about tomorrow, for tomorrow will worry about its own things. Sufficient for the day is its own trouble." (John 14: 31–34 NKJV).*

How often you pray is entirely up to you, but constant prayer means constant contact with God and therefore is highly recommended. Jesus used the parable of the "Persistent Widow" in Luke chapter 18 to show that persistent prayer works.

"There was in a certain city a judge who did not fear God nor regard man. [3] Now there was a widow in that city; and she came to him, saying, 'Get justice for me from my adversary.' [4] And he would not for a while; but afterward he said within himself, 'Though I do not fear God nor regard man, [5] yet because this widow troubles me I will avenge her, lest by her continual coming she weary me.'" [6] Then the Lord said, 'Hear what the unjust judge said. [7] And shall God not avenge His own elect who cry out day and night to Him, though He bears long with them? [8] I tell you that He will avenge them speedily. Nevertheless, when the Son of Man comes, will He really find faith on the earth?' " (Luke 18:2–8 NKJV).

Paul encouraged the church at Thessalonica to:

"Rejoice always, [17] pray without ceasing, [18] in everything give thanks; for this is the will of God in Christ Jesus for you." (1 Thessalonians 5:16–18 NKJV).

He also emphasized prayer when he told the Philippians:

"Be anxious for nothing, but in everything by prayer and supplication, with thanksgiving, let your requests be made known to God; [7] and the peace of God, which surpasses all understanding, will guard your hearts and minds through Christ Jesus." (Philippians 4:6–7 NKJV).

Your approach to prayer should be reflective of the awesome God to whom you are praying. It is therefore important that, no matter what posture you adopt, you should have the correct attitude of heart. Some people ask if there is a right or wrong posture for prayer but there is nothing to indicate such. In fact the Bible shows that people prayed standing, sitting, kneeling, lying on their bed, bowing, or prostrate on their faces.

Some people feel that they should close their eyes to pray, but whether you keep them open or shut is not important. The point is, whether you pray quietly or loudly, as long as you are sincere, comfortable, and not distracted, pray on.

You can pray using Scripture, pray in the Spirit, pray in tongues, or even just groan. When you pray always remember that Jesus has given the assurance, as written in Matthew seven, that you will be heard.

> *"Ask, and it will be given to you; seek, and you will find; knock, and it will be opened to you. [8] For everyone who asks receives, and he who seeks finds, and to him who knocks it will be opened." (Matthew 7:7–8 NKJV).*

The exciting thing about prayer is that God answers when you call. The Bible is replete with instances where people prayed and received what they wanted. Sometimes people were praying about their issues, or groups were in the process of petitioning God about others when the answer came.

The story is told in Acts chapter 12 of how Peter was imprisoned by Herod; but the church was in constant prayer for him. God sent an angel to deliver him from that prison. The irony of this story is that, even though his friends were praying for his release, when they saw him standing at the door they were astonished.

You must always pray with the expectation that your request will be answered. This is called "praying in faith" and has been endorsed by Jesus.

> *"Therefore I say to you, whatever things you ask when you pray, believe that you receive them, and you will have them." (Mark 11:24 NKJV).*

James in chapter five of his epistle says that we could and should pray for specific things.

> *"Is anyone among you suffering? Let him pray. Is anyone cheerful? Let him sing psalms. [14] Is anyone among you sick? Let him call for the elders of the church, and let them pray over him, anointing him with oil in the name of the Lord. [15] And the prayer of faith will save the sick, and the Lord will raise him up. And if he has committed sins, he will be forgiven. [16] Confess your trespasses to one another, and pray for one another, that you may be healed. The effective, fervent prayer of a righteous man avails much." (James 5:13–16 NKJV).*

The Living Bible translates verse 16 this way:

> *"Admit your faults to one another and pray for each other so that you may be healed. The earnest prayer of a righteous man has great power and wonderful results." (James 5:16 TLB).*

You may say that you don't know how to pray, but do not let that worry you. The Holy Spirit, the Comforter who now lives in you, is The Teacher. The writer of Romans in chapter eight reminded the early church that the Holy Spirit helps with this weakness:

> *"For we do not know what we should pray for as we ought, but the Spirit Himself makes intercession for us with groanings which cannot be uttered. [27] Now He who searches the hearts knows what the mind of the Spirit is, because He makes intercession for the saints according to the will of God." (Romans 8:26–27 NKJV).*

There is one aspect of prayer that should never be forgotten, and that is thanksgiving. So often we ask God for things and when we get them we are either ungrateful or just forget to say "thank you". But this is not new. Even Jesus encountered ungrateful people. According to Luke chapter 17, Jesus was on His way to Jerusalem and as He was passing through a village, He met 10 men who were lepers. They called out to Him asking for help:

> *"So when He saw them, He said to them, 'Go, show yourselves to the priests.' And so it was that as they went, they were cleansed. [15] And one of them, when he saw that he was healed, returned, and with a loud voice glorified God, [16] and fell down on his face at His feet, giving Him thanks. And he was a Samaritan. [17] So Jesus answered and said, 'Were there not ten cleansed? But where are the nine? [18] Were there not any found who returned to give glory to God except this foreigner?' " (Luke 17:14–18 NKJV).*

The Old Testament has an interesting story about Daniel, who was sentenced to death for praying to God. Some of King Darius' men had convinced the king that anyone who prayed to any god or person but him would be condemned to the lion's den.

> *"Now when Daniel knew that the writing was signed, he went home. And in his upper room, with his windows open toward Jerusalem, he knelt down on his knees three times that day, and prayed and gave thanks before his God, as was his custom since early days.*
>
> *11 "Then these men assembled and found Daniel praying and making supplication before his God. 12 And they went before the king, and spoke concerning the king's decree: 'Have you not signed a decree that every man who petitions any god or man within thirty days, except you, O king, shall be cast into the den of lions?' The king answered and said, 'The thing is true, according to the law of the Medes and Persians, which does not alter.'*
>
> *13 "So they answered and said before the king, 'That Daniel, who is one of the captives from Judah, does not show due regard for you, O king, or for the decree that you have signed, but makes his petition three times a day.'*
>
> *14 And the king, when he heard these words, was greatly displeased with himself, and set his heart on Daniel to deliver him; and he labored till the going down of the sun to deliver him. 15 Then these men approached*

the king, and said to the king, 'Know, O king, that it is the law of the Medes and Persians that no decree or statute which the king establishes may be changed.'

16 So the king gave the command, and they brought Daniel and cast him into the den of lions. But the king spoke, saying to Daniel, 'Your God, whom you serve continually, He will deliver you.' 17 Then a stone was brought and laid on the mouth of the den, and the king sealed it with his own signet ring and with the signets of his lords, that the purpose concerning Daniel might not be changed.

18 "Now the king went to his palace and spent the night fasting; and no musicians were brought before him. Also his sleep went from him. 19 Then the king arose very early in the morning and went in haste to the den of lions. 20 And when he came to the den, he cried out with a lamenting voice to Daniel. The king spoke, saying to Daniel, 'Daniel, servant of the living God, has your God, whom you serve continually, been able to deliver you from the lions?'

21 "Then Daniel said to the king, 'O king, live forever! 22 My God sent His angel and shut the lions' mouths, so that they have not hurt me, because I was found innocent before ; and also, O king, I have done no wrong before you.'

[23] *"Now the king was exceedingly glad for him, and commanded that they should take Daniel up out of the den. So Daniel was taken up out of the den, and no injury whatever was found on him, because he believed in his God.*

[24] *"And the king gave the command, and they brought those men who had accused Daniel, and they cast them into the den of lions—them, their children, and their wives; and the lions overpowered them, and broke all their bones in pieces before they ever came to the bottom of the den.*

[25] *"Then King Darius wrote: 'To all peoples, nations, and languages that dwell in all the earth: Peace be multiplied to you.*
[26] *I make a decree that in every dominion of my kingdom men must tremble and fear before the God of Daniel.'" (Daniel 6:10–26 NKJV).*

God honors those who honor Him and answers their prayers. You can rest in this assurance; as a born again Christian know that you can go to God in prayer. This was emphasized by the writer of the epistle to the Hebrews:

"Seeing then that we have a great High Priest who has passed through the Heavens, Jesus the Son of God, let us hold fast our confession. [15] *For we do not have a High Priest who cannot sympathize with our weaknesses, but was in all points tempted as we are, yet without sin.* [16] *Let*

> *us therefore come boldly to the throne of grace that we may obtain mercy and find grace to help in time of need." (Hebrews 4:14–16 NKJV).*

God is merciful and there are cases in the Bible where He answered the prayers of sinners. In most of these situations some repentance was involved.

As a Christian pray about everything and anything, and may your prayers be answered.

Chapter 20

What Is Faith?

Faith has been defined as "complete trust or confidence in someone or something." It is also described as belief in the doctrines or teachings of a religion, and belief that is not based on proof.

To the Christian, faith can be either natural or spiritual. Natural faith is what we live by every day as we take things for granted. For instance, when you are about to sit on a chair you never stop to think if it will be able to bear your weight.

Even more astonishing is the fact that we never hesitate to get on an airliner or cruise ship weighing hundreds or even thousands of tons without a thought about the fact that metal isn't supposed to float or fly. We also believe that whoever is controlling these vessels knows how to get us safely to our destination, which could be thousands of miles away.

Spiritual faith is the very foundation of Christianity and is the Christian's most powerful resource. It is the very essence by which we live. Spiritual faith is not only a belief in God but total conviction in His ability, person, and character, and in the loving way He operates.

When you mention faith, most Christians will immediately quote the first verse of Hebrews chapter 11 which says:

> *"Now faith is the substance of things hoped for, the evidence of things not seen." (Hebrews 11:1 NKJV).*

This is even better understood from the New Living Translation:

> *"Faith is the confidence that what we hope for will actually happen; it gives us assurance about things we cannot see." (Hebrews 11:1 NLT).*

Ephesians chapter two, verse eight says that Christians are saved by grace through faith. Chapter 11 of the book of Hebrews also stresses that Christianity is based on faith:

> *"But without faith it is impossible to please Him, for he who comes to God must believe that He is, and that He is a rewarder of those who diligently seek Him." (Hebrews 11:6 NKJV).*

The New Living Translation puts it this way:

> *"And it is impossible to please God without faith. Anyone who wants to come to him must believe that God exists and that he rewards those who sincerely seek him." (Hebrews 11:6 NLT).*

In other words you must have the faith to believe everything about God, including the fact that He is a spirit; He can do any and everything; He is eternal; He is everywhere at the same time, and that He can give you eternal life.

The Bible encourages us to live by faith and Paul, in Galatians chapter three, told the church that ***"the just shall live by faith."*** Jesus in Matthew six told His disciples to have faith that God can supply their everyday needs. All Believers can live with the understanding, faith, and belief that God will take care of them.

> *"Therefore I say to you, do not worry about your life, what you will eat or what you will drink; nor about your body, what you will put on. Is not life more than food and the body more than clothing? [26] Look at the birds of the air, for they neither sow nor reap nor gather into barns; yet your Heavenly Father feeds them. Are you not of more value than they? [27] Which of you by worrying can add one cubit to his stature? [28] So why do you worry about clothing? Consider the lilies of the field, how they grow: they neither toil nor spin; [29] and yet I say to you that even Solomon in all his glory was not arrayed like one of these. [30] Now if God so clothes the grass of the field, which today is, and tomorrow is thrown into the oven, will He not much more clothe you, O you of little faith?" (Matthew 6:25–30 NKJV).*

Jesus also told His disciples that by using faith they could do anything, even the impossible.

> *"Now in the morning, as He returned to the city, He was hungry. [19] And seeing a fig tree by the road, He came to it and found nothing on it but leaves, and said to it, 'Let no fruit grow on you ever again.' Immediately the fig*

> *tree withered away. [20] And when the disciples saw it, they marveled, saying, 'How did the fig tree wither away so soon?' [21] So Jesus answered and said to them, 'Assuredly, I say to you, if you have faith and do not doubt, you will not only do what was done to the fig tree, but also if you say to this mountain, Be removed and be cast into the sea, it will be done. [22] And whatever things you ask in prayer, believing, you will receive.'" (Matthew 21:18–22 NKJV).*

The question of just how much faith you need is sure to arise. Jesus dealt with that in Matthew chapter 17. His disciples had failed in their efforts to heal a boy who was suffering from epilepsy. After chiding them for not doing the job, He rebuked the demon and the boy was healed. His followers were puzzled that they had failed and wanted to know why.

> *So Jesus said to them, "Because of your unbelief; for assuredly, I say to you, if you have faith as a mustard seed, you will say to this mountain, 'Move from here to there,' and it will move; and nothing will be impossible for you." (Matthew 17:20 NKJV).*

Romans 12 says that everybody has what is called "a measure of faith" and that it is this faith that overcomes the world. The question then is, how do we get this faith?

> *"So then faith comes by hearing, and hearing by the word of God." (Romans 10:17 NKJV).*

You can strengthen your faith by studying the Word of God, praying, hearing good preaching, interacting with Christian brothers and friends, and intensifying your relationship with God through Jesus Christ.

To have faith is one thing but to exercise it is another. A man can own the most expensive and luxurious car, but if he never drives it that vehicle is of no use to him. You can have millions of dollars in the bank but if you never use any of it to buy food you could die of starvation. It is the same with faith. If you never use it you have certainly wasted a great gift.

James in his epistle said that faith without works is dead. If you have faith to believe that you can walk on water, that faith can only work when you step out of the boat. Simon Peter had that experience as described in Matthew 14 where in the midst of a storm at sea he and the other disciples saw Jesus walking on the water:

> *"When the disciples saw him walking on the water, they were terrified. In their fear, they cried out, 'It's a ghost!' [27] But Jesus spoke to them at once. "Don't be afraid," he said. "Take courage. I am here!" [28] Then Peter called to him, 'Lord, if it's really you, tell me to come to you, walking on the water.' [29]'"Yes, come,' Jesus said. So Peter went over the side of the boat and walked on the water toward Jesus. [30] But when he saw the strong wind and the waves, he was terrified and began to sink. 'Save me, Lord!' he shouted." [31] Jesus immediately reached out and grabbed him. 'You have so little faith,' Jesus said. 'Why did you doubt me?' " (Matthew 14:26–31 NKJV).*

We are always encouraged to have strong faith, but what really matters is the One in whom you place your faith. Peter had faith to step out of the boat, but when he doubted and took his eyes off of Jesus he started to sink. Only by calling on Jesus was he able to recover and be saved from drowning.

Faith is about trusting God and in Proverbs chapter three we are encouraged to do this:

> *"Trust in the Lord with all your heart, and lean not on your own understanding; [6] In all your ways acknowledge Him, and He shall direct your paths." (Proverbs 3:5–6 NKJV).*

We can also trust God to help us in our time of need, especially if we have been generous to His ministry and to others. Paul pointed out this to the church at Philippi. He was commending the congregation there for their generosity to him and other Christians.

> *"And my God shall supply all your need according to His riches in glory by Christ Jesus." (Philippians 4:19 NKJV).*

The Children of Israel when they were about to enter the Promised Land were given the assurance by Moses that God would be with them and they should trust Him. He reiterated this to his successor:

> *"Then Moses called Joshua and said to him in the sight of all Israel, 'Be strong and of good courage, for you must go with this people to the land which the Lord has sworn to their fathers to give them, and you shall cause them to inherit it. [8] And the Lord, He*

is the One who goes before you. He will be with you, He will not leave you nor forsake you; do not fear nor be dismayed.' " (Deuteronomy 31:7–8 NKJV).

David also reminded us in Psalm 20 that we can trust God because He looks after His own:

"Now I know that the Lord saves His anointed;
He will answer him from His holy Heaven
With the saving strength of His right hand.
7 Some trust in chariots, and some in horses;
But we will remember the name of the Lord
our God. 8 They have bowed down and
fallen; But we have risen and stand upright.
9 Save, Lord! May the King answer us when
we call." (Psalm 20:6–9 NKJV).

One of the greatest faith stories is found in chapter three of the book of Daniel.

The king of Babylon had made a decree that everyone was to worship a golden image that he had created, But three young Hebrew men bluntly refused to bow. The king threatened them with death by burning but they stood firm, stating that their God would deliver them. The king was extremely angry and commanded that they be cast into a furnace.

The king was so incensed by the action of the young men that he commanded that the furnace be heated seven times above normal. It was so hot, that the soldiers assigned to throw them into the fire died.

Later, when the king went to see what had happened, he got the surprise of his life.

" 'Look!' he answered, 'I see four men loose, walking in the midst of the fire; and they are not hurt, and the form of the fourth is like the Son of God.' [26] Then Nebuchadnezzar went near the mouth of the burning fiery furnace and spoke, saying, 'Shadrach, Meshach, and Abed-Nego, servants of the Most High God, come out, and come here.' Then Shadrach, Meshach, and Abed-Nego came from the midst of the fire. [27] And the satraps, administrators, governors, and the king's counselors gathered together, and they saw these men on whose bodies the fire had no power; the hair of their head was not singed nor were their garments affected, and the smell of fire was not on them. [28] Nebuchadnezzar spoke, saying, "Blessed be the God of Shadrach, Meshach, and Abed-Nego, who sent His Angel and delivered His servants who trusted in Him, and they have frustrated the king's word, and yielded their bodies, that they should not serve nor worship any god except their own God!" (Daniel 3:25–28 NKJV).

The first chapter of the book of James indicates that your faith will be tested as you encounter challenges in your life. James says that we should not worry about these struggles but recognize that this strengthens our faith:

"Dear brothers and sisters, when troubles of any kind come your way, consider it an opportunity for great joy. [3] For you know that when your faith is tested, your endurance has a chance to grow. [4] So let it grow,

> *for when your endurance is fully developed, you will be perfect and complete, needing nothing." (James 1:2–4 NLT).*

Strengthen your faith by studying the Bible, listening to good Christian teaching and counseling, and having a full prayer life. Trust God in everything you do.

Chapter 21

What Is the Church?

The word "church" is used to describe several ideas. It may be used to signify the entire body of those who are saved by their relationship with Jesus Christ; a particular Christian denomination; all the people in the Christian ecclesiastical community who profess faith in Jesus Christ; a single organized Christian group; or a building designated for Christian worship.

The truth is that the church is not the physical building or place in which Christians meet to worship. It is not even a particular denomination. The church is really the entire Christian community or the body or group of people who have accepted Jesus Christ as Lord and Savior. The church is therefore the body of Christ with Jesus Christ as the head.

The church can be described as local and universal, with the first referring to any local congregation of Believers who meet at a particular place. The church universal is made up of all born again Christians all over the world. So that when you say you are going to church you are in fact saying that you are going to meet with a group of like-minded people bonded together by the salvation brought through the life, death, and resurrection of Jesus Christ and called to be like Him.

The English word "church" is derived from the Greek translation, which is interpreted as "The Called-Out Ones". The Church is therefore those who have been called out of the world to be in Christ.

Presiding bishop of the Barbados District of the Pentecostal Assemblies of the West Indies, Dr. Gerry Seale, has described the Church as: "A universal community of people in blood covenant with God by faith, being discipled to spiritual maturity and impacting the society in which they live."

The word "Church" was first used by Jesus in the Gospel of Matthew, chapter 16. He was at the time having a discussion with His disciples on who He truly was. This is how the discussion went:

> *"Who do men say that I, the Son of Man, am?" [14] So they said, 'Some say John the Baptist, some Elijah, and others Jeremiah or one of the prophets.' [15] He said to them, 'But who do you say that I am?' [16] Simon Peter answered and said, 'You are the Christ, the Son of the living God.' [17] Jesus answered and said to him, 'Blessed are you, Simon Bar-Jonah, for flesh and blood has not revealed this to you, but My Father who is in Heaven. [18] And I also say to you that you are Peter, and on this rock I will build My church, and the gates of Hades shall not prevail against it.' " (Matthew 16:13–18 NKJV).*

The birth of the Church was dramatic and it all happened on what is known as "The Day of Pentecost". This life-transforming and historic event was promised by Jesus, before His ascension.

> *"These things I have spoken to you while being present with you. [26] But the Helper, the Holy Spirit, whom the Father will send*

in My name, He will teach you all things, and bring to your remembrance all things that I said to you." (John 14:25–26 NKJV).

Acts chapter two records how Jesus' disciples were together in the upper room when they were all filled with the Holy Spirit:

"When the Day of Pentecost had fully come, they were all with one accord in one place.
[2] And suddenly there came a sound from Heaven, as of a rushing mighty wind, and it filled the whole house where they were sitting.
[3] Then there appeared to them divided tongues, as of fire, and one sat upon each of them.
[4] And they were all filled with the Holy Spirit and began to speak with other tongues, as the Spirit gave them utterance." (Acts 2:1– 4 NKJV).

The infilling or the baptism of the Holy Spirit transformed this group of insignificant, fearful people into powerful witnesses. Peter, a fisherman, was the chief spokesman as he preached to the thousands in Jerusalem, many of whom had come from several different parts of the world. The Book of Acts says in chapter two that among those witnessing this event were devout men from every nation under heaven, and even they didn't understand what was happening:

"Then they were all amazed and marveled, saying to one another, 'Look, are not all these who speak Galileans?
[8] And how is it that we hear, each in our own language in which we were born?
[9] Parthians and Medes and Elamites, those dwelling in Mesopotamia,

> *Judea and Cappadocia, Pontus and Asia,*
> *[10] Phrygia and Pamphylia, Egypt and the parts*
> *of Libya adjoining Cyrene, visitors from Rome,*
> *both Jews and proselytes, [11] Cretans and*
> *Arabs—we hear them speaking in our own*
> *tongues the wonderful works of God.' [12] So*
> *they were all amazed and perplexed, saying*
> *to one another, 'Whatever could this mean?'*
> *[13] Others mocking said, 'They are full of new*
> *wine.' " (Acts 2:2–12 NKJV).*

But Peter boldly stood up and explained what was happening:

> *"Men of Judea and all who dwell in Jerusalem, let this be known to you, and heed my words. [15] For these are not drunk, as you suppose, since it is only the third hour of the day. [16] But this is what was spoken by the prophet Joel." (Acts 2:14–16 NKJV).*

Peter was referring to a prophecy by the Old Testament prophet Joel who had, in the second chapter of his book, predicted the outpouring of the Holy Spirit.

> *"And it shall come to pass afterward That I will pour out My Spirit on all flesh; Your sons and your daughters shall prophesy, Your old men shall dream dreams, Your young men shall see visions. [29] And also on My menservants and on My maidservants I will pour out My Spirit in those days." (Joel 2:28–29 NKJV).*

Peter's sermon was so powerful that many were convicted and converted.

> *"Then those who gladly received his word were baptized; and that day about three thousand souls were added to them. [42] And they continued steadfastly in the apostles' doctrine and fellowship, in the breaking of bread, and in prayers. [43] Then fear came upon every soul, and many wonders and signs were done through the apostles. [44] Now all who believed were together, and had all things in common, [45] and sold their possessions and goods, and divided them among all, as anyone had need. [46] So continuing daily with one accord in the temple, and breaking bread from house to house, they ate their food with gladness and simplicity of heart, [47] praising God and having favour with all the people. And the Lord added to the church daily those who were being saved." (Acts 2:41–47 NJKV).*

In the early life of the Church, members did not meet only in Church buildings.

> *"Now all who believed were together, and had all things in common, [45] and sold their possessions and goods, and divided them among all, as anyone had need. [46] So continuing daily with one accord in the temple, and breaking bread from house to house, they ate their food with gladness and simplicity of heart, [47] praising God and having favor with all the people. And the Lord added to the church daily those who were being saved." (Acts 2:44–47 NKJV).*

The Church was created to fulfill God's mission and purpose on earth. It is a place where Christians find fellowship, where they worship, and where they are discipled or trained. The Church is also the place where Christians minister and are ministered to. Like the first Church, today's Church is required to evangelize, and most of all to be fully engaged in prayer.

Being a member of and attending Church regularly is vital to the spiritual growth of the born again Christian. This is contrary to the false belief that you need not be a part of one assembly or another. The Church is not just a denomination or a group meeting together, but an opportunity for people to grow and share with others of similar faith. The Church provides members with the opportunity to be instructed in the word of God so that they have a proper understanding of it and so live their lives accordingly.

The Bible teaches that Christians should support each other.

> *"And let us consider one another in order to stir up love and good works, [25] not forsaking the assembling of ourselves together, as is the manner of some, but exhorting one another, and so much the more as you see the Day approaching." (Hebrews 10:24–25 NKJV).*

The New Living Translation puts it this way:

> *"Let us think of ways to motivate one another to acts of love and good works. [25] And let us not neglect our meeting together, as some people do, but encourage one another, especially now that the day of his return is drawing near." (Hebrews 10:24–25 NLT).*

The Church is the place where the born again Christian will grow and develop to the point where they can become leaders or be a part of what the body of Christ is doing. Believers also find that in the Church there are people who can support and encourage them in times of difficulty. Chapter four of the book of Ecclesiastes explains how there is strength and safety in numbers:

> *"Two are better than one, because they have a good reward for their labour. [10] For if they fall, one will lift up his companion. But woe to him who is alone when he falls, for he has no one to help him up. [11] Again, if two lie down together, they will keep warm; but how can one be warm alone? [12] Though one may be overpowered by another, two can withstand him. And a three-fold cord is not quickly broken." (Ecclesiastes 4:9–12 NKJV).*

The Church, by its very nature, is very diverse, yet with every aspect working together for good. Paul spoke to this in his first epistle to the Corinthians where he used the example of the human body to explain unity in diversity within the Church of Jesus Christ:

> *"For as the body is one and has many members, but all the members of that one body, being many, are one body, so also is Christ. [13] For by one Spirit we were all baptized into one body—whether Jews or Greeks, whether slaves or free—and have all been made to drink into one Spirit. [14] For in fact the body is not one member but many." (1 Corinthians 12:12–14 NKJV).*

Paul even went into more detail to ensure that the members of the Christian Church at Corinth fully understood what he was saying.

> *"But now indeed there are many members, yet one body. [21] And the eye cannot say to the hand, 'I have no need of you'; nor again the head to the feet, 'I have no need of you.' [22] No, much rather, those members of the body which seem to be weaker are necessary. [23] And those members of the body which we think to be less honorable, on these we bestow greater honor; and our unpresentable parts have greater modesty, [24] but our presentable parts have no need. But God composed the body, having given greater honor to that part which lacks it, [25] that there should be no schism in the body, but that the members should have the same care for one another. [26] And if one member suffers, all the members suffer with it; or if one member is honored, all the members rejoice with it." (1 Corinthians 12:20–26 NKJV).*

But Paul did not leave it there; he went on to be even more specific:

> *"Now you are the body of Christ, and members individually. [28] And God has appointed these in the church: first apostles, second prophets, third teachers, after that miracles, then gifts of healings, helps, administrations, varieties of tongues. [29] Are all apostles? Are all prophets? Are all teachers? Are all workers of miracles? [30] Do all have gifts*

of healings? Do all speak with tongues? Do all interpret? [31] But earnestly desire the best gifts. And yet I show you a more excellent way." (1 Corinthians 12:27–31 NKJV).

As the new "babe in Christ" starts his Christian walk he will find that there is so much that he does not know. The best place to find out more is in the company of other born again Believers, and they are found in the Church.

Choosing an assembly or church is a very important decision and you need to pray and ask God to guide you and give you the wisdom to find the place where He wants you to fellowship. The church you choose should teach the truth of the Bible and must be one that encourages you to worship God. The leadership must show an interest in equipping you to grow in knowledge and faith. Your church must also provide good teaching, preaching, and fellowship with other Believers. You, like all other Christians, have been commissioned to bring others to Jesus Christ and your church should therefore be one that is involved in evangelism or reaching the lost.

Once you have become a member of a church, pray and ask God to reveal to you the part He wants you to play. This is sometimes described as "finding your calling". There are many areas in which you can participate and you could consider something in which you can utilize your talents or your gifts. As you learn more and grow, you will recognize that there are many positions in the Church. Your commitment, faithfulness, and seeking and finding God will in time lead you to your place.

Some prefer to be part of a large congregation, while others enjoy the opposite. The main thing about going to church is it is one place where a Christian can be in the presence of the Lord. Jesus told His disciples that numbers did not matter when it came to being in His presence.

> *"Again I say to you that if two of you agree on earth concerning anything that they ask, it will be done for them by My Father in Heaven. [20] For where two or three are gathered together in My name, I am there in the midst of them." (Matthew 18:19–20 NKJV).*

Find a good Bible-teaching and Bible-believing church where you can be comfortable and grow.

Chapter 22

Water Baptism

The term "to be baptized" comes from a Greek word that means to immerse in or wash with water. It involves immersing a person in water, submerging him for a moment, and then taking him out. This process is used to describe John's baptism and Christian baptism. Simply stated, to baptize is to totally immerse an object in another substance and then bring it out again.

The tradition of Christian baptism goes back to the days when Jesus was baptized by John the Baptist.

Jesus stressed baptism's importance as part of the new birth when He said in the Gospel of John, chapter three:

> *"Most assuredly, I say to you, unless one is born of water and the Spirit, he cannot enter the kingdom of God. [6] That which is born of the flesh is flesh, and that which is born of the Spirit is spirit." (John 3:5–6 NKJV).*

Baptism is considered to be symbolic of Christ's death, burial, and resurrection and our identification with Him in them. It is a symbol of death simply because you have to hold your breath; burial in that you are put under water or into the grave. Resurrection is symbolized when you are brought up out of the water. Baptism also testifies to your new life in Christ and tells the world that you are now committed to Him.

Water baptism is an experience after salvation to confirm and strengthen your commitment to live a godly life. It gives the Believer the opportunity to openly testify to others of his born again experience. It serves as an outward sign and testimony of an inward grace. The Believer has been crucified with Christ, buried with Him and raised together with Him to walk in the newness of life.

The baptismal waters represent a grave or burial ground. When you are buried with Christ in baptism, you are proclaiming to Heaven, earth, and hell that the old you no longer exists. To be buried with Jesus means that your old self died to sin just as Jesus did when He was made sin for us.

Coming up out of the water signifies being raised to a new life in Christ. This means making Him Lord of every area of your life.

John the Baptist, who is known as the "forerunner of Jesus", probably got his moniker because of his role in baptizing probably thousands of people. Matthew chapter three says:

> *"Then Jerusalem, all Judea, and all the region around the Jordan went out to him and were baptized by him in the Jordan, confessing their sins." (Matthew 3:5 NKJV).*

John also told them that there was a greater baptism than his when he hinted about the coming of Jesus:

> *"I indeed baptize you with water unto repentance, but He who is coming after me is mightier than I, whose sandals I am not worthy to carry. He will baptize you with the Holy Spirit and fire." (Matthew 3:11 NKJV).*

In the New Testament Jesus' disciples and apostles preached to sinners that they should repent from their sins and be baptized. The first 22 verses of chapter three of the Gospel of Luke tell the story of Jesus' baptism.

Jesus gave His followers instructions for baptism just before He ascended into Heaven. In Matthew chapter 28, verse 19, known as the Great Commission, He told His disciples exactly how they should evangelize the world:

> *"Go ye therefore, and teach all nations, baptizing them in the name of the Father, and of the Son, and of the Holy Ghost." (Matthew 28:19 KJV).*

The giving of the Great Commission as recorded in the sixteenth chapter of Mark's Gospel also speaks to this. Verse 16 says in part:

> *"Go into all the world and preach the gospel to every creature. 16 He who believes and is baptized will be saved; but he who does not believe will be condemned." (Mark 16:16 NKJV).*

Chapter two of the book of the Acts of the Apostles shows that the very first Christians and founders of the early Church practiced baptism. Peter on the Day of Pentecost invited all ***"to repent and be baptized."*** Throughout the New Testament there are accounts where people received Jesus Christ as Savior and were baptized or submerged in water.

The importance of baptism was preached by the writer of Romans:

> *"What shall we say then? Shall we continue in sin that grace may abound? 2 Certainly not! How shall we who died to sin live any longer in it? 3 Or do you not know that as many of us as were baptized into Christ Jesus were baptized into His death? 4 Therefore we were buried with Him through baptism into death, that just as Christ was raised from the dead by the glory of the Father, even so we also should walk in newness of life. 5 For if we have been united together in the likeness of His death, certainly we also shall be in the likeness of His resurrection, 6 knowing this, that our old man was crucified with Him, that the body of sin might be done away with, that we should no longer be slaves of sin. 7 For he who has died has been freed from sin. 8 Now if we died with Christ, we believe that we shall also live with Him, 9 knowing that Christ, having been raised from the dead, dies no more. Death no longer has dominion over Him. 10 For the death that He died, He died to sin once for all; but the life that He lives, He lives to God. 11 Likewise you also, reckon yourselves to be dead indeed to sin, but alive to God in Christ Jesus our Lord." (Romans 6:1–11 NKJV).*

Baptism is therefore considered one of the pillars of the Christian religion. It is, however, vital to understand that baptism alone will not get you to Heaven. It will not save you. You must be born again. The process then is first you must repent and turn away from your sin and, having accepted Jesus Christ as Savior, you qualify for baptism.

Water baptism must be undertaken with sincerity, faith, and commitment to Jesus Christ. The story of Philip and the Ethiopian eunuch in Acts chapter eight is testimony to this. The man was reading the Scriptures but he did not understand. Philip, led by the Holy Spirit, was taken to him and after learning that he wanted information was able to explain to the point where the man received Jesus Christ as Savior.

> *"Now as they went down the road, they came to some water. And the eunuch said, 'See, here is water. What hinders me from being baptized?' [37] Then Philip said, 'If you believe with all your heart, you may.' And he answered and said, 'I believe that Jesus Christ is the Son of God.' [38] So he commanded the chariot to stand still. And both Philip and the eunuch went down into the water, and he baptized him." (Acts 8:36–38 NKJV).*

This Scripture is also testimony to the act of baptism being done in a body of water.

There is also the story where Peter had an encounter with Cornelius and his family. The Holy Spirit led Cornelius to send for Peter, who preached Jesus Christ, and he and his family accepted Jesus Christ as Savior.

> *"While Peter was still speaking these words, the Holy Spirit fell upon all those who heard the word. [45] And those of the circumcision who believed were astonished, as many as came with Peter, because the gift of the Holy Spirit had been poured out on the Gentiles also. [46] For they heard*

> *them speak with tongues and magnify God. Then Peter answered, [47] "Can anyone forbid water, that these should not be baptized who have received the Holy Spirit just as we have?" [48] And he commanded them to be baptized in the name of the Lord." (Acts 10:44–48 NKJV).*

Over the years there has been some debate over baptism. Some denominations believe in the baptism of infants soon after birth through the sprinkling of water on them. Others have insisted that baptism is for those who have made a conscious decision to follow Jesus Christ and are then immersed in, or put under water.

There is nothing in Scripture to indicate that babies should be baptized by sprinkling them with water. In fact there are no records of infants being baptized. It therefore seems conclusive that baptism is for those who understand what it is to repent of sin and ask God for forgiveness.

What Jesus did was to bless the children. Matthew 19 records where little children were brought to Jesus so that He could pray for them. His disciples objected to this but Jesus insisted:

> *" 'Let the little children come to Me, and do not forbid them; for of such is the kingdom of Heaven.' [15] And He laid His hands on them and departed from there." (Matthew 19:14–15 NKJV).*

Mark also records an instance where Jesus blessed children:

> *"Then they brought little children to Him, that He might touch them; but the disciples rebuked those who brought them. [14] But when Jesus saw it, He was greatly displeased and said to them, 'Let the little children come to Me, and do not forbid them; for of such is the kingdom of God. [15] Assuredly, I say to you, whoever does not receive the kingdom of God as a little child will by no means enter it.' [16] And He took them up in His arms, laid His hands on them, and blessed them." (Mark 10:13–16 NKJV).*

Water baptism should be a very significant event in the life of a Believer. It is a time of fully committing to obeying and following Jesus, and being willing to fulfill the purpose and plan of Almighty God for your life. This is not something just for super-Christians but a basic requirement for building your faith and showing your commitment to Jesus Christ.

The fact that Jesus chose and demanded to be baptized should be more than enough reason to convince the born again Believer that it is important and necessary.

You are probably wondering just how this water baptism is done. It is performed by the pastor or other leaders of a local church and usually takes place in a body of water, whether it is the sea, a river, a lake, a pool, or a specially constructed font. The Believer who is being baptized goes into the water with the person or people who are doing the baptism. He or she is then "dunked" backward under the water and quickly brought back up.

A pastor or church leader should be more than happy to speak with you about baptism.

Chapter 23

Baptism in The Holy Spirit

Baptism in the Holy Spirit is the empowering of the Christian for ministry and service in the Kingdom of God. It is also described as "being filled with the Spirit". It is a life-changing experience and is available only to those who repent of their sins and turn to Jesus Christ.

Baptism in the Holy Spirit fills the Believer with the Spirit of God, brings power to the ministry and lifestyle or witness of the Christian. It opens the way for them to receive spiritual gifts from God.

When a sinner is converted, he or she receives the Holy Spirit. This indwelling of the Spirit reproduces the life of Jesus in the Believer. But there is more. Baptism in the Holy Spirit comes afterward. It is the outpouring of the Spirit that reproduces the ministry and power of Jesus in the life of the Believer, igniting the ability to do the things the Savior did while He was on earth.

While water baptism is done by man, baptism in the Holy Spirit comes from Jesus Christ. John the Baptist prophesied that there was someone coming after him through whom there would be a different baptism.

"And John bore witness, saying, 'I saw the Spirit descending from Heaven like a dove, and He remained upon Him. [33] I did not know Him, but He who sent me to baptize with water said to me, Upon whom you see the Spirit descending, and remaining on Him, this is He who baptizes with the Holy Spirit. [34] And I have seen and testified that this is the Son of God.' " (John 1:32–34 NKJV).

John was also recorded in Luke's Gospel testifying that Jesus would baptize with the Holy Spirit.

"Now as the people were in expectation, and all reasoned in their hearts about John, whether he was the Christ or not, [16] John answered, saying to all, 'I indeed baptize you with water; but One mightier than I is coming, whose sandal strap I am not worthy to loose. He will baptize you with the Holy Spirit and fire.'" (Luke 3:15–16 NKJV).

Later, Jesus went to John and requested that He be baptized. John at first refused, stressing that Jesus should be the one baptizing him. But Jesus told him that he must do it.

"When He had been baptized, Jesus came up immediately from the water; and behold, the Heavens were opened to Him, and He saw the Spirit of God descending like a dove and alighting upon Him. [17] And suddenly a voice came from Heaven, saying, 'This is My beloved Son, in whom I am well pleased.' " (Matthew 3:16–17 NKJV).

The baptism in the Holy Spirit came on what is known as "The Day of Pentecost". The entire event is recorded in chapter two of the book of the Acts of the Apostles.

Just before He ascended into Heaven, Jesus told His disciples that He would soon send the "Promise of His Father" on them and they would be endued with power from on high.

> *"And being assembled together with them, He commanded them not to depart from Jerusalem, but to wait for the Promise of the Father, 'which,' He said, 'you have heard from Me; [5] for John truly baptized with water, but you shall be baptized with the Holy Spirit not many days from now.' [6] Therefore, when they had come together, they asked Him, saying, 'Lord, will You at this time restore the kingdom to Israel?' [7] And He said to them, 'It is not for you to know times or seasons which the Father has put in His own authority. [8] But you shall receive power when the Holy Spirit has come upon you; and you shall be witnesses to Me in Jerusalem, and in all Judea and Samaria, and to the end of the earth.'" (Acts 1:4–8 NKJV).*

After Jesus ascended into Heaven, the disciples assembled in an upper room where they prayed together and waited, as Jesus had instructed. And then it happened.

> *"When the Day of Pentecost had fully come, they were all with one accord in one place. [2] And suddenly there came a sound from Heaven, as of a rushing mighty wind, and it filled the whole house where they were sitting. [3] Then there appeared to them divided*

tongues, as of fire, and one sat upon each of them. [4] And they were all filled with the Holy Spirit and began to speak with other tongues, as the Spirit gave them utterance." (Acts 2:1–4 NKJV).

The New Living Translation describes the event this way:

"On the day of Pentecost all the Believers were meeting together in one place. [2] Suddenly, there was a sound from Heaven like the roaring of a mighty windstorm, and it filled the house where they were sitting. [3] Then, what looked like flames or tongues of fire appeared and settled on each of them. [4] And everyone present was filled with the Holy Spirit and began speaking in other languages, as the Holy Spirit gave them this ability." (Acts 2:1–4 NLT).

The baptism in the Holy Spirit instantly transformed a group of individuals from ordinary to extraordinary. This was very evident to the people who were in Jerusalem at the time.

"And there were dwelling in Jerusalem Jews, devout men, from every nation under Heaven. [6] And when this sound occurred, the multitude came together, and were confused, because everyone heard them speak in his own language. [7] Then they were all amazed and marveled, saying to one another, 'Look, are not all these who speak Galileans? [8] And how is it that we hear, each in our own language in which we were

> *born? [9] Parthians and Medes and Elamites, those dwelling in Mesopotamia, Judea and Cappadocia, Pontus and Asia, [10] Phrygia and Pamphylia, Egypt and the parts of Libya adjoining Cyrene, visitors from Rome, both Jews and proselytes, [11] Cretans and Arabs—we hear them speaking in our own tongues the wonderful works of God.' [12] So they were all amazed and perplexed, saying to one another, 'Whatever could this mean?' " (Acts 2:5–12 NKJV).*

The event was so dramatic that some people accused the disciples of drunkenness. But this was quickly and vehemently rejected by Simon Peter.

> *"But Peter, standing up with the eleven, raised his voice and said to them, 'Men of Judea and all who dwell in Jerusalem, let this be known to you, and heed my words. [15] For these are not drunk, as you suppose, since it is only the third hour of the day. [16] But this is what was spoken by the prophet Joel: [17] And it shall come to pass in the last days, says God, That I will pour out of My Spirit on all flesh; Your sons and your daughters shall prophesy, Your young men shall see visions, Your old men shall dream dreams. [18] And on My menservants and on My maidservants I will pour out My Spirit in those days; And they shall prophesy. [19] I will show wonders in Heaven above and signs in the earth beneath: Blood and fire and vapor of smoke. [20] The sun shall be turned into darkness, and the moon into blood, before the*

> *coming of the great and awesome day of the Lord.* [21] *And it shall come to pass that whoever calls on the name of the Lord shall be saved.' "* (Acts 2:14–20 NKJV).

That day Peter preached to the crowd about Jesus, recalling His ministry, death, resurrection, and ascension.

> *"People of Israel, listen! God publicly endorsed Jesus the Nazarene by doing powerful miracles, wonders, and signs through him, as you well know.* [23] *But God knew what would happen, and his prearranged plan was carried out when Jesus was betrayed. With the help of lawless Gentiles, you nailed him to a cross and killed him.* [24] *But God released him from the horrors of death and raised him back to life, for death could not keep him in its grip.* [25] *King David said this about him: 'I see that the Lord is always with me. I will not be shaken, for he is right beside me.* [26] *No wonder my heart is glad, and my tongue shouts his praises! My body rests in hope.* [27] *For you will not leave my soul among the dead or allow your Holy One to rot in the grave.* [28] *You have shown me the way of life, and you will fill me with the joy of your presence.'* [29] *"Dear brothers, think about this! You can be sure that the patriarch David wasn't referring to himself, for he died and was buried, and his tomb is still here among us.* [30] *But he was a prophet, and he knew God had promised with an oath that one of David's own descendants would sit on his throne.* [31] *David was looking into the*

> *future and speaking of the Messiah's resurrection. He was saying that God would not leave him among the dead or allow his body to rot in the grave. [32] 'God raised Jesus from the dead, and we are all witnesses of this. [33] Now he is exalted to the place of highest honour in Heaven, at God's right hand. And the Father, as he had promised, gave him the Holy Spirit to pour out upon us, just as you see and hear today. [34] For David himself never ascended into Heaven, yet he said, 'The Lord said to my Lord, Sit in the place of honor at my right hand [35] until I humble your enemies, making them a footstool under your feet.' [36] 'So let everyone in Israel know for certain that God has made this Jesus, whom you crucified, to be both Lord and Messiah!" (Acts 2:22–36 NLT).*

Peter's sermon was so powerful and convicting that many of the people were pricked in their hearts and wanted to know what they should do.

> *"Peter replied, 'Each of you must repent of your sins and turn to God, and be baptized in the name of Jesus Christ for the forgiveness of your sins. Then you will receive the gift of the Holy Spirit. [39] This promise is to you, to your children, and to those far away—all who have been called by the Lord our God.' [40] Then Peter continued preaching for a long time, strongly urging all his listeners, 'Save yourselves from this crooked generation!'" (Acts 2:38–40 NLT).*

There was a swift response to Peter's invitation and about three thousand people were saved.

Baptism in the Holy Spirit equipped the disciples to carry out the Great Commission that Jesus had given them. He had also said that those who believe in Him would do even greater things than He had done.

> *"And He said to them, 'Go into all the world and preach the gospel to every creature. [16]He who believes and is baptized will be saved; but he who does not believe will be condemned. [17] And these signs will follow those who believe: In My name they will cast out demons; they will speak with new tongues; [18] they will take up serpents; and if they drink anything deadly, it will by no means hurt them; they will lay hands on the sick, and they will recover.'" (Mark 16:15–18 NKJV).*

After the disciples were baptized in the Holy Spirit they began to work many miracles. This power is still available to the Believer today as Jesus continues to baptize His people in the Holy Spirit.

To be baptized in the Holy Spirit, the born again Believer must earnestly ask God for it. It is a gift from Him. Jesus said that all you need to do is ask.

> *"You fathers—if your children ask for a fish, do you give them a snake instead? [12] Or if they ask for an egg, do you give them a scorpion? Of course not! [13]So if you sinful people know how to give good gifts to your children, how much more will your Heavenly Father give the Holy Spirit to those who ask Him." (Luke 11:11–13 NLT).*

The Christian must earnestly desire the baptism in the Holy Spirit, which brings with it the power that Jesus described as "living water". He and His disciples were attending the Jewish Feast of Tabernacles and He had been teaching in the temple and answering questions from the people.

> *"On the last day, that great day of the feast, Jesus stood and cried out, saying, 'If anyone thirsts, let him come to Me and drink. [38] He who believes in Me, as the Scripture has said, out of his heart will flow rivers of living water.' [39] But this He spoke concerning the Spirit, whom those believing in Him would receive; for the Holy Spirit was not yet given, because Jesus was not yet glorified." (John 7:37–39 NKJV).*

To be baptized in the Holy Spirit you first have to accept Jesus Christ as your Lord and Savior. The power can fall on the Believer at that instant, as happened in the Bible, but more often than not it comes some time afterward.

The Believer must ensure that he or she has the right motives before asking God for the baptism in the Holy Spirit. Some may selfishly see the gift as making them more important than others or may want it just because their friends have it.

It will do well to remember the story of Simon the Sorcerer, as told in chapter eight of the Acts of the Apostles. Peter, John, and some of the other apostles were preaching and ministering in Samaria where there were people who had accepted Jesus as Savior, but had not yet received the baptism of the Holy Spirit. Simon the Sorcerer was among those who had been saved and he was amazed by the miracles and signs that were happening through the apostles.

When the apostles laid hands on the people and they received the baptism in the Holy Spirit, Simon wanted that same power, but for the wrong reasons.

> *"And when Simon saw that through the laying on of the apostles' hands the Holy Spirit was given, he offered them money, [19] saying, 'Give me this power also, that anyone on whom I lay hands may receive the Holy Spirit.' [20] But Peter said to him, 'Your money perish with you, because you thought that the gift of God could be purchased with money! [21] You have neither part nor portion in this matter, for your heart is not right in the sight of God. [22] Repent therefore of this your wickedness, and pray God if perhaps the thought of your heart may be forgiven you. [23] For I see that you are poisoned by bitterness and bound by iniquity.' [24] Then Simon answered and said, 'Pray to the Lord for me, that none of the things which you have spoken may come upon me.'" (Acts 8:18–24 NKJV).*

The disciples who were in the upper room on the Day of Pentecost were not the only people to be baptized in the Holy Spirit. One such occasion was in Samaria where Philip the apostle was preaching.

> *"When the apostles in Jerusalem heard that the people of Samaria had accepted God's message, they sent Peter and John there. [15] As soon as they arrived, they prayed for these new Believers to receive the Holy Spirit. [16] The Holy Spirit had not yet come*

> *upon any of them, for they had only been baptized in the name of the Lord Jesus. [17] Then Peter and John laid their hands upon these Believers, and they received the Holy Spirit." (Acts 8:14–17 NLT).*

The Holy Spirit was also poured out on people who were not with the apostles. Peter, after a vision from God, was invited to the home of a Roman army officer named Cornelius in a place called Caesarea.

> *"Even as Peter was saying these things, the Holy Spirit fell upon all who were listening to the message. [45] The Jewish Believers who came with Peter were amazed that the gift of the Holy Spirit had been poured out on the Gentiles, too. [46] For they heard them speaking in other tongues and praising God. Then Peter asked, [47] 'Can anyone object to their being baptized, now that they have received the Holy Spirit just as we did?' [48] So he gave orders for them to be baptized in the name of Jesus Christ." (Acts 10:44–48 NLT).*

Paul the apostle also had an encounter with a group of Believers who had no idea about the Holy Spirit.

> *"While Apollos was in Corinth, Paul travelled through the interior regions until he reached Ephesus, on the coast, where he found several Believers. [2] 'Did you receive the Holy Spirit when you believed?' he asked them. 'No,' they replied, 'we haven't even heard that there is a Holy Spirit.'*

> [3] *'Then what baptism did you experience?' he asked. And they replied, 'The baptism of John.'* [4] *Paul said, 'John's baptism called for repentance from sin. But John himself told the people to believe in the one who would come later, meaning Jesus.'* [5] *As soon as they heard this, they were baptized in the name of the Lord Jesus.* [6] *Then when Paul laid his hands on them, the Holy Spirit came on them, and they spoke in other tongues and prophesied. 7 There were about twelve men in all." (Acts 19:1–7 NLT).*

Baptism in the Holy Spirit is not only available to every Christian but is vital, as the Believer serves and ministers in the Kingdom of God. Jesus knew that the disciples needed this power to carry out the Great Commission.

> *"And then he told them, "Go into all the world and preach the Good News to everyone.* [16] *Anyone who believes and is baptized will be saved. But anyone who refuses to believe will be condemned.* [17] *These miraculous signs will accompany those who believe: They will cast out demons in my name, and they will speak in new languages.* [18] *They will be able to handle snakes with safety, and if they drink anything poisonous, it won't hurt them. They will be able to place their hands on the sick, and they will be healed." (Mark 16:15–18 NLT).*

As long as you're living a Christian life, the outpouring of the Holy Spirit can be activated through prayer, praise, and worship.

There was an occasion when apostles Peter and John were arrested and taken before the authorities for preaching about Jesus and His resurrection. They were later forbidden to preach about Jesus and released without conviction. They returned to their friends and together they started to pray, praise, and worship God.

> *"And when they had prayed, the place where they were assembled together was shaken; and they were all filled with the Holy Spirit, and they spoke the word of God with boldness." (Acts 4:31 NKJV).*

Baptism in the Holy Spirit is seen in the lives of Believers who demonstrate the love of Jesus. These virtues are described as "the Fruit of the Spirit".

> *"But the Holy Spirit produces this kind of fruit in our lives: love, joy, peace, patience, kindness, goodness, faithfulness, [23] gentleness, and self-control. There is no law against these things! [24] Those who belong to Christ Jesus have nailed the passions and desires of their sinful nature to his cross and crucified them there. [25] Since we are living by the Spirit, let us follow the Spirit's leading in every part of our lives. [26] Let us not become conceited, or provoke one another, or be jealous of one another." (Galatians 5:22–26 NLT).*

Every Believer is encouraged to live by the power of the Holy Spirit.

> *"So be careful how you live. Don't live like fools, but like those who are wise. [16] Make the most of every opportunity in these evil days. [17] Don't act thoughtlessly, but understand what the Lord wants you to do. [18] Don't be drunk with wine, because that will ruin your life. Instead, be filled with the Holy Spirit, [19] singing psalms and hymns and spiritual songs among yourselves, and making music to the Lord in your hearts. [20] And give thanks for everything to God the Father in the name of our Lord Jesus Christ." (Ephesians 5:15–20 NLT).*

The baptism in the Holy Spirit, and all of the gifts that come with this experience, truly empower the Believer to show the world the power of God, as exhibited on earth through His Son, Jesus Christ.

Not having the baptism in the Holy Spirit does not mean that you are not saved, and not having it will not stop you from going to Heaven. The thief on the cross, who asked for forgiveness, was told by Jesus that he would be in Paradise that same day. You must recognize that you are not saved by the baptism in the Holy Spirit. Salvation comes through believing in Jesus Christ and His shed blood.

> *"For by grace you have been saved through faith, and that not of yourselves; it is the gift of God, [9] not of works, lest anyone should boast." (Ephesians 2:8–9 NKJV).*

Not having the baptism in the Holy Spirit will not prevent you from doing great works and having a successful ministry. There are several Christians who do not speak in tongues and are doing good work in healing and other areas of ministry.

While they may be doing well, just think of how much more could be achieved if they were "endued with power from on high".

Believers need to continually seek the presence, direction, and blessings of God even though their circumstances may not be the best. Even Timothy, Paul's protégé, had his struggles, but thankfully he had the support of and the encouragement from that apostle. Paul advised him to ***"stir up the gift of God which is in you"***, encouraging him to develop the anointing of the Holy Spirit that had been placed on him.

The born again Christian must continually seek to go deeper in God. Every day is another step on this spiritual journey. Legendary evangelist Smith Wigglesworth was quoted as saying that if you do not "grow in Christ" you are backslidden.

Do everything in your power to seek the baptism in the Holy Spirit and, if you already have it, strive for even more anointing of the Holy Spirit. With this anointing you will certainly do great things for the kingdom of God.

Baptism in the Holy Spirit will also provide you with excellent opportunities to help your church and those with whom you come into contact. Strive for it. Pray for it. Trust and believe God for it.

Get the gift of the baptism in the Holy Spirit and watch your ministry explode.

Chapter 24

The Gifts of The Holy Spirit

With baptism in the Holy Spirit comes spiritual gifts. This power is the same that Jesus exhibited while He was on earth.

Paul the apostle told the people at Corinth about these special gifts. He reminded them that at one time they worshipped idols but stressed that it is through the Holy Spirit that these special abilities are activated.

> *"There are different kinds of spiritual gifts,*
> *but the same Spirit is the source of them all.*
> *5 There are different kinds of service, but*
> *we serve the same Lord. 6 God works in*
> *different ways, but it is the same God who*
> *does the work in all of us. 7 A spiritual gift is*
> *given to each of us so we can help each other.*
> *8 To one person the Spirit gives the ability*
> *to give wise advice; to another the same*
> *Spirit gives a message of special knowl-*
> *edge. 9 The same Spirit gives great faith to*
> *another, and to someone else the one Spirit*
> *gives the gift of healing. 10 He gives one*
> *person the power to perform miracles, and*
> *another the ability to prophesy. He gives*

someone else the ability to discern whether a message is from the Spirit of God or from another spirit. Still another person is given the ability to speak in unknown languages, while another is given the ability to interpret what is being said. [11] It is the one and only Spirit who distributes all these gifts. He alone decides which gift each person should have." (1 Corinthians 12:4–11 NLT).

God has also given special spiritual gifts for the leadership of the Church. These are to, among other things, prepare Believers for service and ministry and help in the spiritual growth of the Church. Paul identified these gifts to the church at Ephesus:

"Now these are the gifts Christ gave to the church: the apostles, the prophets, the evangelists, and the pastors and teachers. [12] Their responsibility is to equip God's people to do his work and build up the church, the body of Christ. [13] This will continue until we all come to such unity in our faith and knowledge of God's Son that we will be mature in the Lord, measuring up to the full and complete standard of Christ. [14] Then we will no longer be immature like children. We won't be tossed and blown about by every wind of new teaching. We will not be influenced when people try to trick us with lies so clever they sound like the truth. [15] Instead, we will speak the truth in love, growing in every way more and more like Christ, who is the head of his body, the church. [16] He makes the whole

> *body fit together perfectly. As each part does its own special work, it helps the other parts grow, so that the whole body is healthy and growing and full of love." (Ephesians 4:11–16 NLT).*

Speaking in Tongues

There has been quite a lot of debate on how Believers would know that they have received the baptism in the Holy Spirit. It is to be noted that in the New Testament on most occasions, when there was an outpouring of the Spirit, the Believers spoke "in tongues" or a strange language.

Where this was not reported at that time, certain information indicated that at some time some did have the experience of speaking in tongues. One such case was Paul the apostle, who said that he spoke in tongues more than anyone else, but there is no record of when he started.

Jesus Himself said that speaking in tongues will be part of the Believer's ministry. He made this quite clear when He gave the Great Commission.

> *"And these signs will follow those who believe: In My name they will cast out demons; they will speak with new tongues; [18] they will take up serpents; and if they drink anything deadly, it will by no means hurt them; they will lay hands on the sick, and they will recover." (Mark 16:17–18 NKJV).*

Speaking in tongues, sometimes referred to as a Heavenly language, is a vehicle the Believer uses in speaking to God. This language is usually used in private devotions and prayer.

There is also the gift of tongues, which is for the Church, and for which there should be an interpreter.

Paul the apostle had a lot to say about how Believers should use tongues. In 1 Corinthians, chapter 14 he stressed that the Believer who spoke in tongues spoke to God. He also pointed out that while speaking in tongues was important, there were other things that the born again Christian should desire.

> *"He who speaks in a tongue edifies himself, but he who prophesies edifies the church. 5 I wish you all spoke with tongues, but even more that you prophesied; for he who prophesies is greater than he who speaks with tongues, unless indeed he interprets, that the church may receive edification.*
>
> *6 "But now, brethren, if I come to you speaking with tongues, what shall I profit you unless I speak to you either by revelation, by knowledge, by prophesying, or by teaching? 7 Even things without life, whether flute or harp, when they make a sound, unless they make a distinction in the sounds, how will it be known what is piped or played? 8 For if the trumpet makes an uncertain sound, who will prepare for battle?*
>
> *9 "So likewise you, unless you utter by the tongue words easy to understand, how will it be known what is spoken? For you will be speaking into the air. 10 There are, it may be, so many kinds of languages in the world, and none of them is without significance. 11 Therefore, if I do not know the meaning of*

*the language, I shall be a foreigner to him
who speaks, and he who speaks will be a foreigner to me. [12] Even so you, since you are
zealous for spiritual gifts, let it be for the edification of the church that you seek to excel.*

*[13] "Therefore let him who speaks in a tongue
pray that he may interpret. [14] For if I pray
in a tongue, my spirit prays, but my understanding is unfruitful. [15] What is the conclu-
sion then? I will pray with the spirit, and I
will also pray with the understanding. I will
sing with the spirit, and I will also sing with
the understanding. [16] Otherwise, if you bless
with the spirit, how will he who occupies the
place of the uninformed say "Amen" at your
giving of thanks, since he does not understand what you say? [17] For you indeed give
thanks well, but the other is not edified.*

*[18] "I thank my God I speak with tongues
more than you all; [19] yet in the church I would
rather speak five words with my understanding, that I may teach others also, than
ten thousand words in a tongue. [20] Brethren,
do not be children in understanding; however, in malice be babes, but in understanding be mature.*

*[21] "In the law it is written: 'With men of other
tongues and other lips I will speak to this
people; And yet, for all that, they will not
hear Me,' says the Lord.*

[22] "Therefore tongues are for a sign, not to those who believe but to unbelievers; but prophesying is not for unbelievers but for those who believe. [23] Therefore if the whole church comes together in one place, and all speak with tongues, and there come in those who are uninformed or unbelievers, will they not say that you are out of your mind? [24] But if all prophesy, and an unbeliever or an uninformed person comes in, he is convinced by all, he is convicted by all. [25] And thus the secrets of his heart are revealed; and so, falling down on his face, he will worship God and report that God is truly among you.

[26] "How is it then, brethren? Whenever you come together, each of you has a psalm, has a teaching, has a tongue, has a revelation, has an interpretation. Let all things be done for edification. [27] If anyone speaks in a tongue, let there be two or at the most three, each in turn, and let one interpret. [28] But if there is no interpreter, let him keep silent in church, and let him speak to himself and to God. [29] Let two or three prophets speak, and let the others judge. [30] But if anything is revealed to another who sits by, let the first keep silent. [31] For you can all prophesy one by one, that all may learn and all may be encouraged. [32] And the spirits of the prophets are subject to the prophets. [33] For God is not the author of confusion but of peace, as in all the churches of the saints." (1 Corinthians 14:4–33 NLT).

The Christians at Rome were also reminded that it is the Holy Spirit who is involved when the Believer speaks in tongues.

> *"Likewise the Spirit also helps in our weaknesses. For we do not know what we should pray for as we ought, but the Spirit Himself makes intercession for us with groanings which cannot be uttered. [27] Now He who searches the hearts knows what the mind of the Spirit is, because He makes intercession for the saints according to the will of God." (Romans 8:26–27 NKJV).*

It should be noted that speaking in tongues is not the baptism in the Holy Spirit but happens when the Believer receives the baptism.

The Assemblies of God (AOG) is the world's largest Pentecostal denomination, with over 67 million members and followers around the globe. This denomination is committed to the doctrine of the baptism in the Holy Spirit with the initial evidence of speaking in tongues.

There are other denominations, some Pentecostal, that do not adhere to that same doctrine, teaching that Believers can receive the baptism in the Holy Spirit without the evidence of tongues.

The Assemblies of God says it is concerned that some Pentecostals look on the baptism and tongues as ends in themselves rather than as means to a much greater end. According to the AOG, the baptism is the entry experience, introducing the Believer to the beauty and power of the Spirit-filled life.

The Assemblies of God says it believes the Spirit is at work in all Christians, whether they have been baptized in the Spirit or not. It adds that God can also use and does use

Christians who, for one reason or another, have not received the baptism experience. The organization has stressed that the ministry of these Christians should never be depreciated. Rather, it must be recognized that baptism in the Holy Spirit will make the Christian's life and ministry even more effective.

Christians who do not speak in tongues should not feel any less than other Believers. Paul the Apostle indicated that not everyone speaks in tongues:

> *"Now you are the body of Christ, and members individually. [28] And God has appointed these in the church: first apostles, second prophets, third teachers, after that miracles, then gifts of healings, helps, administrations, varieties of tongues. [29] Are all apostles? Are all prophets? Are all teachers? Are all workers of miracles? [30] Do all have gifts of healings? Do all speak with tongues? Do all interpret? [31] But earnestly desire the best gifts. And yet I show you a more excellent way." (1 Corinthians 12:27–31 NKJV).*

Chapter 25

What Is the Holy Communion or Eucharist?

The Holy Communion takes several names. They include the Lord's Supper, the Eucharist (from the Greek *eukharistia*, meaning thanksgiving or gratitude), the Sacrament of Communion, the Bread and Wine, and the Breaking of Bread.

The Holy Communion is a very important part of Christian worship. Among other things, it stresses the union between God and Christians and also between Christians and other Christians.

This sacrament was instituted by Jesus and involves Christians coming together at church or in other groups to partake of bread and wine, symbolizing the last supper Jesus Christ had with His disciples. The bread symbolizes the body of Jesus while the wine symbolizes His blood.

Jesus and His disciples were in a room observing the feast of the Passover when He told them that it would be His last meal with them. The details of this event are recorded in the Gospel of Luke, chapter 22:

> *"When the hour had come, He sat down, and the twelve apostles with Him. [15] Then He said to them, 'With fervent desire I have desired to eat this Passover with you*

> *before I suffer; [16] for I say to you, I will no longer eat of it until it is fulfilled in the kingdom of God.' [17] Then He took the cup, and gave thanks, and said, 'Take this and divide it among yourselves; [18] for I say to you, I will not drink of the fruit of the vine until the kingdom of God comes.' [19] And He took bread, gave thanks and broke it, and gave it to them, saying, 'This is My body which is given for you; do this in remembrance of Me.' [20] Likewise He also took the cup after supper, saying, 'This cup is the new covenant in My blood, which is shed for you.' " (Luke 22:14–20 NKJV).*

After Jesus' crucifixion, death, resurrection, and ascension, the early Church was obedient to His command to continue this activity. Paul in his first epistle to the Corinthians had this to say:

> *"For I received from the Lord that which I also delivered to you: that the Lord Jesus on the same night in which He was betrayed took bread; [24] and when He had given thanks, He broke it and said, 'Take, eat; this is My body which is broken for you; do this in remembrance of Me.' [25] In the same manner He also took the cup after supper, saying, 'This cup is the new covenant in My blood. This do, as often as you drink it, in remembrance of Me.' [26] For as often as you eat this bread and drink this cup, you proclaim the Lord's death till He comes." (1 Corinthians 11:23–26 NKJV).*

The Holy Communion is one of the most important requirements of the Christian faith and should therefore not be taken lightly. Every Believer should participate and should prayerfully prepare before receiving it. Paul was careful to point out this to the Corinthian church.

> *"Therefore whoever eats this bread or drinks this cup of the Lord in an unworthy manner will be guilty of the body and blood of the Lord. [28] But let a man examine himself, and so let him eat of the bread and drink of the cup. [29] For he who eats and drinks in an unworthy manner eats and drinks judgment to himself, not discerning the Lord's body. [30] For this reason many are weak and sick among you, and many sleep. [31] For if we would judge ourselves, we would not be judged. [32] But when we are judged, we are chastened by the Lord, that we may not be condemned with the world." (1 Corinthians 11:27–32 NKJV).*

The Bread and Wine

The bread and wine used in the Lord's Supper are usually referred to as "the elements" and there are differing views among some Christian denominations about their significance and meaning.

Some believe that these elements become the actual body and blood of Christ, something the Roman Catholic Church terms *transubstantiation.* Other denominations believe that the bread and the wine are unchanged, but Christ's presence by faith is made spiritually real in and through them. There is also the conviction by some that the elements are unchanged and are used as symbols, representing Christ's body and blood, in remembrance of his enduring sacrifice.

The observation of the Holy Communion also signifies the participation of Christians in the Body of Christ or the Church. Paul in first Corinthians, chapter 10 observed:

> *"Is not the cup of thanksgiving for which we give thanks a participation in the blood of Christ? And is not the bread that we break a participation in the body of Christ? Because there is one loaf, we, who are many, are one body, for we all partake of the one loaf." (1 Corinthians 10:16–17 NIV).*

So participation in the Lord's Supper shows that we remember Jesus; that we have examined ourselves to ensure that we are in right standing: that we are continuing to proclaim His death and that we recognize that we are part of the body of Christ or the Church.

The Bread of Life

Jesus, during the Last Supper, referred to the bread as His body. This is significant since He had earlier told His followers that He was the Bread of Life.

> *"Most assuredly, I say to you, he who believes in Me has everlasting life. [48] I am the bread of life. [49] Your fathers ate the manna in the wilderness, and are dead. [50] This is the bread which comes down from Heaven, that one may eat of it and not die. [51] I am the living bread which came down from Heaven. If anyone eats of this bread,*

> *he will live forever; and the bread that I shall give is My flesh, which I shall give for the life of the world." (John 6:47–51 NKJV).*

There is no limit to the number of times that the Lord's Supper could be celebrated. During the life of the early church, members gathered at homes for meetings and it was there and in synagogues that they participated. In Acts chapter two it is written that the Believers continued steadfastly in the apostles' doctrine and fellowship and in breaking of bread.

Some churches observe the Lord's Supper every week; others once a month or twice a month or as often as they can. Make sure that you are a part of this celebration.

Chapter 26

What Is Worship and Praise?

Mankind is obligated to praise and worship God the Father. There are Scriptures throughout the Bible that indicate this.

The call to worship God is brought sharply into context during what is known as "the temptation of Jesus" by Satan. Jesus had just come out of a 40-day fast when He was approached by the devil, who made three attempts to get Him to obey. But the Son of God refused to fall for his tricks.

The devil first appealed to Jesus' natural desires when, knowing that He was hungry, suggested that He turn stones into bread. He next invited Christ to show off by jumping from the top of the temple.

It was Satan's third temptation that brought out the fact that God the Father is the only one that deserves worship.

> *"Again, the devil taketh him up into an exceeding high mountain, and sheweth him all the kingdoms of the world, and the glory of them; [9] And saith unto him, All these things will I give thee, if thou wilt fall down and worship me. [10] Then saith Jesus unto him, Get thee hence, Satan: for it is written, Thou shalt worship the Lord thy God, and him only shalt thou serve." (Matthew 4:8–10 KJV).*

Webster's online dictionary describes worship as the "act of paying divine honors to the Supreme Being; religious reverence and homage; adoration, or acts of reverence paid to God, or a being viewed as God." It also says it is to "pay divine honors to; to reverence with supreme respect and veneration; to perform religious exercises in honor of; to adore; to venerate."

Worshipping God is spiritual and could be described as an attitude or way of life. You first have to know God or have a relationship with Him through Jesus Christ before you can worship Him.

Jesus had to explain this to Thomas and His other disciples.

> *"Jesus said to him, 'I am the way, the truth, and the life. No one comes to the Father except through Me. [7] If you had known Me, you would have known My Father also; and from now on you know Him and have seen Him.' " (John 14:6–7 NKJV).*

Jesus in His conversation with the Samaritan woman, as recorded in John's Gospel, chapter four, said that God wants people to worship Him. He told the woman that her people, who were idol worshippers, were ignorant about worship.

> *"You worship what you do not know; we know what we worship, for salvation is of the Jews. [23] But the hour is coming, and now is, when the true worshippers will worship the Father in spirit and truth; for the Father is seeking such to worship Him. [24] God is Spirit, and those who worship Him must worship in spirit and truth." (John 4:22–24 NKJV).*

This verse makes it clear that God wants His children to worship Him and He wants it to be genuine.

Because God is a spirit He can only be worshipped in Spirit, and this suggests that there must be a relationship between His Spirit and that of anyone worshipping Him. That connection comes when a person is born again and has the Holy Spirit living in him or her.

Worship must be true and must come from a heart that has a genuine love for God. The worshipper must recognize God as Everlasting Father and must approach Him with adoration, reverence, trust, and a true belief in the doctrine of Jesus Christ.

The born again Christian can worship God personally, when you are alone, and corporately, while you are in a church setting. It is interwoven into every aspect of the Christian walk. In other words worship goes beyond the formal church setting and expands to everything you do whether in church, at work, at home, or at play.

While worship is internal and could be described as an attitude, there are outward manifestations. This could be in posture; whether you are kneeling, bowing, lying prostrate, lifting up hands, praying, crying, or singing. Whatever you do, remember that worship must come from the heart.

A. W. Tozer, a famous and celebrated man of God, has been quoted as saying that: "True worship is to be so personally and hopelessly in love with God, that the idea of a transfer of affection never even remotely exists."

In worshipping God we genuinely express our faith, love, and devotion to Him. This is done not only by our actions in church but also in the way we live our Christian lives.

While God expects His people to worship Him, He will not accept just any worship. Psalm 24 indicates that He will not hear those who do evil.

> *"Who may ascend into the hill of the Lord? Or who may stand in His holy place? [4] He who has clean hands and a pure heart, who has not lifted up his soul to an idol, nor sworn deceitfully." (Psalm 24:3–4 NKJV).*

Worship and praise are similar but while the former is more in the spirit, praise is mostly external.

Webster's online dictionary says praise is: "To extol in words or song; to magnify; to glorify on account of perfections or excellent works; to do honor to; to display the excellence of; applied especially to the Divine Being." The dictionary also calls praise: "The act of glorifying or extolling the Creator; worship, particularly worship by song, distinction from prayer and other acts of worship; as, a service of praise."

Praise could be described as the outward manifestation of worship and we are encouraged to praise God at all times.

> *"Praise the Lord! Praise God in His sanctuary; Praise Him in His mighty firmament! [2] Praise Him for His mighty acts; Praise Him according to His excellent greatness! [3] Praise Him with the sound of the trumpet; Praise Him with the lute and harp! [4] Praise Him with the timbrel and dance; Praise Him with stringed instruments and flutes! [5] Praise Him with loud cymbals; Praise Him with clashing cymbals! [6] Let everything that has breath praise the Lord. Praise the Lord!" (Psalm 150:1–6 NKJV).*

The psalmist in Psalm 47 also encouraged the singing of praises to God:

> *"Sing praises to God, sing praises! Sing praises to our King, sing praises! [7] For God is the King of all the earth; Sing praises with understanding." (Psalm 47:6–7 NKJV).*

The idea of praising God and extolling His virtues can also be found in 1 Chronicles, chapter 16:

> *"Sing to the Lord, all the earth; Proclaim the good news of His salvation from day to day. [24] Declare His glory among the nations, His wonders among all peoples. [25] For the Lord is great and greatly to be praised; He is also to be feared above all gods. [26] For all the gods of the peoples are idols, But the Lord made the Heavens. [27] Honour and majesty are before Him; Strength and gladness are in His place. [28] Give to the Lord, O families of the peoples, give to the Lord glory and strength. [29] Give to the Lord the glory due His name; bring an offering, and come before Him. Oh, worship the Lord in the beauty of holiness!" (I Chronicles 16:23–29 NKJV).*

There are several psalms that encourage us to praise and worship God. Psalm 147 says this is a good thing. In Psalm 100 there is some indication about how to praise God:

> *"Make a joyful shout to the Lord, all you lands! [2] Serve the Lord with gladness; Come before His presence with singing. [3] Know that the Lord, He is God; It is He who has made us, and not we ourselves; we are His people and the sheep of His pasture. [4] Enter into His gates with thanksgiving, and into His courts*

> *with praise. Be thankful to Him, and bless His name. [5] For the Lord is good; His mercy is everlasting, and His truth endures to all generations." (Psalm 100:1–5 NKJV).*

Psalm 96 also talks about how we should praise God:

> *"Oh, sing to the Lord a new song! Sing to the Lord, all the earth. [2] Sing to the Lord, bless His name; proclaim the good news of His salvation from day to day. [3] Declare His glory among the nations, His wonders among all peoples. [4] For the Lord is great and greatly to be praised; He is to be feared above all gods." (Psalm 96:1–4 NKJV).*

Psalm 100 reveals that praising God can get us into His presence. Verse four says we should:

> *"Enter into His gates with thanksgiving, And into His courts with praise. Be thankful to Him, and bless His name." (Psalms 100:4 NKJV).*

The story of Paul and Silas in the Philippian prison as set out in Acts chapter 16, shows clearly that praise and worship can result in miracles. They had been beaten and not only thrown into the inner prison, but also had their feet bound.

> *"But at midnight Paul and Silas were praying and singing hymns to God, and the prisoners were listening to them. [26] Suddenly there was a great earthquake, so that the foundations of the prison were shaken; and immediately all the doors were opened and everyone's chains were loosed. [27] And the keeper of the*

> *prison, awaking from sleep and seeing the prison doors open, supposing the prisoners had fled, drew his sword and was about to kill himself. [28] But Paul called with a loud voice, saying, "Do yourself no harm, for we are all here." (Acts 16:25–28 NKJV).*

The epistle to the Hebrew church stressed the need to praise God vocally:

> *"Therefore by Him let us continually offer the sacrifice of praise to God, that is, the fruit of our lips, giving thanks to His name." (Hebrews 13:15 NKJV).*

Praise and worship are intertwined but they are different. Although we praise and thank God for all the things that He has done for us we also praise others who for one reason or another are deserving of such.

Praising and worshipping God invites His presence. When Solomon dedicated the Temple, as written in Second Chronicles, chapter five, there was a great ceremony that involved praise, worship, music, and prayer, and God came on the scene.

> *"Indeed it came to pass, when the trumpeters and singers were as one, to make one sound to be heard in praising and thanking the Lord, and when they lifted up their voice with the trumpets and cymbals and instruments of music, and praised the Lord, saying: 'For He is good, for His mercy endures forever," that the house, the house of the Lord, was filled with a cloud, [14] so that the priests could not continue*

ministering because of the cloud; for the glory of the Lord filled the house of God." (2 Chronicles 5:13–14 NKJV).

Praising God is essential and Jesus himself endorsed it. Luke records His triumphant entry into Jerusalem where He was riding on a young donkey and the people were spreading their clothes on the road and praising Him:

"Then, as He was now drawing near the descent of the Mount of Olives, the whole multitude of the disciples began to rejoice and praise God with a loud voice for all the mighty works they had seen, [38] saying: 'Blessed is the King who comes in the name of the Lord! Peace in Heaven and glory in the highest!' [39] And some of the Pharisees called to Him from the crowd, 'Teacher, rebuke Your disciples.' [40] But He answered and said to them, 'I tell you that if these should keep silent, the stones would immediately cry out.' " (Luke 19:37–40 NKJV).

Christians say that God inhabits the praises of His people. There is no specific Scriptural reference to this, but verse three of Psalm 22 in the King James Version says:

"But thou art holy, O thou that inhabitest the praises of Israel." (Psalm 22:3 KJV).

It seems reasonable that, since all Christians are considered like Israel to be God's people, He therefore inhabits their praises as well.

Worship goes beyond praise and is an act of the heart reserved exclusively for God. Worship can be described as a lifestyle because it relates to everything we do. Praise and worship should be continuous and Psalm 34 speaks to this.

> *"I will bless the Lord at all times; His praise shall continually be in my mouth." (Psalm 34:1 NKJV).*

Praising the Lord can bring great blessings to His people. Psalm 67 shows that by sending up praise we can prosper materially.

> *"Let the peoples praise You, O God; Let all the peoples praise You. [6] Then the earth shall yield her increase; God, our own God, shall bless us. [7] God shall bless us, and all the ends of the earth shall fear Him." (Psalm 67:5–7 NKJV).*

Several postures can be adopted during worship and they include bowing, kneeling, and lifting hands, all of which project an attitude of humility that is so essential to worshipping God.

Praise includes, among other things, prayer, music, dancing, singing, shouting, hand-clapping, making "a joyful noise", and any other expression of adoration, worship, or submission to God.

Some congregations use joyous songs and loud music to praise God, while for worship the music is usually more sedate and introspective.

Praising and worshipping God will be the very essence of Heaven.

> *"And the twenty-four elders and the four living creatures fell down and worshiped God who sat on the throne, saying, 'Amen! Alleluia!' [5] Then a voice came from the throne, saying, 'Praise our God, all you His servants and those who fear Him, both small and great!' [6] And I heard, as it were, the voice of a great multitude, as the sound of many waters and as the sound of mighty thunderings, saying, 'Alleluia! For the Lord God Omnipotent reigns! [7] Let us be glad and rejoice and give Him glory, for the marriage of the Lamb has come, and His wife has made herself ready.'" (Revelation 19:4–7 NKJV).*

Praise must also include thanksgiving. Some people ask God for things and when He grants them, they forget to say "Thank you". The case of the 10 leprous men in Luke 17 is a perfect example of this. Jesus had healed these men but only one returned to show his gratitude.

Prayer is a very important part of worship and must be accompanied by thanksgiving. The Christian in worshipping God must also confess his or her sins and ask forgiveness.

Reading and preaching the Word of God are other elements of worship. This was done in the Old Testament and in the early Church.

Giving to God is also an act of worship. Giving back to God a portion of what you have received is not only required but is rewarding. Jesus told His disciples to love their enemies and to lend to others, not expecting any return. But He went even further.

> *"Give, and it will be given to you: good measure, pressed down, shaken together, and running over will be put into your bosom. For with the same measure that you use, it will be measured back to you." (Luke 6:38 NKJV).*

Praising God in difficult times can bring the awesome power of God rushing to the rescue of His children. The story of Jehoshaphat in 2 Chronicles, chapter 20 tells about a large army that was preparing to attack his people. He sought the Lord and got unbelievable results:

> *"So they rose early in the morning and went out into the Wilderness of Tekoa; and as they went out, Jehoshaphat stood and said, 'Hear me, O Judah and you inhabitants of Jerusalem: Believe in the Lord your God, and you shall be established; believe His prophets, and you shall prosper.' [21] And when he had consulted with the people, he appointed those who should sing to the Lord, and who should praise the beauty of holiness, as they went out before the army and were saying: 'Praise the Lord, For His mercy endures forever.' [22] Now when they began to sing and to praise, the Lord set ambushes against the people of Ammon, Moab, and Mount Seir, who had come against Judah; and they were defeated. [23] For the people of Ammon and Moab stood up against the inhabitants of Mount Seir to utterly kill and destroy them. And when they had made an end of the inhabitants of Seir, they helped to destroy*

> *one another. [24] So when Judah came to a place overlooking the wilderness, they looked toward the multitude; and there were their dead bodies, fallen on the earth. No one had escaped." (2 Chronicles 20: 20–24 NKJV).*

As a born again Believer do not neglect to praise and worship God.

Chapter 27

What Born Again Christians Can Expect

Do not believe for one moment that by becoming born again, life will be easier. Rather, you can expect challenges to your newfound faith from every side. But while that may be the case, rest assured that the God that you have chosen to serve will be faithful and help you to triumph.

When Jesus was about to leave this earth, He had a conversation with His disciples about what would happen to them. He told them that they would have problems.

> *"These things I have spoken to you, that in Me you may have peace. In the world you will have tribulation; but be of good cheer, I have overcome the world." (John 16:33 NKJV).*

The situation is simple; Satan recognizes that he has lost a soul and he will do everything to get you back. The challenges will come and, like the early Church, they will take the form of persecution. There are several organizations committed to eliminating Christianity and their onslaught is already known around the world.

Paul in his letter to his protégé, Timothy, warned that this time would come.

> *"Yes, and everyone who wants to live a godly life in Christ Jesus will suffer persecution. [13] But evil people and impostors will flourish. They will deceive others and will themselves be deceived. [14] But you must remain faithful to the things you have been taught. You know they are true, for you know you can trust those who taught you. [15] You have been taught the holy Scriptures from childhood, and they have given you the wisdom to receive the salvation that comes by trusting in Christ Jesus. (2 Timothy 3:12–15 NLT).*

Paul's colleague Peter also told the early Church that Believers will face challenges, something he described as "fiery trials".

> *"Dear friends, don't be surprised at the fiery trials you are going through, as if something strange were happening to you. [13] Instead, be very glad—for these trials make you partners with Christ in his suffering, so that you will have the wonderful joy of seeing his glory when it is revealed to all the world. [14] If you are insulted because you bear the name of Christ, you will be blessed, for the glorious Spirit of God rests upon you. [15] If you suffer, however, it must not be for murder, stealing, making trouble, or prying into other people's affairs. [16] But it is no shame to suffer for being a Christian. Praise God for the privilege of being called by his name! (1 Peter 4:12–16 NLT).*

The Believer has been given the assurance by Jesus that he should not let challenges such as these be a source of worry, because He has a plan.

> *"Let not your heart be troubled; you believe in God, believe also in Me. [2] In My Father's house are many mansions; if it were not so, I would have told you. I go to prepare a place for you. [3] And if I go and prepare a place for you, I will come again and receive you to Myself; that where I am, there you may be also." (John 14: 1–3 NKJV).*

Later in that same chapter Jesus reiterated that Believers should be calm.

> *"Peace I leave with you, My peace I give to you; not as the world gives do I give to you. Let not your heart be troubled, neither let it be afraid." (John 14:27 NKJV).*

Doubt is the first test that is likely to come. This is one of Satan's strongest tools to weaken or destroy your confidence in God's Word and the salvation that you have gained through His Son, Jesus Christ. The devil will put thoughts in your mind about whether you have made the right decision to walk away from your sinful past and accept Jesus Christ as Savior.

There will be some confusion about exactly what you have done and what it means. You may even question if you are really saved. But John gives this bold assurance in the first chapter of his first epistle:

"If we confess our sins, He is faithful and just to forgive us our sins and to cleanse us from all unrighteousness." (1 John 1:9 NKJV).

This assurance is also found in the epistle to the Romans:

"That if you confess with your mouth the Lord Jesus and believe in your heart that God has raised Him from the dead, you will be saved.
[10] For with the heart one believes unto righteousness, and with the mouth confession is made unto salvation. [11] For the Scripture says, 'Whoever believes on Him will not be put to shame.' [12] For there is no distinction between Jew and Greek, for the same Lord over all is rich to all who call upon Him. [13] For "whoever calls on the name of the Lord shall be saved".'" (Romans 10:9–13 NKJV).

Satan will remind you about the "good times" you may have had and will question your ability to remain on the path that you have chosen. Family, friends, and work colleagues will have their say, some negatively. Others will predict that you will soon be back to your old ways. The good news is that you can overcome doubt. The remedy is faith. You have to believe, trust, and depend on the God to whom you have given your life.

Proverbs chapter three, verses five to six states exactly what you should do:

"Trust in the Lord with all your heart, and lean not on your own understanding; [6] in all your ways acknowledge Him, and He shall direct your paths." (Proverbs 3:5–6 NKJV).

Another good way to overcome doubt is to find an experienced Christian friend or counselor who can encourage you and explain some of the early pitfalls.

Temptation will be another challenge and this will most likely be in areas of your greatest weakness. If you have been a womanizer, the enemy will put the most desirable women in your path. He may even bring back into your life some of your old lovers. Opportunities for partying, drinking, and similar activities will come for those who have found these things to be enjoyable.

You must understand that temptation WILL come. Even Jesus was tempted by none other than Satan himself. The full account of this can be found in the first part of chapter four of Matthew's Gospel. In that passage Jesus resisted and rebuked Satan. James the apostle has said in chapter four of his epistle that Christians should do the same.

> *"Therefore submit to God. Resist the devil and he will flee from you. [8] Draw near to God and He will draw near to you. Cleanse your hands, you sinners; and purify your hearts, you double-minded." (James 4:7–8 NKJV).*

The Christian also has the assurance that, even in the face of temptation, God is watching. Paul made this clear in chapter 10 of his first epistle to the Corinthians:

> *"No temptation has overtaken you except such as is common to man; but God is faithful, who will not allow you to be tempted beyond what you are able, but with the temptation will also make the way of escape, that you may be able to bear it." (1 Corinthians 10:13 NKJV).*

When you give your life to Jesus Christ some of your family and friends may even desert you or in some way slight you. This could lead to discouragement and, if you are not strong enough, could make you think about walking away from the new life that you have chosen. Discouragement comes when you start to think that you may not be able to handle the criticism and therefore may be uncomfortable in your new circumstances.

One of the good things about the Christian walk is that while some old friends may distance themselves from you, at the same time you will find new friends in the Church. The members of the early Church were instructed to encourage one another.

> *"Let us hold fast the confession of our hope without wavering, for He who promised is faithful. [24] And let us consider one another in order to stir up love and good works, [25] not forsaking the assembling of ourselves together, as is the manner of some, but exhorting one another, and so much the more as you see the Day approaching." (Hebrews 10:23–25 NKJV).*

The Living Bible translates that passage this way:

> *"Now we can look forward to the salvation God has promised us. There is no longer any room for doubt, and we can tell others that salvation is ours, for there is no question that he will do what he says. [24] In response to all he has done for us, let us outdo each other in being helpful and kind to each other and in doing good. [25] Let us not neglect our church meetings, as some people do, but*

> *encourage and warn each other, especially now that the day of his coming back again is drawing near." (Hebrews 10:23–25 TLB).*

If you are not inclined to make friends easily, you could talk to a counselor, pastor, or senior person at your church about how best you could establish a relationship with other members in that assembly.

Although the new convert will have challenges, be assured that God is with you at all times. Though you may be by yourself, you are never alone. When Jesus gave His final instructions to His disciples to go and make converts, He told them that they would not be alone.

> *"And Jesus came and spoke to them, saying, 'All authority has been given to Me in Heaven and on earth. [19] Go therefore and make disciples of all the nations, baptizing them in the name of the Father and of the Son and of the Holy Spirit, [20] teaching them to observe all things that I have commanded you; and lo, I am with you always, even to the end of the age.'" (Matthew 28:18–20 NKJV).*

This promise was reiterated in the book of Hebrews:

> *"Let your conduct be without covetousness; be content with such things as you have. For He Himself has said, 'I will never leave you nor forsake you.' [6] So we may boldly say: 'The Lord is my helper; I will not fear. What can man do to me?' (Hebrews 13:5–6 NKJV).*

When he was handing over leadership of Israel to Joshua, Moses told his followers that they should go forward, knowing that God was with them.

> *"Be strong and of good courage, do not fear nor be afraid of them; for the Lord your God, He is the One who goes with you. He will not leave you nor forsake you." (Deuteronomy 31:6 NKJV).*

The Christian can claim that same assurance, which is repeated in the book of Revelation:

> *"Because you have kept My command to persevere, I also will keep you from the hour of trial which shall come upon the whole world, to test those who dwell on the earth." (Revelation 3:10 NKJV).*

The new convert could find himself or herself worrying about one thing or another. But Jesus has told his children not to worry:

> *"Therefore I say to you, do not worry about your life, what you will eat or what you will drink; nor about your body, what you will put on. Is not life more than food and the body more than clothing? [26] Look at the birds of the air, for they neither sow nor reap nor gather into barns; yet your Heavenly Father feeds them. Are you not of more value than they? [27] Which of you by worrying can add one cubit to his stature? [28] So why do you worry about clothing? Consider the lilies of the field, how they grow: they neither toil*

nor spin; [29] and yet I say to you that even Solomon in all his glory was not arrayed like one of these. [30] Now if God so clothes the grass of the field, which today is, and tomorrow is thrown into the oven, will He not much more clothe you, O you of little faith? [31] Therefore do not worry, saying, 'What shall we eat?' or 'What shall we drink?' or 'What shall we wear?' [32] For after all these things the Gentiles seek. For your Heavenly Father knows that you need all these things. [33] But seek first the kingdom of God and His righteousness, and all these things shall be added to you. [34] Therefore do not worry about tomorrow, for tomorrow will worry about its own things. Sufficient for the day is its own trouble." (Matthew 6: 25–34 NKJV).

Paul also encouraged the church at Philippi not to worry:

"Be anxious for nothing, but in everything by prayer and supplication, with thanksgiving, let your requests be made known to God; [7] and the peace of God, which surpasses all understanding, will guard your hearts and minds through Christ Jesus." (Philippians 4:6–7 NKJV).

The Believer has also been given the assurance that no matter what the struggle may be he or she can depend on God to be faithful.

"Now He who searches the hearts knows what the mind of the Spirit is, because He makes intercession for the saints according to the

> *will of God. [28] And we know that all things work together for good to those who love God, to those who are the called according to His purpose." (Romans 8:27–28 NKJV).*

God's promise to deliver His children from any situation brings comfort and strengthens their faith in Him. They can be at peace knowing that in the face of their greatest adversity, He will provide the solution.

> *"No weapon formed against you shall prosper, and every tongue which rises against you in judgment You shall condemn. This is the heritage of the servants of the Lord, and their righteousness is from Me," says the Lord." (Isaiah 54:17 NKJV).*

God also used the prophet Isaiah to assure His people that He would protect them in any situation.

> *"But now, O Jacob, listen to the Lord who created you. O Israel, the one who formed you says, 'Do not be afraid, for I have ransomed you. I have called you by name; you are mine. [2] When you go through deep waters, I will be with you. When you go through rivers of difficulty, you will not drown. When you walk through the fire of oppression, you will not be burned up; the flames will not consume you. [3] For I am the Lord, your God, the Holy One of Israel, your Saviour.' " (Isaiah 43:1–3 NLT).*

The Christian can expect that there will be suffering and this could be in several forms. Do not be surprised if you encounter sickness, misery, pain, poverty, persecution, disappointments, sorrow, and trouble of some kind. Jesus would have at one time or another felt these oppressions and His followers have been told that they will suffer with Him.

Paul had this encouragement for the Corinthians:

> *"We are pressed on every side by troubles, but we are not crushed. We are perplexed, but not driven to despair. [9] We are hunted down, but never abandoned by God. We get knocked down, but we are not destroyed. [10] Through suffering, our bodies continue to share in the death of Jesus so that the life of Jesus may also be seen in our bodies. [11] Yes, we live under constant danger of death because we serve Jesus, so that the life of Jesus will be evident in our dying bodies. [12] So we live in the face of death, but this has resulted in eternal life for you. [13] But we continue to preach because we have the same kind of faith the psalmist had when he said, 'I believed in God, so I spoke.' [14] We know that God, who raised the Lord Jesus, will also raise us with Jesus and present us to himself together with you. [15] All of this is for your benefit. And as God's grace reaches more and more people, there will be great thanksgiving, and God will receive more and more glory. [16] That is why we never give up. Though our bodies are dying, our spirits are being renewed every day. [17] For our present troubles are small and won't last very long. Yet they produce for us a glory that vastly outweighs*

> *them and will last forever! [18] So we don't look at the troubles we can see now; rather, we fix our gaze on things that cannot be seen. For the things we see now will soon be gone, but the things we cannot see will last forever." (2 Corinthians 4:8–18 NLT).*

The Church at Rome also had similar encouragement and assurances:

> *"For as many as are led by the Spirit of God, these are sons of God. [15] For you did not receive the spirit of bondage again to fear, but you received the Spirit of adoption by whom we cry out, 'Abba, Father.' [16] The Spirit Himself bears witness with our spirit that we are children of God, [17] and if children, then heirs—heirs of God and joint heirs with Christ, if indeed we suffer with Him, that we may also be glorified together. [18] For I consider that the sufferings of this present time are not worthy to be compared with the glory which shall be revealed in us." (Romans 8:14–18 NKJV).*

Being born again could even lead to death as apostles Paul, Peter, and some of the others found out. But you must be strong in Christ.

> *"Then they will deliver you up to tribulation and kill you, and you will be hated by all nations for My name's sake. [10] And then many will be offended, will betray one another, and will hate one another. [11] Then many false prophets will rise up and deceive many. [12] And because lawlessness will abound, the love of many will*

> *grow cold. [13] But he who endures to the end shall be saved." (Matthew 24:9–13 NKJV).*

While Believers have been told to expect trouble, they have also been assured of God's peace.

> *"Then justice will dwell in the wilderness, and righteousness remain in the fruitful field. [17] The work of righteousness will be peace, and the effect of righteousness, quietness and assurance forever. [18] My people will dwell in a peaceful habitation, in secure dwellings, and in quiet resting places, [19] Though hail comes down on the forest, and the city is brought low in humiliation." (Isaiah 32:16–19 NKJV).*

The assurance that God will take care of His children has also been confirmed by Paul in his letter to the Philippians.

> *"I thank my God upon every remembrance of you, [4] always in every prayer of mine making request for you all with joy, [5] for your fellowship in the gospel from the first day until now, [6] being confident of this very thing, that He who has begun a good work in you will complete it until the day of Jesus Christ." (Philippians 1:3–6 NKJV).*

John also stressed to the early Christians that they could depend on their God.

> *"Now this is the confidence that we have in Him, that if we ask anything according to His will, He hears us. [15] And if we know that*

He hears us, whatever we ask, we know that we have the petitions that we have asked of Him." (1 John 5:14–15 NKJV).

The Christians at Rome were also assured that God would be faithful at all times and with Him on their side they could not fail. Today's Believer can also be confident in that conviction.

> *"Who shall separate us from the love of Christ? Shall tribulation, or distress, or persecution, or famine, or nakedness, or peril,*
> *or sword? [36] As it is written 'For Your sake we are killed all day long; We are accounted*
> *as sheep for the slaughter.' [37] Yet in all these things we are more than conquerors through*
> *Him who loved us. [38] For I am persuaded that neither death nor life, nor angels nor principalities nor powers, nor things*
> *present nor things to come, [39] nor height nor depth, nor any other created thing, shall be able to separate us from the love of God which is in Christ Jesus our Lord." (Romans 8:35–39 NKJV).*

Christians can be assured of God's protection in times of physical danger and spiritual need. This was echoed by the psalmist in Psalm 91:

> *"Surely He shall deliver you from the snare of the fowler and from the perilous pestilence.*
> *[4] He shall cover you with His feathers, and under His wings you shall take refuge; His*
> *truth shall be your shield and buckler. [5] You*
> *shall not be afraid of the terror by night, nor*

> *of the arrow that flies by day, [6] nor of the pestilence that walks in darkness, nor of the destruction that lays waste at noonday. [7] A thousand may fall at your side, and ten thousand at your right hand; but it shall not come near you. [8] Only with your eyes shall you look, and see the reward of the wicked. [9] Because you have made the Lord, who is my refuge, even the Most High, your dwelling place, [10] no evil shall befall you, nor shall any plague come near your dwelling; [11] For He shall give His angels charge over you, to keep you in all your ways. [12] In their hands they shall bear you up, lest you dash your foot against a stone. [13] You shall tread upon the lion and the cobra, the young lion and the serpent you shall trample underfoot." (Psalm 91:3–16 NKJV).*

In that Scripture the psalmist writes about what the child of God can expect when he puts his trust in Him. The rest of the passage shows God speaking to those who love and obey Him.

> *"Because he has set his love upon Me, therefore I will deliver him; I will set him on high, because he has known My name. [15] He shall call upon Me, and I will answer him; I will be with him in trouble; I will deliver him and honor him. [16] With long life I will satisfy him, and show him My salvation." (Psalm 91:14–16 NKJV).*

This entire passage is put in more modern language in the New Living Translation:

> *"For he will rescue you from every trap and protect you from deadly disease. 4He will cover you with his feathers. He will shelter you with his wings. His faithful promises are your armor and protection. 5 Do not be afraid of the terrors of the night, nor the arrow that flies in the day. 6 Do not dread the disease that stalks in darkness, nor the disaster that strikes at midday. 7 Though a thousand fall at your side, though ten thousand are dying around you, these evils will not touch you. 8 Just open your eyes, and see how the wicked are punished. 9 If you make the Lord your refuge, if you make the Most High your shelter, 10 no evil will conquer you; no plague will come near your home. 11 For he will order his angels to protect you wherever you go. 12 They will hold you up with their hands so you won't even hurt your foot on a stone. 13 You will trample upon lions and cobras; you will crush fierce lions and serpents under your feet! 14 The Lord says, 'I will rescue those who love me. I will protect those who trust in my name. 15 When they call on me, I will answer; I will be with them in trouble. I will rescue and honor them. 16 I will reward them with a long life and give them my salvation.' " (Psalm 91:3–16 NLT).*

God promised the children of Israel that He would bless them if they obeyed Him and these same promises are extended to the Christian. They are spelled out in chapter 28 of the book of Deuteronomy:

"If you fully obey the Lord your God and
carefully keep all his commands that I am
giving you today, the Lord your God will set
you high above all the nations of the world.
2 You will experience all these blessings if
you obey the Lord your God: 3 Your towns
and your fields will be blessed. 4 Your chil-
dren and your crops will be blessed. The
offspring of your herds and flocks will be
blessed. 5 Your fruit baskets and bread-
boards will be blessed. 6 Wherever you go
and whatever you do, you will be blessed.
7 The Lord will conquer your enemies when
they attack you. They will attack you from
one direction, but they will scatter from you
in seven! 8 The Lord will guarantee a blessing
on everything you do and will fill your store-
houses with grain. The Lord your God will
bless you in the land he is giving you. 9 If you
obey the commands of the Lord your God
and walk in his ways, the Lord will estab-
lish you as his holy people as he swore he
would do. 10 Then all the nations of the world
will see that you are a people claimed by
the Lord, and they will stand in awe of you.
11 The Lord will give you prosperity in the
land he swore to your ancestors to give you,
blessing you with many children, numerous
livestock, and abundant crops. 12 The Lord
will send rain at the proper time from his
rich treasury in the Heavens and will bless
all the work you do. You will lend to many
nations, but you will never need to borrow
from them. 13 If you listen to these com-
mands of the Lord your God that I am giving

> *you today, and if you carefully obey them, the Lord will make you the head and not the tail, and you will always be on top and never at the bottom. [14] You must not turn away from any of the commands I am giving you today, nor follow after other gods and worship them." (Deuteronomy 28:1–14 NLT).*

In that same chapter God also warned that those who disobey Him could find themselves facing no fewer than 120 curses.

Christians can take great comfort in the words of Psalm 23, which is probably one of the most popular and well known portions of Scripture.

> *"The Lord is my shepherd; I shall not want. [2] He makes me to lie down in green pastures; He leads me beside the still waters. [3] He restores my soul; He leads me in the paths of righteousness For His name's sake. [4] Yea, though I walk through the valley of the shadow of death, I will fear no evil; For You are with me; Your rod and Your staff, they comfort me. [5] You prepare a table before me in the presence of my enemies; You anoint my head with oil; My cup runs over. [6] Surely goodness and mercy shall follow me all the days of my life; And I will dwell in the house of the Lord forever." (Psalm 23 NKJV).*

One thing that could be of concern to the new convert is the behavior of other Christians. You must remember that Christians are people and therefore will have all sorts of different personalities and challenges. Do not let the bad behavior of others dishearten you. Choose those who best exemplify Christian qualities.

The newly converted Believer will face the challenge of deciding which denomination to join. There are so many choices these days and so many differing doctrines, that even some experienced Christians are changing from one to another.

One of the most intimidating experiences is living in an environment where you are the only Christian. Sometimes this could be a hostile situation with circumstances that could discourage. This is where your faith and resolve to live a Christian life will be tested. Your success or failure will impact those around you. Your lifestyle and resolution to serve Jesus Christ will attract others to do the same while, should you fail, Satan would have triumphed. Do not let this happen.

One of the best ways to ensure that you strengthen your Christian walk is to get involved in ministry or some other aspect of church life. All Christians are called to minister, according to the Great Commission to "go into all the world and make disciples". However, finding the specific area to which you as an individual have been called is vital to your spiritual growth. Everything that is done in church or for God is ministry and this includes teaching, preaching, evangelizing, caregiving, testifying, using your talent in singing or music, and a host of other things. Pray and ask God to show you where He wants you to serve and use your talents or gifts. Remember that your gift is for His glory and is based on your talent or some skill at which you are particularly good. The intention is to serve God with everything that you have.

While the Believer has been given many wonderful promises, there is a stern warning for those who are less than genuine. Jesus told His followers that they had to be righteous and not hypocritical like some of the religious leaders of that day.

Matthew chapter seven quotes Him as making what could be described as one of the saddest statements in the Bible.

> *"Not everyone who says to Me, 'Lord, Lord,' shall enter the kingdom of heaven, but he who does the will of My Father in heaven. [22] Many will say to Me in that day, 'Lord, Lord, have we not prophesied in Your name, cast out demons in Your name, and done many wonders in Your name?' [23] And then I will declare to them, 'I never knew you; depart from Me, you who practice lawlessness!' (Matthew 7:21–23 NKJV).*

Here is how the New Living Translation puts it.

> *"Not everyone who calls out to me, 'Lord! Lord!' will enter the Kingdom of Heaven. Only those who actually do the will of my Father in heaven will enter. [22] On judgment day many will say to me, 'Lord! Lord! We prophesied in your name and cast out demons in your name and performed many miracles in your name.' [23] But I will reply, 'I never knew you. Get away from me, you who break God's laws.' (Matthew 7:21–23 NLT).*

Every born again Believer can rest in the words of Paul the Apostle to the Colossian Christians.

> *"I want them to be encouraged and knit together by strong ties of love. I want them to have complete confidence that they understand God's mysterious plan, which is Christ himself. [3] In him lie hidden all the*

treasures of wisdom and knowledge. [4] *I am telling you this so no one will deceive you with well-crafted arguments.* [5] *For though I am far away from you, my heart is with you. And I rejoice that you are living as you should and that your faith in Christ is strong.* [6] *And now, just as you accepted Christ Jesus as your Lord, you must continue to follow him.* [7] *Let your roots grow down into him, and let your lives be built on him. Then your faith will grow strong in the truth you were taught, and you will overflow with thankfulness.* [8] *Don't let anyone capture you with empty philosophies and high-sounding nonsense that come from human thinking and from the spiritual powers of this world, rather than from Christ.* [9] *For in Christ lives all the fullness of God in a human body.* [10] *So you also are complete through your union with Christ, who is the head over every ruler and authority". (Colossians 2:2–10 NLT).*

Peter the apostle also had some advice. He told the members of the early Church that knowing that they are born again makes them much better people and has provided the resources to make them more productive.

By his divine power, God has given us everything we need for living a godly life. We have received all of this by coming to know him, the one who called us to himself by means of his marvelous glory and excellence. [4] *And because of his glory and excellence, he has given us great and precious promises. These are the promises that enable you to share*

> *his divine nature and escape the world's corruption caused by human desires. [5] In view of all this, make every effort to respond to God's promises. Supplement your faith with a generous provision of moral excellence, and moral excellence with knowledge, [6] and knowledge with self-control, and self-control with patient endurance, and patient endurance with godliness, [7] and godliness with brotherly affection, and brotherly affection with love for everyone. [8] The more you grow like this, the more productive and useful you will be in your knowledge of our Lord Jesus Christ. [9] But those who fail to develop in this way are shortsighted or blind, forgetting that they have been cleansed from their old sins. [10] So, dear brothers and sisters work hard to prove that you really are among those God has called and chosen. Do these things, and you will never fall away. [11] Then God will give you a grand entrance into the eternal Kingdom of our Lord and Savior Jesus Christ. (2 Peter 1:3–11 NLT).*

Peter also stressed that accepting Jesus Christ as Savior has great benefits, while those who reject Him face grave consequences.

> *Therefore, to you who believe, He is precious; but to those who are disobedient, "The stone which the builders rejected Has become the chief cornerstone," [8] and "A stone of stumbling And a rock of offense." They stumble, being disobedient to the word, to which they also were appointed.*

> *[9] But you are a chosen generation, a royal priesthood, a holy nation, His own special people, that you may proclaim the praises of Him who called you out of darkness into His marvelous light; [10] who once were not a people but are now the people of God, who had not obtained mercy but now have obtained mercy. (1 Peter 2:7–10 NKJV).*

The New Living Translation puts that same passage this way:

> *Yes, you who trust him recognize the honor God has given him. But for those who reject him, "The stone that the builders rejected has now become the cornerstone." [8] And, "He is the stone that makes people stumble, the rock that makes them fall." They stumble because they do not obey God's word, and so they meet the fate that was planned for them. [9] But you are not like that, for you are a chosen people. You are royal priests, a holy nation, God's very own possession. As a result, you can show others the goodness of God, for he called you out of the darkness into his wonderful light. (1 Peter 2:7–10 NLT).*

There is one challenge that the Christian will face that will certainly test him or her to the utmost. Jesus Christ has told His followers that they must love their enemies. Some may say this is impossible but Jesus says it must be done.

> *"You have heard the law that says, 'Love your neighbor' and hate your enemy. [44] But I say,*

> *love your enemies! Pray for those who persecute you! [45] In that way, you will be acting as true children of your Father in heaven. For he gives his sunlight to both the evil and the good, and he sends rain on the just and the unjust alike. [46] If you love only those who love you, what reward is there for that? Even corrupt tax collectors do that much. If you are kind only to your friends, how are you different from anyone else? Even pagans do that. [48] But you are to be perfect, even as your Father in heaven is perfect. (Matthew 5:43–48 NLT).*

Love is the very bedrock of Christianity and Jesus said that exhibiting love will be the way to show that we belong to Him.

> *So now I am giving you a new commandment: Love each other. Just as I have loved you, you should love each other. [35] Your love for one another will prove to the world that you are my disciples." (John 13:34–35 NLT).*

But while Christians are encouraged to love others, they should not expect everyone to reciprocate.

> *So don't be surprised, dear brothers and sisters, if the world hates you. [14] If we love our brothers and sisters who are believers, it proves that we have passed from death to life. But a person who has no love is still dead. [15] Anyone who hates another brother or sister is really a murderer at heart. And you know that murderers don't have eternal life within*

> *them. [16] We know what real love is because Jesus gave up his life for us. So we also ought to give up our lives for our brothers and sisters. [17] If someone has enough money to live well and sees a brother or sister in need but shows no compassion—how can God's love be in that person? [18] Dear children, let's not merely say that we love each other; let us show the truth by our actions. [19] Our actions will show that we belong to the truth, so we will be confident when we stand before God. [20] Even if we feel guilty, God is greater than our feelings, and he knows everything. [21] Dear friends, if we don't feel guilty, we can come to God with bold confidence. [22] And we will receive from him whatever we ask because we obey him and do the things that please him. (1 John 3:13–22 NLT).*

Christians must make sure they know the Word of God so that they can counteract false teaching. Peter the apostle has stressed in his second epistle, that false prophets can mislead the Believer into going against his or her Christian principles. This could lead to serious consequences.

> *And when people escape from the wickedness of the world by knowing our Lord and Savior Jesus Christ and then get tangled up and enslaved by sin again, they are worse off than before. [21] It would be better if they had never known the way to righteousness than to know it and then reject the command they were given to live a holy life. [22] They prove the truth of this proverb: "A dog returns to*

> *its vomit." And another says, "A washed pig returns to the mud." (2 Peter 2:20–22 NLT).*

Chances are that you have read this book but you have never committed your life to Christ and are therefore NOT born again. Based on what you have discovered here you have perhaps been convicted and recognize that you need to be converted. This is your opportunity to take the first step toward becoming a Christian.

The process of becoming born again is very simple and is outlined in the book of Romans.

> *If you openly declare that Jesus is Lord and believe in your heart that God raised him from the dead, you will be saved. [10] For it is by believing in your heart that you are made right with God, and it is by openly declaring your faith that you are saved. [11] As the Scriptures tell us, "Anyone who trusts in him will never be disgraced." (Romans 10:9–11 NLT).*

You have a very important choice to make. It all starts with admitting that you are a sinner, and asking God to forgive you. Your next step is to accept Jesus Christ as your Savior and see Him help you make a drastic change from doing the things that have been identified as sin.

The question is: Can you afford not to make that choice? Do you really want to take that chance? Are you ready to make that decision and ask Jesus Christ to come into your life? If so, pray the following prayer from your heart, believing every word of it.

> *"Heavenly Father,*

> *I come to You asking for the forgiveness of my sins. I confess with my mouth and believe with my heart that Jesus is your Son, and that He died on the Cross at Calvary that I might be forgiven and have eternal life in the Kingdom of Heaven. Father, I believe that Jesus was born of a virgin, rose from the dead, and is now in Heaven with You. I ask you right now to come in to my life and be my personal Lord and Savior. I repent of my sins and will worship You all the days of my life! Because Your Word is truth, I confess with my mouth that I am born again and cleansed by the Blood of Jesus! In Jesus' Name I pray. Amen."*

If you have prayed that prayer, you have made the first step as a born again Christian. Be faithful to what you have prayed and find a Bible-believing church to attend. Pray daily, read and study the Bible, and, if possible, contact a friend or someone who is a Christian and share the news of your decision.

May God richly bless you. I pray Jesus The Christ may dwell in your heart through faith as you are being rooted and grounded in His love.

About the Author

Michael L. Goddard is a multi-award-winning Caribbean journalist with nearly 50 years' experience.

He has been inducted into the Barbados Association of Journalists' Hall of Fame and has also been recognized by several other national organizations.

Mike Goddard, as he is better known, is a legend, having at one time been dubbed "the voice of horse racing in Barbados".

He could be described as the complete journalist, having worked in every area of the media.

He has published and edited The Messenger, a Christian newspaper, along with several magazines and newsletters.

Michael L. Goddard was born again in 2001 and has transferred the excitement and passion of his journalistic career to not only living the Christian life but also introducing people to Jesus Christ.

Mike is an elder and head of Men's Ministry at The People's Cathedral, the largest Pentecostal Church in Barbados. He has also served as general men's director of the Pentecostal Assemblies of the West Indies International.

Michael L. Goddard has been a featured speaker in churches, Christian denominations, and organizations in Barbados and the Caribbean. His testimony of walking away from the exciting world of the media to serve Jesus Christ is awesome. He says he not only loves and serves God, but has experienced Him, and "there is nothing like it."